"With his typical flair and remarkable clarity Philip Jenkins takes the reader on a global tour to explore the intimate relationship between religion and fertility. This book offers an engaging exploration of the implications this relationship holds for the future. It is highly accessible and will be of interest to a general audience."
—**Roger Finke**, Professor of Sociology, Religious Studies, and International Affairs, Pennsylvania State University

"Religious leaders have spent decades debating strategies for global evangelism or combating (post)modernism, convinced that the key to religious growth lies in perfecting techniques or ideas. Yet scholars of religion have long observed that 'demography is destiny' when it comes to religious groups. In this accessible book, Philip Jenkins synthesizes a wealth of research on the vital connection between fertility and faith worldwide. He argues persuasively that, for religious groups to thrive, they must adjust to the emerging reality of a low-fertility world, along with all of its tumultuous cultural, political, and economic implications. For scholars, faith leaders, and laypersons alike, this is an important book."
—**Samuel L. Perry**, Assistant Professor, University of Oklahoma

"True to form, in another well-researched and well-written book, Philip Jenkins breaks new ground by examining the influences of traditional religions and secularization on fertility and the reciprocal influence of fertility patterns on future developments in religion and society. Taking an in-depth look at nation states and religious institutions he utilizes extensive data as he considers the influences of cultures, economics, politics, attitudes toward sexuality, gender and family, and thoughtfully analyzes the complex configurations they produce. His conclusions are thought-provoking and compelling."
—**Anthony J. Pogorelc**, Sociology Scholar in Residence, School of Humanities and Social Sciences, St. Mary's University

"In this riveting new book, Philip Jenkins masterfully navigates the disciplines of demography, history, economics, sociology, and psychology in order to systematically capture the startling relationship between faith and fertility. Jenkins demonstrates how faith and fertility are related to each other as well as the many seismic ways in which this relationship will influence what the world will look like in generations to come. Academics and popular audiences will find this book compelling, as will clergy, lay leaders, policy makers, and even futurists."
—**Byron R. Johnson**, Distinguished Professor of the Social Sciences and Director of the Institute for Studies of Religion and the Program on Prosocial Behavior, Baylor University

FERTILITY AND FAITH

The Demographic Revolution and the
Transformation of World Religions

Philip Jenkins

BAYLOR UNIVERSITY PRESS

Cover design by Claudine Mansour, Claudine Mansour Design
Book design by Kasey McBeath
Cover image: Alexander Spatari/Moment Collection via Getty Images

Hardcover ISBN 978-1-4813-1131-1
Library of Congress Control Number: 2020008635

CONTENTS

Part II

ACKNOWLEDGMENTS

I am as always deeply grateful to my colleagues at Baylor University's Institute for Studies of Religion (ISR), who have offered such helpful advice and encouragement throughout the process of research. I particularly thank Jeff Levin and Byron Johnson. Thanks also to Cade Jarrell and David Aycock at Baylor University Press. Carey Newman was another great source of encouragement.

Thanks to Kathryn Hume for her valuable comments on the MS.

Greatest thanks, as always, to my wife, Liz Jenkins.

At several points in this book, it will be apparent that I do not discuss the present or future impact of the COVID-19 crisis that became so powerful a factor in our affairs. This is because the present book was completed and in production before the major impact of this threat became so strongly apparent in March 2020, and I decided not to make any further revisions.

INTRODUCTION

1

FERTILITY AND FAITH

I n the past half century, many countries have been transformed by a sweeping demographic change, which shows no signs of diminishing in pace. Around the globe, fertility rates have fallen precipitously, family sizes have contracted, and populations have stabilized or contracted. We are still coming to terms with the many ramifications of that change, which echo through economic, social, political, and cultural life. But for all the discussions of these issues, all the projections of what it will be like living in a low-fertility world, one critical area remains largely neglected, and that is religion and religious behavior.[1]

Rarely remarked even by expert observers, a direct relationship exists between the fertility rates of a community—the number of children that a typical woman bears during her lifetime—and that society's degree of religious fervor and commitment. High-fertility societies, like most of contemporary Africa, tend to be fervent, devout, and religiously enthusiastic. Conversely, the lower the fertility rate, and the smaller the family size, the greater the tendency to detach from organized or institutional religion. Fertility rates provide an effective gauge for religious behavior and commitment, and rapid changes should serve as an alarm bell about incipient secularization and the decline of institutional religion. As I will explain, the term *secularization* oversimplifies the process substantially, but we may let that stand presently.

Of itself, such an idea is not new, and it has been explored to some degree as a causal factor in the dramatic decline of institutional faith in contemporary Western Europe. Recent projections, though, show that European-style rapid declines in fertility are now affecting much of the globe, and that those trends will become ever more marked over the coming decades. That is true whether we look at East Asia or Latin America, or at many Islamic nations. We would thus expect the religious character of those areas to alter—whether that means the decline and contraction of traditional structures, as in Europe itself, or some parallel development in tune with the distinctive traditions of other world faiths. Not just within the Christian world, contemporary religion is incomprehensible without appreciating that demographic dimension—of the shifting makeup and composition of populations.[2]

In recent years, news media have regularly reported the sharp drop in fertility rates within the United States, to levels that are now below those of Scandinavia. That story receives wide coverage, but largely lacking are the religious implications. A great deal of precedent suggests that such a change at long last heralds in this country the kind of secular drift—of secularization—that we associate with Western Europe. If so, the fertility drop is one of the most significant and newsworthy developments in modern American religion.[3]

These bald statements about the relationship between fertility and religious behavior raise critical questions of interpretation. Merely to speak of a correlation between two phenomena says nothing necessarily about causation, but the fact of that linkage offers a valuable interpretive tool, which does have predictive value. If we look at the fertility rate of any society over the past few decades, we can form some likely hypotheses concerning that society and make predictions about how it will develop in the near future. We can make plausible statements about general social conditions—about the status of women or attitudes to family and to specific issues such as homosexuality—but we can also discuss religious conditions, concerning the state of organized religion in that society, or the status of clergy and religious professionals. Our deductions will not be infallible, and some exceptional societies demand detailed analysis and discussion, but in the great majority of cases, our assertions will prove broadly correct. In studying religious developments, demographic change is a bellwether statistic. To that extent God is (and always has been) in the numbers. Or, to adapt the celebrated maxim of Auguste Comte, in the realm of religion, demography is indeed destiny.[4]

A world with the very low fertility rates that we are now observing is almost historically unprecedented—not wholly, but earlier examples are few. But although this is uncharted territory, we can reasonably project that such a low-fertility world will offer a deeply inhospitable environment for institutional religion and for many traditional approaches to religion itself. That does not of itself supply any kind of death warrant for the great religions, either in Europe or beyond, or for supernatural faith as such. Rather, in order to accommodate to new social trends, religions have to evolve new means of presenting their views, to address and accommodate societies where large families with abundant children are no longer the norm and where concepts of "family" are in flux. Of necessity, and in many different ways, those institutions will develop different emphases concerning morality and sexuality, gender and family, and also about the relative roles of clergy and laity in the institutional structures of a given faith. Demographic change is creating wholly new social and religious conditions. Institutions or faiths that hope to succeed and survive have no option but to take account of them and to adapt, accordingly.

Measuring Fertility

Central to these changes is the question of fertility, a factor that can be measured in different ways. The General Fertility Rate (GFR) counts the number of live births per thousand women of reproductive age in a population each year. That reproductive age is defined as 15–44 years (or sometimes 15–49). In the contemporary United States, the GFR is about sixty births per thousand women aged 15 to 44—which is, as I will discuss, significantly down from what it was half a century ago. Much more commonly cited for international comparisons is the Total Fertility Rate (TFR), which is what I will chiefly be using here. The TFR measures the average number of children who would be born to a woman over her lifetime, assuming that she survives to the end of her reproductive life. To take some examples, France's TFR is presently 2.06, while Egypt's is 3.5. In West Africa, the figure for Burkina Faso is 5.7.[5]

At that point, an obvious question should arise, namely how do we actually know how a woman's record of childbearing at the present day can be used to predict her behavior over the whole span of her fertile years? The answer is that we do not know this exactly, but we can make projections with fair confidence. Theoretically, if we want to know about the lifetime fertility of women who are sexually active today, the only way to be certain is to wait until after they have finished their childbearing years, which might mean in twenty years' time. But because fertility issues are so significant for the present day, we have to use some method to obtain a snapshot of behavior at any given time. Demographers thus take the number of women who bore a child in the previous year, then distribute the proportion of women according to their age. Based on what we know from that society, we can then make plausible predictions about those women over their life span and the number of children they will bear in all. The TFR is thus a synthetic figure. Like many social statistics, it involves a measure of extrapolation and projection, and there will be errors, particularly if a large cohort of women suddenly changes its behavior—for instance, to having children significantly earlier or later in life. This can produce misleading impressions of a baby boom, or bust. Generally, the TFR is an excellent guide to trends, and it offers a solid basis for international comparisons.[6]

The Great Change

By itself, the fertility rate does not determine a country's population, but it does have vital consequences, both in terms of the overall size of the population and (scarcely less important) its age distribution. If that TFR figure for a particular country is around 2.1 children per woman (roughly the present French situation), then the population will remain broadly stable, and that level is termed *replacement rate*. If the rate is much higher than that, say 4 or 5 per woman, then we will see an expanding population with many young people and young adults, with all the restlessness and turbulence that suggests. A fertility rate below 2.1—what we call *sub-replacement*—results in a contracting population and an aging society.[7]

The contrast might be illustrated by taking two countries that stand at opposite ends of the spectrum of behavior and that offer wildly different models of possible demographic worlds. In contemporary Germany, which has a sub-replacement TFR of 1.6, the median age of the population is 47.4. In central Africa, Uganda's TFR is 5.8, and the median age is 15.9. Uganda has an extremely young population, with 48 percent of the people aged 14 or younger; the comparable figure for Germany is under 13 percent. One particular number that social scientists pay attention to is the proportion of the population who are teenagers or young adults, aged between 15 and 24—a stage of life often associated with unrest and, sometimes, violence. When that figure for any given society is much over 15 percent or so, demographers speak of a *youth bulge* and expect that fact to be manifested in various forms of conflict, instability, or economic strains. The Ugandan figure is 21 percent, compared to below 10 percent in Germany. At the other end of the scale, 22 percent of Germans are aged over 65, as against 2 percent in Uganda. However crude the raw numbers, they suggest a great deal about the respective societies, not least about the demands on government and the relative importance of one's family in supplying essential needs. These are very different social worlds. For some decades, demographers have explored these divergent models as ideal types, respectively named Fertilia and Sterilia; but real examples are not hard to find.[8]

Over the span of history, fertility rates can rise or fall, but in modern times—mainly since the 1960s—they have fallen noticeably. In this regard, the present German situation has become typical of much of the advanced world. When the fertility decline first attracted serious notice in the 1960s, the illustrations used to describe it were usually Scandinavian societies like Denmark, although later years have shown that these would not in fact be the most extreme examples of change. Denmark's TFR fell from 2.67 in 1963 to just 1.38 by 1983, although it has now recovered to 1.71. Such an apparent rebound is a little misleading in that much of the growth is found among newer immigrant communities, while the fertility of old-stock residents continues to be very low. In the economically advanced nations of the Organisation for Economic Co-operation and Development (OECD), the average TFR is now 1.7, down from 2.7 in 1970.[9]

Japan offers an extreme example of the process at work. Since 1960, Japan's TFR fell from 2.0 to bottom out at 1.25 in 2005, before rebounding to its present rate of 1.4. Even with that limited recovery, such a rate betokens a dramatic rise in the country's average age. The median age of Japan's population is 47.7, the highest in the world with the exception of the tiny European principality of Monaco. By some estimates, the country's population over the next thirty years could drop from its present 127 million to below 100 million. To put that in perspective, as recently as 2002, Japan and Nigeria both had a similar population size, of around 130 million. By 2050 Japanese numbers will have fallen to at most 100 million, while Nigeria's will have ballooned to over 400 million.[10]

Demographic Transitions

Social scientists have long understood the demographic effects of industrialization and economic progress, which promote a shift away from high death rates and high fertility. As far back as 1929, the idea of such a demographic transition was formulated by American scholar Warren Thompson, and the theory has been substantially developed in later years. Today that demographic transition is one of the most commonly used concepts in the study of populations. Since the 1980s the fast-accelerating rate of change in family structures and sexual attitudes has led scholars to speak of a Second Demographic Transition, at least as dramatic as the first, and with consequences far beyond the old developed world. So standard has the concept become in recent years that it has acquired its own familiar acronym, SDT.[11]

What was not immediately clear was how the economically advanced societies that pioneered the demographic transition stood in relation to the rest of the world, which remained far less developed. In the 1960s and 1970s, commentators were alarmed by the growing demographic gulf between low- and high-fertility societies—between richer and poorer parts of the world. Many warned of a population explosion, the seemingly uncontrollable rise in the populations of poor and (then) undeveloped nations like India, Mexico, or Uganda. Western stereotypes imagined those "Third World" nations in terms of teeming legions of starving children and famished cities, and the racist undertones of the analysis were often thinly disguised. In a notorious work of fantasy fiction, *The Camp of the Saints* (1973), Jean Raspail imagined those beggarly South Asian masses pouring west to swamp and conquer the white world in an apocalyptic act of judgment and vengeance. That book has subsequently become something like a sacred text for the racist Right and for anti-immigration campaigners. So evident was the threat to planetary security that when the Vatican pronounced against artificial contraception in 1968, liberals and secularists widely criticized the decision as something like an act of treason against the human race. In 1989 the United Nations instituted World Population Day to raise awareness of continuing population growth.[12]

But the spread of low-fertility patterns worldwide makes such images now look almost ludicrously outdated. Since 1970 Mexico's TFR has fallen from almost 7 children per woman to 2.2—in other words, to just above replacement. In the same years, Vietnam's rate fell from 6.4 to 1.9, Indonesia's from 5.4 to 2.3, and India's from 5.5 to 2.3. South Korea's fell quite spectacularly from 4.5 to just under 1.0, which is one of the lowest figures on the planet. The change is still more marked in some regions within countries. Around half the states of India presently have TFRs below replacement rate, and such populous and influential states as Punjab and West Bengal have fertility rates below Denmark's. Most observers think that these recent plunges will continue over the next decade or two, to spread something like what are presently German demographic conditions around much of the non-European world. To put all this in context, I have noted how nervously Europeans in the 1960s viewed the explosive fertility rates of many Asian countries. Today, however, those same so-called Third World countries have TFRs that are actually lower than the European nations did in that earlier era, often by a sizable margin. One problem for anyone seeking to write about this process is that in many countries, rates are falling so fast that it is difficult to keep up with the latest numbers.[13]

Looking broadly at the continents of Africa, Asia, and Latin America, some regions do indeed still have very high fertility rates—Uganda and

Burkina Faso are examples—but many others do not. Moreover, different areas vary enormously in their degree of prosperity and economic development. In demographic terms at least, the whole Third World notion is obsolete, and only somewhat more valuable is the less judgmental successor to that concept, the Global South.

New Worlds

The reasons for the fertility decline are complex and will only be sketched here. (I will discuss these topics at greater length in chapter 2.) As we will see, changes in birth rates and mortality rates both play a role, especially rates of infant mortality, and the interactions between these various factors make it hard to determine an exact path of causation. Throughout these transformations, it is all but impossible to determine the relative role played by social and ideological factors: changes in society and the economy created new ideological attitudes, which in turn drove new social revolutions. Beyond the general levels of wealth in a given society, technology and medicine are both critical.

The most obvious change involves the status of women in any given society and the life chances available to them. So many of the changes that I will describe here form part of a global gender revolution, a move toward broad gender equity that constitutes a sweeping transformation of social attitudes and relationships. To appreciate this imagine a preindustrial or premodern society in which young women have few available opportunities in the form of higher education or a career. The prospect of early death also makes it imperative that women begin their reproductive life early, so that they can have a realistic prospect of seeing their children reach adulthood. They begin bearing children in their teens and might well bear six or eight over their life span. That is all the more probable if the technological and legal environment restricts ways of limiting fertility. In Western Europe or North America, that older pattern was revolutionized even before the twentieth century. Gender roles were further transformed by the growing availability of contraceptives that were both effective and easy to use and that gave women the decisive say in deploying them. In the United States, the "Pill" was approved for contraceptive use in 1960, and thereafter it became widely popular around the world. Economics played its role, with the rapid growth of service sectors as the most developed societies moved toward a mature postindustrial economy. Opportunities for women's employment grew dramatically, as did female participation in higher education. Time and again, we will encounter those three closely linked drivers of change: women's education, women's employment, and contraception.[14]

With new aspirations and opportunities in life, with a new commitment to education and career, women determined to postpone childbearing until later in life or even to forego parenthood altogether. A woman who postpones childbearing until her mid-thirties or later is unlikely to begin a large family on anything like the older model. New social attitudes also meant declining disapproval of couples who chose to live together outside traditional structures of marriage and family, with or without children. For large sections of the population, founding a family and raising children ceased to be the central and defining goal of life, and were replaced by other concepts of personal and career fulfillment. The demographic revolution is above all a gender revolution. When scholars study the Second Demographic Transition in a particular region or nation, they measure crucial trends such as female participation in the labor force, rises in premarital cohabitation and the number of children born to cohabiting couples, and the postponement of both marriage and parenthood. Gradually such changes have spread beyond the traditionally developed world, to transform new lands, and they are continuing to do so.[15]

Whatever their origins, those demographic changes have vast consequences. Just to take Japan as an example, that country's workforce could by 2040 be 20 percent smaller than it is today, and a falling number of taxpayers will be available to support the needs of a fast-growing population of retired elderly people. An aging population and a scarcity of children echo through the whole economy. They determine how businesses market goods and services, how they build and furnish apartments or houses, how they organize public transportation. Demographic change correlates with shifts in mores and attitudes—although the direction of causation is open to discussion. A society that moves away from traditional views of the child-centered nuclear family is likely to be open to nontraditional views of sexual behavior and the rights of sexual minorities. Seemingly eternal and inevitable structures of family, gender, and sexuality are all in flux.[16]

Religious Impact

Each of these changes has its impact on religious structures and behavior, and migration offers one powerful example. When a society makes the decisive move to sub-replacement fertility, it faces pressing needs for labor, which is commonly imported from poorer high-fertility nations, often far afield. But despite its strictly economic motivations, that immigration cannot fail to have broad cultural effects. It often serves to spread particular forms of religion, by importing new faith traditions, or new denominations, into a society where they did not exist before. We naturally think of the new Islamic presence in post-1960s Europe, but new Christian communities have also established themselves across the continent. Less noticed than the European story, a similar process has brought sizable Christian populations into the Arab Gulf nations that not long since were almost monolithically Muslim. In all these cases, migrants often return to their home countries, whether temporarily or permanently, and they bring with them the religious ideas and attitudes of those wealthier and more advanced nations. That further accelerates the process of religious cross-pollination and of globalization. If we just consider migration alone, demographic change drives religious transformations.[17]

But the demographic impact is much more extensive and more pervasive. In whatever era we are considering, the history of religion and religious change has to take account of issues of demography. Depending on its demographic character, a society might have a high or low birth rate; its members might expect a long or short lifespan; people might be prone to disease or unusually healthy. A society might be homogeneous in terms of race, ethnicity, and language or very diverse. Any or all of these issues have wider effects in terms of the stability of a particular society, the rate of social change, and the concentration of settlement and urbanization. Such factors can change over time, often quite swiftly. Whatever its exact demographic profile, those features have a profound effect on religion, in shaping the audiences that are available for particular messages and approaches. As many scholars have noted, religious behavior can usefully be explored through the analogy of a marketplace, in which suppliers and providers succeed or fail depending on how far they take account of shifting patterns of consumption and consumer tastes. This applies to the kind of religious faith that gains the most followers, the means by which it is practiced, and the most popular forms of religiosity and devotion.[18]

A society with a great many teenagers and young adults—a youth bulge—offers particular opportunities to revivalist and evangelistic movements preaching a fiery, enthusiastic faith. An older, more stable society has quite different needs and interests. Cities, again, offer opportunities and challenges quite different from those of villages and small towns, and that is especially true when those cities are growing quickly. Changes in the role and autonomy of women offer particular challenges and opportunities for religious institutions. A substantial scientific literature now amply confirms that women are more religious than men, and that distinction holds good across societies, so that any loss of female adherents has a uniquely damaging effect on a church or institution. Wise religious organizations tailor their activities and rhetoric to the communities that they have to deal with, and if they do not do so effectively, they will lose influence to newer and more efficient rivals who have a better sense of audience and marketplace. Demographics shape religious life and behavior, and they always have.[19]

In the modern context, we repeatedly find a potent correlation between fertility and faith, so that a list of the world's nations by fertility rates will be very similar to a ranking of countries by their degree of religious belief and behavior. To say that Denmark (for example) is at once a low-fertility and a low-faith society is to make an interesting observation, just as it is to point out that Nigeria represents very high fertility, and intense faith, expressed in different traditions. But when such correlations occur frequently and examples accumulate, it is probable that we are dealing with a real relationship between the two elements.

A society that falls significantly below replacement rates is likely to face a steep decline in institutional religious forms, and often of religiosity more generally. As is well known, the low-fertility societies of Europe also rank at the bottom of any listing of countries in terms of religious commitment and belief. A change in one of those elements, demographic or religious, will be followed by a development in the other. Historically, the European shift toward very low fertility from the 1960s onward coincides exactly with the precipitous drop in religious behavior in those same years, and both patterns spread together to new regions of the continent. More recently we observe the twin shifts occurring in many different parts of the world, beyond Europe. The accumulation of evidence strongly suggests that demographic transitions also mark religious transformations—that fertility and faith travel together.[20]

Causation and Correlation

Such a statement raises well-known questions about identifying the chain of causation, a problem familiar to anyone who ever took an introductory statistics class. If two trends follow each other closely on a graph, we can interpret their relationship in various ways. Perhaps trend A is influencing and driving trend B; or else B is influencing A; or else both A and B are both driven by another factor, C. Alternatively, perhaps the apparent linkage between A and B is coincidental, and there is no linkage whatever. That final explanation becomes ever less likely as we find more and more examples of the two trends running together, in multiple different settings and eras. That then leaves us with the three basic narratives about causation.

In the contemporary context, we can see several possible reasons why lower fertility rates should be connected to declining religiosity. I discuss these factors at greater length in chapter 3 but will sketch them briefly here.

One path of explanation suggests that religiosity declines first, and that then leads to declining fertility and smaller families. As is commonly noted, larger families do tend to be more connected to religious institutions and more committed to religious practice. Perhaps conservative and traditionalist believers tend to be more family oriented, more committed to continuity and posterity, and thus they have more children; or else people in large families tend to be more conservative, more vested in traditional religious faith. To take one example of many, one American study described the completed fertility of women in their forties in the period 2013–2015, and that was based on the actual number of children born in their lives, rather than any projections or estimates. The religious conclusion was clear. The rate for fundamentalist Protestants was 2.6 children per woman, with Catholics at 2.2 and mainline Protestants at 2.0. Those of "no religion" had a rate of 1.5. Again, if this was one isolated example, it would be a suggestive tidbit, but it is not: such findings are commonplace (although in recent years, even these once solidly rooted assumptions might finally be changing). Indeed, the association between conservative or traditionalist religion and high fertility is often used to explain the relative success of conservative denominations in modern U.S. history, at the expense of liberal mainliners. What separates the winners and losers in the religious economy is not the soundness of their theology but their fertility rates.[21] But now let us imagine conditions changing so that levels of religious belief decline and the number of people with no religion grows; then we would naturally expect a consequent fall in fertility.

Alternatively, we might suggest that fertility declines first and that this has its impact on religiosity. We note for example that smaller families reduce their ties to organized religious institutions, as there are simply fewer children to put through religious school and First Communion classes, or the equivalent training and socialization that exists in other religions. As religious ties diminish, ordinary people increasingly define their values in individualistic and secular terms, and are more willing to oppose churches or religious institutions on social and political issues of gender and morality. Even in once solidly Catholic countries, we see the advance of contraception, abortion, and same-sex marriage, and a precipitous decline in church attendance and participation. In many nations the decline in fertility correlates neatly to the fast-growing acceptance of the practice of same-sex marriage, which was a near-unthinkable concept just a few decades ago. Around the world we regularly see a dependable pattern: as fertility rates fall, so gay rights grow.

But it is scarcely necessary to determine an exact sequence of change, as the two factors, fertility and religiosity, work so closely together, and developments occur within a short time span. We might imagine a community that becomes increasingly detached from traditional religious-based concepts of gender roles. That reduces the ideological pressure to define one's role in terms of family, parenthood, and posterity. As women become emancipated from familiar roles, they become more deeply involved in the workforce and do not have time to contemplate the large families of their mothers' generation. That in turn reduces ties to religious institutions. A shift to lower fertility encourages declining religiosity, which in turn would discourage religious enthusiasm, and so on, in a kind of feedback loop. The two factors—family size and religiosity—work intimately together in ways that are difficult to disentangle. If the correlation between fertility and faith is strong and easily demonstrated, the precise nature of causation is not so clear, nor need it be.

As I have remarked, any discussion of fertility rates also has to take account of mortality. The fertility transition involves birth and death rates changing more or less simultaneously, with infant mortality an excellent gauge of the shift in process. Again, these trends are inextricable and interdependent, but they are also essential to understanding religious change. As advanced societies no longer live in the midst of death—at least, in the constant presence of visible and frequent death—so their attitudes to life and the afterlife are both in transition. Again, I will discuss this at greater length in chapter 3.

In Search of Security

Changes in both fertility and faith might be driven by an additional factor—the element C from my sketch above—which we can term a sense of existential security, both individual and collective. (I am here drawing on the crucial work of social scientists Pippa Norris and Ronald Inglehart.) As societies become more advanced and economically sophisticated, ordinary people benefit from greater stability, improving medicine, and a better social safety net. Reinforcing and globalizing these trends are critical changes in technology, which open new employment opportunities and offer easy access to effective contraception. Among other things, this new world allows families to be more confident that children they have are likely to grow to healthy adulthood. Accordingly, they no longer face the need to have many children to contribute labor to subsistence economic activities and to support them in old age. Of themselves security and stability tend to reduce fertility.[22]

At the same time, those same factors undermine many of the attractions of religion. Just to take one factor, a medically advanced society is much less likely to be afflicted by endemic diseases and ill health of the kind that so often inspires religions based on healing. In modern societies, such miracles become unnecessary and obsolete. This does not mean that healing churches or sects are unknown in advanced societies, but they occupy a far smaller part of the spectrum of religious behavior. Often, too, such modern healing movements focus not on obvious material complaints but on the healing of psychological conditions or personal failings. That move away from the healing role of religion is a historic shift. Indeed, in counting the key figures whose work massively reduced the appeal of religion, we should probably pay less attention to Marx, Freud, or Darwin than to Louis Pasteur, for his pioneer work in medical innovation and the germ theory. Similarly, a state with a sophisticated social welfare system is far less troubled by extreme and widespread poverty or by life-threatening hunger. No longer do religious institutions occupy a key role as the faces of the charitable endeavors that keep people alive. Doctors, states, and social workers appropriate many of the functions long held to be the terrain reserved for clergy and holy people.

To appreciate the power of these security factors, we need only imagine a society where they are conspicuously absent, a society marked by pervasive poverty and deprivation, by widespread diseases and ill health, and by social turmoil. In such communities, economic structures offer little role for women beyond the most basic forms of physical labor, and they will bear and raise many children. As we will note in many cases in Africa and the Middle East, a very fertile society is likely to experience endemic conflict, partly because it is unable to cope with its cohort of young adults. The longer such conflicts last, the harder it is for that country to make the kind of economic progress that will provide jobs for women, and that in turn reinforces the patterns that produce and sustain high fertility. It is not hard to see how existential insecurity would be associated with high fertility and with high levels of faith.

The argument linking religion to security undoubtedly has much to recommend it, and I will often have occasion to return to these general themes. At the same time, we cannot simply draw a deterministic link between levels of prosperity and technological sophistication and the decline of religion. If that were true, then (for example) the United States would have led the way in secularization over the past century, rather than being long celebrated for its stubbornly high degree of faith and religious expression, not least in politics. That may well be changing in recent years, but even if it is, the long delay raises serious questions about any neat equations we might construct. So do other examples from different parts of the globe. Economic change always has to be considered in the context of cultural developments.

Shifting Frontiers

The consequences of the fertility/faith revolution are open to debate. At first sight so much about the low-fertility scenario is attractive, even utopian, and the spread of Western models worldwide could presage a global decline in extreme poverty and immiseration. Ideally we are imagining societies that are far more prosperous and healthier than any of their predecessors, more equal in terms of gender, more secular, and above all, more stable. We would generally see a diminution of factors making for aggression and violence, and for some traditional expressions of masculinity. Ideally too, a society with a dearth of young adults would likely be more careful about engaging in military conflicts, at least in ways that threatened mass casualties. Domestic political violence also becomes less likely when there are fewer young adults to fight for causes. An eventual lowering of population levels would reduce the strain on global resources and even limit damage to the climate. Taken together the scenario sounds like a real-world rendering of John Lennon's song "Imagine," with its total absence of any religious dimension: above us, only sky. Religious believers might even face the dilemma of whether the near extinction of their faiths is a reasonable price to pay for so much evident improvement in the living conditions of the hitherto impoverished. In fact, anyone who objected to such a scenario would face an obvious question: What do they not like about the new world, the peace, the health, or the prosperity?

But problems are also apparent, and it remains open to question just how long a sub-replacement-fertility society can remain economically viable. If commentators of the 1960s panicked about the thronging cohorts of children and young adults pouring forth from the Third World, modern-day observers are much more concerned about the menace to social services and care facilities posed by many millions of the old and very old, with all that implies for fiscal well-being. Such problems are already evident in Japan, as in much of Europe. Some writers have spoken of Europe's demographic future as a "geriatric peace." This is a highly ambiguous concept that at once points to the virtues of stability while warning of stagnation and weakness.[23] For all its prosperity, all the measures of the health and longevity of its people—unimaginably high by the standard of previous generations—contemporary Western Europe still falls far short of a Utopia.

At the same time, rapid demographic change of the kind I am describing opens the way to multiple conflicts of varying degrees of severity, to tensions both domestic and international. The problem lies not in the fact of demographic change but in its patchy and sporadic nature. Differential rates of change can create profound imbalances and tensions, and even result in violence. A comment attributed to esteemed science fiction author William Gibson observes that "the future is already here. It's just not very evenly distributed," and that caveat applies strongly to demographic realities.[24] If the great fertility shift will eventually transform the whole world, it has not done so yet. It would be convenient if all societies in the world shared identical demographic trends, but they do not. Besides the regions of declining fertility, many other parts of the world retain very high fertility patterns and the demographics we traditionally think of as Third World, as in Uganda. In the vast Democratic Republic of the Congo, the TFR today stands much where it did in 1960, at over 6 children per woman. Such societies are characterized by strong religiosity, sternly traditional gender roles, and (often) sharply defined concepts of masculinity and honor. Those societies also tend to be more turbulent and unstable, with weak states and high levels of violence. Although such countries will presumably pass through the demographic transition and fertility decline, it could be several decades before this happens.

Such international disparities would matter less in a world of poorer transportation and communication, lacking the globalization that is now so advanced. If Europe (say) has definitively made the transition to a new social and demographic world, then large portions of North Africa and the Near East have not. In terms of social realities, that is a world decades or centuries removed from modern Europe, but only a few hundred miles in geographical distance. People literally can walk and sail from Syria or Burkina Faso to Germany, and a great many have done just this in the refugee wave of recent years. Those refugees share demographic patterns, and the associated values, radically different from those of the host nations, and culture clashes are inevitable. Commonly, those differences take the form of religious identities and resentments.

Something like the European refugee crisis is an extreme event, but other less spectacular outbreaks can cause tensions between very different demographic worlds. In many countries the high fertility pattern and strong religiosity of new immigrant populations set them apart from old-stock communities. Disparities that emerge often take a mild form, but they can become severe. Differential fertility rates make existing conflicts over race, ethnicity, and identity still more acute, adding a poisonous new element of generational resentment. Nor is this a simple story of Muslims from an older demographic world confronting a socially advanced Christian or post-Christian Europe. In terms of demographic patterns and religious outlook, Global South Christians are in many ways more akin to their Muslim neighbors than their European coreligionists.[25]

Also, demographic decline is by no means a straight-line uniform process, even within a single country, and it can affect communities to different degrees. Around the world many nations are divided between high- and low-fertility areas, with different communities having very disparate levels of access to wealth and education. Those distinctions might be geographical, dividing regions, or they might divide classes living in near physical proximity. Generally, the low-fertility communities tend to be wealthier and more economically developed, and more secular; their high-fertility compatriots are poorer and more religious. So stark are divisions between different communities as to make them appear almost like rival societies, if not competing nations. In recent years, populist and sometimes authoritarian regimes have emerged in various nations, basing their power in socially conservative regions, or populations marked by high fertility and high faith: Turkey and India are conspicuous examples (see chapter 8 below).

The world will not, therefore, evolve neatly and homogeneously into an idyllic secular society of low fertility and low tension, but nor will it be partitioned neatly between high- and low-fertility societies, between old and new world orders. There will be constant adjustments and evolutions, as the shifting fault lines between societies and religious outlooks mark the borderlands of conflict. Aggression, violence, and tension are to be found in the essence of neither the old world nor the new, but along the constantly fluctuating boundaries between the two. Those boundaries divide continents, nations, and regions. When old and new social orders do come into conflict, their struggles are expressed in a common currency of very contemporary technologies and social media. The old world fights with very new weapons. In demographic and cultural terms, the world is anything but flat.

Scholarship

This present book is certainly not the first to propose a linkage between demographic change and religious behavior, but it is unusual in exploring it systematically and on a global scale. Few observers have explored the implications of fertility decline that run across confessional lines. If Western Christians are indeed suffering the effects of demographic change, then so in their various ways are Muslims, Buddhists, and others.

Popular accounts of demographic change tend to doomsaying, and occasionally to the apocalyptic. When authors do address the religious side of matters, it is usually with the assumption that a sharply declining Judeo-Christian West confronts a high-fertility outside world—whether that means the Third World or, often, the world of Islam—and the potential for polemic is troublingly high. This was true of the population explosion literature of an earlier generation, and some of the contemporary literature of fertility decline faces similar problems. Such trends—whether upward or downward—offer a rich vein of rhetorical themes for commentators and moralists, who can use the processes they describe to blame a range of human failings and foibles. If fertility is declining, then this must indicate that people are selfish, materialistic, and hedonistic, unwilling to serve the needs of their nation or society, and likely that women (or men) have lost a sense of their proper role in life. Such critiques are not new. As far back as the second century BC, the Greek historian Polybius described what he believed to be a move to sub-replacement fertility, and he complained, "For as men had fallen into such a state of pretentiousness, avarice, and indolence that they did not wish to marry, or if they married to rear the children born to them, or at most as a rule but one or two of them, so as to leave these in affluence and bring them up to waste their substance, the evil rapidly and insensibly grew." In different forms such rhetoric is familiar today.[26]

Since the 1960s changes in population and fertility have attracted many authors and inspired popular fiction. For many years *overpopulation* inspired widespread fears of famine and social collapse, on the lines originally proposed by Thomas Malthus in the eighteenth century. That core idea of soaring population outstripping resources supplied the foundation for Paul Ehrlich's 1968 work *The Population Bomb*. Such ideas in turn inspired many apocalyptic science fiction novels, the theme of which is neatly summarized by the title of Harry Harrison's *Make Room! Make Room!* (1966). That in turn supplied the basis for the dystopian 1973 film *Soylent Green*, which imagined an agonizingly overpopulated world driven to surreptitious cannibalism. Such visions suffered from the common habit of taking a contemporary trend and extrapolating it as if it would go on unchecked, ad infinitum, which is improbable.[27]

A subset of this literature involved the disparity between the global population explosion and the increasingly apparent fertility decline in advanced countries—what Ben Wattenberg in 1987 called the "birth dearth." That theme long occupied center stage in jeremiads on contemporary Europe, where issues of religion are so critical. Many books and magazine articles focused on the disparity between old-stock populations (white and notionally Christian) and newer immigrants (mainly Muslim) and the Islamic countries from which they derived. In the grimmest and most polemical visions, demographic change thus lay the foundation for an Islamization of Europe, the creation of a dystopian Eurabia. Conservative critics regularly placed the blame for such a prospect on the lack of will or self-confidence that supposedly beset Christians and other Westerners, which led directly to their reproductive failures, a kind of white Christian suicide. That scenario envisaged religious change as one component of a larger racial nightmare.[28]

By the end of the century, both scholars and social observers went beyond the specific dilemmas of Europe as they became keenly aware of global fertility decline, or indeed a population implosion. Again, popular writers and novelists were vital to popularizing the underlying ideas. In 1985 Margaret Atwood used the prospect of a worldwide collapse of fertility to imagine a radically different kind of dystopia in her novel *The Handmaid's Tale*. Women's personal and political rights are extinguished in order to restore the birth rate and preserve the species. In 1992, in *The Children of Men*, P. D. James likewise explored the consequences of populations collapsing due to mass infertility, to the point of presaging the possible extinction of humanity. That in turn became a landmark film in 2006. Although *The Children of Men* was not the first popular book to treat such themes, the title established itself in popular culture to express these ideas at their most extreme.[29]

More recently visions of a baby bust have been addressed by many strictly respectable outlets, journalistic and technical, and quite apart from any racial concerns. Since 2005 books on this theme have proliferated almost as abundantly as the "explosion" literature of half a century ago. Some recent accounts include Fred Pearce's *The Coming Population Crash* and Phillip Longman's *The Empty Cradle*. Darrell Bricker and John Ibbitson have provocatively envisaged an *Empty Planet*, resulting from *The Shock of Global Population Decline*. Particularly unnerving were the consequences for the age profiles of low-fertility nations, and the prospect of a general graying. In his book *Shock of Gray*, Ted C. Fishman comprehensively discussed *The Aging of the World's Population and How It Pits Young against Old, Child against Parent, Worker against Boss, Company against Rival and Nation against Nation*. Jonathan V. Last epitomized the task of projecting a low-fertility future with the evocative title of his 2013 book *What to Expect When No One's Expecting*. Several authors have explored the implications of the fertility change for military arrangements and for the future structure of international conflicts.[30]

But if the idea of a graying (or even empty) planet is not new and has even become established in mainstream discourse, the religious side of that demographic story has received short shrift (with the exception of the Islamization nightmares). Social scientists studying the Second Demographic Transition do indeed pay attention to secularization, but scholars of religion scarcely repay the compliment. The proliferating library of books on secularization tackles the subject from a wide variety of angles, including social, political, and philosophical; the theme of demography features very rarely. A handful of really distinguished authors stand out as exceptions to that statement, namely Callum Brown, Mary Eberstadt, David Goldman, and Eric Kaufmann.[31]

Brown's most significant contribution was his 2012 book *Religion and the Demographic Revolution*, which centrally (and incontestably) emphasized the role of women in the ongoing transitions in fertility and secularization. He likewise pays due attention to the role of the sexual revolutions from the 1960s onward. The book remains a touchstone for thinking about the topic. Its focus was however limited to four specific nations—the United States, Canada, Britain, and Ireland—leaving abundant room for discussion of the truly global scale on which these trends have developed. Also, both demographic and religious trends have developed and accelerated so much even in the quite brief intervening years that a great deal of new observation and analysis remains to be added to Brown's work.[32]

In 2013 Mary Eberstadt powerfully addressed the role of shrinking family size in secularization, in the story of *How the West Really Lost God.* Even so, I will disagree with her suggestion that the changes she describes are effectively confined to the Euro-American world. As I will show, those trends are global, and their effects will run far beyond Western Christianity.[33]

Another significant author is David Goldman, long famous as the exceedingly well-informed journalist and commentator "Spengler." Goldman writes forcefully about the impact of demographic decline as a force subverting civilizations and cultures, and his book *How Civilizations Die* features chapters with titles like "Faith, Fertility and the World's Future." Very unusually among commentators, Goldman tracks the demographic contraction within the Islamic world: "The Closing of the Muslim Womb." Where I differ from him is in the wider relationship between demography and religion, and in issues of causation. Appropriately enough, given the pen name Spengler, he attributes the fertility decline to a metaphysical loss of faith in civilization, whereas I look to more specific changes in attitudes to gender and sexuality and to work and employment.[34]

The other influential scholar who acutely addresses issues of demography, religion, and politics is Eric Kaufmann, author of (among other works) *Shall the Religious Inherit the Earth?* Kaufmann presents a sophisticated and well-argued thesis. While acknowledging the steep declines in fertility worldwide, he suggests that this trend will in the long run produce a much more actively religious world. Yes, he says, secular households will have few children, but they will be outnumbered by highly religious families who will continue to have large numbers of offspring. That process is best exemplified by the amazing growth of Orthodox and ultra-Orthodox communities among Jewish populations both within the nation of Israel and worldwide. Traditionalist Catholic families follow quite similar patterns, as do some Mormons. Making such a distinction is a vital contribution to the argument, but it does involve some difficulties on a global scale, not least that nations and communities that currently have very high fertility tend to change swiftly in the opposite direction—and indeed, that trend has become increasingly evident just over the past decade. If some specific highly religious communities currently hold out against the general trend, then this resistance may be at best temporary and might last for a generation or so. It will not detract from long-term declines in institutional faith and in some areas, from outright secularization.[35]

But for any caveats I might make about specific points, such scholars must be recognized for their pioneering analyses of demographic trends that must be treated much more centrally in any projections of future realities. That is true above all of any considerations of the future of faith and of particular faiths.

The Book

Part I of *Fertility and Faith* describes how the demographic revolution that began in Europe transformed religious faith and practice worldwide.

Already in the 1960s, scholars were noting the steep declines in fertility rates in Europe, changes that were all the more marked coming as they did so soon after the baby boom of the post–World War II era. In retrospect, we can now see that European trend as the opening stage of a critically important demographic revolution—the Second Demographic Transition—which forms the theme of *chapter 2*.

That demographic change coincided with a marked decline in religious behavior and institutional structures, indeed, a collapse of religious practice across much of the continent. The intimate relationship between these two trends, religious and demographic, is described in *chapter 3*, in which we will also seek more precise definitions of secularization. If demography does not offer a complete account of Europe's religious transformations over the past half century, then it is an essential component of the story that we neglect at our peril. In many instances demographic change was accompanied by new concepts of identity, by the politics of the personal, with the attendant controversies over morality and sexuality—struggles that are fought along generational lines. Perversely, weakening religious behavior can be accompanied by a growing ferocity of culture war politics.

Initially those European trends appeared to be strongly localized and distinctive, but by the end of the century, they were manifesting around the world. European and even "Danish" conditions became widespread, originally in the fast-modernizing boom nations of the Pacific Rim, but then more widely, across South Asia and Latin America. Clearly, the transition was no simple diffusion of European or Western ways—a simplistic "Westernization"—but was rather a worldwide convergence owing to similar economic changes. *Chapter 4* describes this global transformation, and especially its impact on religion. As in Europe, fertility declines in Asia and Latin America have been reliably followed by sweeping religious changes, as religious institutions have faced growing crises.

In all the global discussions of fertility and secularization, one very prominent exception long appeared to challenge most hypotheses, and that was the United States—an advanced and wealthy nation that was nevertheless marked by high fertility and strong religiosity. Recent developments, though, show the United States synchronizing with global norms in matters of both fertility and faith, a trend discussed in *chapter 5*. If that interpretation is correct, that could well portend the secularization that scholars have long expected in the United States, but which (by some views) has been so unaccountably delayed.

Part II of the book explores how contemporary global politics are shaped by conflicts between regions of high and low fertility, with their attendant religious patterns. Many of these tensions arise from developments proceeding at unequal rates in different regions and nations. To adapt a famous comment made about race, the problem of the twenty-first century is the fertility line.

Although the demographic change has indeed transformed much of the globe, some areas retain stubbornly traditional patterns. As we will see in *chapter 6*, those high-fertility societies remain very religious, and their sharply growing numbers mean that they will occupy an ever-larger share of the world's faithful believers. Africa, above all, will be pivotal to the intertwined futures of both Christianity and Islam. Such high-fertility patterns are especially common in the region that Western policy makers have called the "Arc of Crisis," which stretches from North Africa across the Middle East and into South Asia. These areas represent the antithesis of the pacific and secular trends we have witnessed in Europe. The notorious Arc of Crisis, in fact, looks very much like an Arc of Fertility.

Although Western observers often see the Islamic world as uniform, matters of fertility and family size in fact draw sharp divisions between some countries that are strongly "European" in character and those that are resolutely traditional. Even more surprising, Iran emerges as the setting for an astonishing drop in fertility rates. As recently as 1982, Iran's TFR was around 6.5 children per woman, but today it stands below 1.7, below that of Denmark. Other countries are following suit, even including Saudi

Arabia. *Chapter 7* describes the rapidly growing divisions within "Two Tier Islam" and asks whether the fertility decline in some critical regions might augur a hitherto unexpected secularization.

As remarked earlier, the world is not going through the transition in fertility rates in anything like an even way, a smooth trajectory. We observe enormous disparities between demographic profiles, between neighboring countries, and also within major countries. As we see in *chapter 8*, differential fertility rates within particular nations go far toward explaining some of the thorniest and most troubling situations in the modern world. Through the manipulation of religious symbols and historical ideologies, populist governments draw support from poorer and high-fertility groups, drawing groups together in a common national cause. In their various ways, we can see such patterns at work in Turkey and Russia, and even in such democratic nations as Israel and India.

A concluding *chapter 9* discusses the dilemma of religious institutions and individuals coping with a low-fertility world. How, in fact, can religions cope with a demographic order utterly different from most of human history?

PART I

2

EUROPE'S REVOLUTION

Viewed on a global scale, the growth of Europe has been one of the most important trends in modern history. As the birthplace of modern industrial civilization, Europe's population naturally boomed during the nineteenth century, in both absolute and relative terms. Depending on the exact limit we assign the continent, Europe roughly doubled in population in the nineteenth century, growing from some 200 million people in 1800 to 400 million in 1900 and to 700 million by the start of the new millennium. The figure today is about 740 million. But that growth is not projected to continue. In 2050 there should be somewhat fewer Europeans than there are today, and that number will fall as the century advances. The change is even more marked as a share of overall world population. In 1900 Europeans made up around a quarter of humanity, compared to just 10 percent today, and that proportion will fall in coming decades. That shrinkage has occurred despite the greatly expanded life spans that characterize modern European societies and the substantial numbers of immigrants entering the continent, a pattern that is unlikely to change in coming decades. In terms of the natural growth of its older-stock populations, Europe has for some years ceased to expand and instead has moved to decline and contraction. As we have seen, that reflects a sharp fall in fertility rates from the 1960s onward.

Initially, commentators interpreted these changes as distinctive to Europe, at a time when the continent was undergoing such social turbulence, with a widespread challenge to older assumptions about gender and sexuality. It also seemed likely that the trends were peculiar to Northern Europe, with its

Protestant roots, and would not affect Catholic countries. At the time it was not obvious that the "revolution" was a more general European event, and indeed the harbinger of a global phenomenon. The new society emerging in Europe provided a blueprint that eventually was reproduced, with many local variations, around the world. In retrospect the religious implications of the European story have become ever more evident.[1]

The Long Twentieth Century

At the end of the nineteenth century, most European countries still recorded total fertility rates of around 5.0, a rate equivalent to that of many African countries today. Drawing on such figures, in 1907, commentator Emil Reich extrapolated that the population of the German Empire would grow rapidly from its current level of around 60 million to reach 150 million by 1980 and possibly 200 million by the start of the new century. (The actual modern figure is 83 million, and the 2050 figure might be only 75 million or less.) Such projections gave potent ammunition to advocates of European imperial expansion overseas as the only means to escape the Malthusian population trap. Not just in Germany, old-world demographics coupled with new-world technology to foster serious aggression. At the time this was the demographic nightmare that troubled European leaders and thinkers, but change was not far off.[2]

The Netherlands illustrates the demographic transformation in progress. Through the nineteenth century, the country recorded a TFR of around 5.0, much the same level as Italy or Germany. The Dutch figure fell steadily during the twentieth century, and for some years in the 1930s it dipped below 3.0. During the post–World War II baby boom, the figure touched 3.2, which is actually higher than we would find today in countries like India or Indonesia. But an obvious decline then set in, as the TFR halved between 1962 and 1983. By 1973 the TFR was 2.04, just below replacement, and it bottomed out below 1.5 in the early 1980s. The modern figure is around 1.8. As I noted earlier in the case of Denmark, that recent rebound does not primarily represent a new enthusiasm for parenthood among old-stock Dutch people but rather reflects the presence of major immigrant populations. Fifteen percent of the population trace their background to non-Western countries, chiefly Turkey, Morocco, and Indonesia.[3]

The Dutch case epitomizes the forces at work in Europe at large, with the level of economic development as the major variable. Agricultural societies demanded that families produced multiple children to work and to provide support for parents in old age, a function for which state mechanisms were quite inadequate. Until modern times, also, those societies were deeply vulnerable to seasonal fluctuations and blights, which might cause starvation or subsistence crises, killing vulnerable children. That old world changed dramatically with the expansion of industry and growing urbanization, a surge in agricultural productivity, and the opening of global trade networks. From the late nineteenth century, both birth and death rates generally fell together. In England and Wales, typical life expectancies rose from the low forties in the mid-nineteenth century to over seventy a century later and to over eighty by 2000. In each era women tended to outlive men by a few years.[4]

Declining infant mortality rates were particularly significant, and as we will see, these correlate closely to overall fertility rates (the rate tracks the number of deaths before the age of 1 year). Falling infant mortality meant that families did not have to produce several children in the hope that one or two might survive. In 1900 Scandinavian countries were still recording infant mortality rates of 100 per thousand live births, compared to an appalling 200 or more in Germany or Austria. Rates then began to tumble generally, with improvements in medical knowledge, reinforced by public health programs and social welfare. The decline of epidemic diseases further reduced grim expectations about child survival. By the 1950s the customary European rates for infant mortality were between 20 and 50 deaths per thousand live births. In the Netherlands itself, the figure stood at 25 in 1950, compared to the modern figure of 3. That decline in infant mortality was of much wider significance in shaping how we understand demographic trends. As I noted, life expectancies have risen powerfully over recent decades, and much of that general increase results directly from drops in infant and maternal deaths. Yes, people in Western countries are indeed living longer, but the growing number of child survivors has had a vast effect on raising overall averages.[5]

Collapsing infant mortality rates were accompanied by sweeping improvements in child nutrition and maternal health, and by improving health care across the life span. During the twentieth century, Dutch people grew significantly in height and physical size, to the point of becoming stereotypically tall in a way that had simply not been true in earlier eras. We actually witness parallel developments today with East Asian peoples like the Chinese and Japanese following some decades of prosperity in those countries.

The First Baby Bust

As I noted, the Netherlands experienced a brief but significant dip in fertility rates during the late 1920s and 1930s, and this was part of a larger

European phenomenon. In many ways it foreshadowed the post-1960s fertility decline. Although this older phenomenon is barely known to nonspecialists, it was a significant portent of later developments, and it profoundly affects how we tell the story of the more recent fertility plunge.[6]

One key factor here was the First World War, which not only killed some ten million in combat but resulted in millions more deaths through associated hunger and diseases. At least officially, military campaigns ended in 1918, but mass violence continued for several years in parts of Europe, accompanied by revolutionary upsurges and economic chaos. Wartime slaughter had a disproportionate impact on young men, massively reducing the available supply of marriage partners for women over the following decades. The strict moral codes of the time made it difficult to contemplate women bearing children outside wedlock.[7]

But other factors were also at work. The Netherlands, for instance, was a noncombatant in the Great War, but it still noted a fertility dip. Across Europe attitudes to gender and sexuality were in flux, following the social turbulence of the war years. At the same time, women's demands for equality had their effects, as did greatly expanded access to education. Greater knowledge about contraception played its part, galvanizing many different churches to crusade against what they saw as a grave social evil. In 1930 the Vatican issued a stern encyclical prohibiting artificial contraception, an act that brings to mind the better-known restatement of that doctrine in 1968, in the papal encyclical *Humanae Vitae*. (We will discuss this further in the next chapter.) Many Anglicans and other Protestants were as perturbed by the rise of contraception as were Catholics, and to the degree that they felt that contraception could launch a social revolution, they were correct.[8]

For multiple reasons young people postponed setting up households and having children. The rate of population growth plummeted in the 1920s—in Europe, by about a third.[9] Such a shift could not fail to have wider consequences, and it has been plausibly argued that the sudden shrinkage of new households in both Europe and North America contributed powerfully to the overall lack of demand that provoked the 1929 Crash and the ensuing Great Depression. Those events in turn further reinforced the dip in fertility, as the 1930s were a brutally unpromising environment in which to start families. In some countries—notably France—that shift for some years brought the country to sub-replacement rates, a noteworthy historical first. Very unusually the country was recording more deaths than births. Early perceptions of the demographic transition paid special attention to French conditions, as the country gave researchers a standard model for study and comparison.[10]

Demographic decline was alarming at a time of international tensions, when each major power needed young men for its armed forces and also wished to justify maintaining colonial empires. Apart from threatening the supply of potential cannon fodder, the demographic decline roused eugenic fears. If better-off and educated people were the ones refusing to have children, then the gene pool would increasingly be dominated by the offspring of the ignorant, of social and racial inferiors, and according to the pseudo-science of the time, that would degrade both race and nation. In the words of one eugenic-based fictional piece from midcentury, society would be overrun with the "marching morons." Through the 1920s and 1930s, fertility became a lively political issue in many nations. Especially in the totalitarian dictatorships of the time, governments worked to raise birth rates through various pro-family or natalist policies, offering rewards or even medals for prolific families. Hitler's Germany offered a Mother's Medal of different grades, depending on how many children the woman had successfully raised—all, of course, with acceptable racial credentials. In 1934 the low birth rate in democratic Sweden was the subject of an influential book on the *Crisis in the Population Question*, by sociologists Alva and Gunnar Myrdal. The solutions they proposed gave a new impetus to the Swedish model of social welfare, which was widely imitated.[11]

Although it is difficult to speculate about the "roads not taken" in history, it is notable that already in the 1930s, some European societies had briefly begun to make that critical move to the kind of low-fertility world that would reappear at the end of the century. We do not know how that trend might have developed without the catastrophic intervention of the Second World War. Although we rightly pay attention to the baby boom of the postwar years, that phenomenon should rather be seen as the product of a particular era, rather than as representing standard historical normality.[12]

A Baby Boom

The Second World War caused an overwhelming disruption in family life, removing tens of millions of men to the armed forces or to various forms of servitude. When peace was restored, survivors were desperately anxious to build or rebuild families, and conditions were set for the baby boom that continued apace into the 1960s. Although exact estimates vary between countries, the boom dated from 1945 through the early to mid-1960s, with the years 1963–1965 as conspicuous points of transition. In Germany the TFR peaked in 1964 at 2.53. The French rate for that year was 2.87; Sweden's was 2.47; Italy's was 2.65. The Spanish rate also peaked in 1964, at 3.01. Denmark's peak year was 1963 (2.67).[13]

At this point we need to explain why matters were so completely different from conditions after 1918, the Armageddon of an earlier generation. As I have suggested, the 1920s witnessed a baby bust rather than a boom. The political mood was different in the two eras, with a real upsurge of optimism about the future from the late 1940s, and that was rooted in economic circumstances. If the mid-1920s were generally good for most countries, that prosperity was nothing like as sustained, or as widespread in its impact, as the boom experienced by the next generation. Post-1945 demographic growth was a side effect of far-reaching economic expansion, in the era that the French recalled as the *trente glorieuses*, the "thirty glorious years" of 1945–1975. Partly the contrasting circumstances reflected a conscious attempt by government and planners to avoid the errors of the post-1918 era, with its crushing austerity. Also in the post-1945 era, a triumphant United States poured in aid for European reconstruction, which helped build up flourishing consumer economies as living standards soared. Italians spoke of *il miracolo economico*, as the country's GDP doubled between 1950 and 1962. Widespread prosperity across Western Europe allowed the creation of generous governmental services, social welfare systems, and safety nets, encouraging family formation among all classes.[14]

Yet for all the new opportunities after 1945, social and legal restraints conspired to minimize female participation in the workforce. In many countries there was a powerful expectation that women would give up their jobs when they married or became pregnant. Even by the standards of Americans, who are accustomed to the long struggle that women faced for full legal equality, many European countries were considerably more reactionary. Only in 1944 did French women receive the right to vote, with Italy following in 1945, and various forms of legal discrimination lasted long after that. Until as recently as 1981, Italy allowed men an honor killing defense in murder cases. Gender discrimination strongly encouraged women to define their role in terms of motherhood. States systematically encouraged high birth rates, seeing large populations as a visible sign of success and national greatness. French leader Charles de Gaulle called for policies that would produce twelve million "beaux bébés," and even leftist parties saw no reason to disagree. The powerful French Communist Party long opposed contraception, to the horror of socialist feminists.[15]

In a society with many large families, couples faced powerful social pressures to reproduce, while having many friends with children offered an effective network for support and childcare. The image of large families—the natalist dream—was also presented widely through mass media, through films and popular songs. And as more children were born, the number surviving to adulthood was far larger than might have been imagined some decades earlier.

Across Europe the baby boom had cascading effects through society, politics, and the economy. We see the impact in the tremendous boom in educational institutions, especially with the enormous demand for higher education, with all that implied for life expectations. Through the 1960s the leading countries of Western Europe recorded an *annual* average growth rate of university and college enrollments of between 7 and 11 percent.[16]

The baby boom cohort provided the foundation for an explosive youth culture and for new political and social movements across the continent. Although many of the best-known artists and performers were strictly speaking a little older than the boomers—the Beatles and Rolling Stones are cases in point—it was the generation born after 1945 that provided the core of their market. Youth cultures reached a height between 1965 and the economic downturn of 1973–1974, as did the interlocking network of radical movements and protests. The growth of television—and the global nature of music cultures—promoted the global spread of images and ideologies, with minimal time lags between continents. European nations rapidly encountered and absorbed American styles and ideas, including new attitudes to gender and sexuality, and surging movements promoting feminism and gay rights.[17]

The availability of sexually explicit media provided an index of change and of greater social freedom. Pornography was strictly prohibited or regulated across Europe prior to the 1950s but became increasingly available in the 1960s, and in ever more explicit forms. By the mid-1960s, hard-core pornography became the basis of thriving industries in Northern European nations like Denmark and the Netherlands, and that pattern thereafter spread across much of the continent. Meanwhile sexual themes and images became ever more acceptable in mainstream media and culture. In retrospect feminists in particular would find such a development troubling, but at the time this was seen as a fundamental component of sexual liberation.[18]

Those changes of the baby boom era provide a direct segue into the subsequent time of very low fertility. To oversimplify, the baby boom produced boomers, who demanded new freedoms and opportunities, which in turn produced the baby bust. The baby boom was a self-limiting phenomenon.

The New Baby Bust

From the late 1960s, that baby boom swiftly went into reverse, as many countries dipped below the replacement fertility rate of 2.1 children per woman. That change was most marked in Scandinavian countries like Denmark. Germany fell below replacement fertility in 1971 and has never returned above that level. Its rate cratered in 2006 at 1.33, although it has subsequently rebounded to around 1.6. The fertility collapse was even higher in particular regions, and some eastern German areas had disturbing rates as low as 0.8. Rates for urban areas were particularly striking, with Italian centers like Milan and Bologna at barely 1.0 by the turn of the century. Taking the half-billion people of the European Union as a whole—the twenty-eight countries, which then included Great Britain—the average TFR by 2016 was just 1.6.[19]

In the early stages of the change, observers noted a sharp contrast between the Protestant and Catholic regions of the continent and speculated about the influence of Protestant traditions of individualism. Contradicting such interpretations, from the mid-1970s onward, Catholic areas shared in the larger transition, including countries that had once been legendary for prolific families. By the end of the century, Italy, Spain, Austria, Portugal, and even Ireland were all moving toward Danish-style rates or sinking below them. In 1964 a typical Spanish woman would have three children in her lifetime, a rate that fell to 1.1 by 1997. In the space of a single generation—between 1964 and 1995—Italy's TFR fell from 2.65 to 1.19 (it is now 1.45); the figure for Catholic Austria was comparable. Today, the contraceptive prevalence rate in predominantly Catholic countries like Spain, Italy, or Austria runs only slightly below that for Protestant nations like the Netherlands. As demographers wryly note, the closer a woman lives to Rome, the fewer children she has.[20]

Historically, Catholic areas of Southern and Eastern Europe had been slower to modernize and industrialize than their Protestant counterparts. That difference faded rapidly in post–World War II Europe, with Italy especially undergoing swift modernization. Between 1955 and 1971, some nine million Italians migrated within the country, overwhelmingly leaving villages and small towns for major cities like Milan and Turin. Urban and industrial successes were reflected in the growing depopulation of rural areas, the villages that had historically been marked by high-fertility societies of peasants and smallholders. Those long-enduring peasant societies effectively dissolved. By the end of the century, large areas of Italy and Spain had population densities as low as Lapland and were regularly described as "emptied" or "hollowed out." Although many villages later revived, it was as second homes and summer homes for prosperous city dwellers. The physical landscape changed as fast as the social environment.[21]

Ireland offers another telling Catholic example. This was the long-familiar center of a fervent and usually conservative culture, where Catholic policies often found expression in the law of the land. Even when Catholics world-wide despaired at the liberalization of their church from the 1960s onward, they commonly assumed that Ireland would remain as a heroic last bastion of conservative faith. As recently as the early 1970s, the country's TFR was barely below 4.0, and it long remained high by Western European standards. Only in the 1990s did the rate drift below replacement, and even a decade ago it was usually around that level. Subsequently though the decline has been more marked, and in recent years it has generally ranged between 1.9 and 2.0, which is stunningly low in light of Irish social history.[22]

The Communist East

From 1945 through 1989, the political division of Europe between Com-munist and non-Communist regions was a fundamental fact of political life. Communist-ruled nations shared some of the same trends as the West, including the move to industrialization, but levels of growth and prosperity were of course far lower. Even so, Eastern nations experienced compara-ble demographic patterns of boom and bust, although following a some-what different chronology. Poland still had a TFR of 3.0 in 1960, falling to replacement level in 1990. More prosperous nations like Hungary and Czechoslovakia reached their highest fertility levels in the mid-1970s, before beginning a comparable decline. The Communist taste for state intervention led several states to quite draconian measures to try to stem the decline, including limiting access to oral contraceptives, and Romania in particular enforced quite fierce pro-natalist policies. But at most these only delayed the overall decline.[23]

It was only after the collapse of Communism that the scale of the baby bust became most evident, during an era of revolutionary economic and political change. In some regions the failure of old and failing industries caused many years of decline and despair, while some countries suffered mass emigration. Across the region exposure to Western media and social arrangements inspired rising social aspirations over and above traditional concepts of family. For whatever reason, the former Communist countries now entered a period of demographic decline that was alarming even by the standards of Western Europe. In the former East Germany, TFRs reached an astonishing 0.8 before recovering from the mid-1990s onward. Today fertil-ity rates across the region are as low as any in the West: 1.46 in the Czech Republic, 1.4 in Hungary. Curiously, in light of its very strong Catholic her-itage, even Poland's rate fell precipitously, to just 1.22 by 2003, and today it stands at only 1.37. (I will discuss Poland's idiosyncratic conditions more in the next chapter.) Despite the long separation, most of Eastern Europe now shares the common demographic fate of the rest of the continent.

Europe's Future

On any map of global fertility, Europe stands out clearly. In 2017 a ranking of the world's 224 nations by their TFR demonstrated the scale of these changes, and as we will see, the highest rates were found in Africa and South Asia. Not until position 109 do we find a European nation, namely France, with its near-replacement fertility rate, followed by Ireland at position 125 and Sweden at 141. Most European nations found themselves among the lowest forty, with rates below 1.6. At the bottom of the ranking, we find 28 countries with TFRs at or below 1.50. Most of the major European nations are in this category of extremely low fertility, including Italy, Spain, Poland, Portugal, Hungary, Austria, Romania, Bulgaria, and the Balkan successor states of the former Yugoslavia.[24]

Demographers offer varying estimates for how these trends will continue in future years. In the early years of this century, several countries noted an uptick in their fertility rates, arousing some hopes that the birth dearth might be ending. Any such hopes soon faded, as the economic crisis of 2008 shattered hopes and reduced opportunities. The number of babies born in the EU in 2013 was 7 percent below the figure for 2008. By present projections, over the next thirty years, Germany's population will shrink from its current level of 83 million to between 70 and 74 million. The population of Italy will dip from its present 60.3 million to 58.6 million but with a steeper fall in subsequent years, to below 54 million by 2065. In some countries projected losses appear extreme to the point of disastrous. Between 2000 and 2050, Romania should contract from 22.5 million to 16.4 million; Bulgaria will shrink from 8.2 million to 5.4 million. In the same time span, Latvia's population will probably contract from 2.4 million to 1.5 million. Not only will Europe's overall population contract somewhat by 2050, but this will be a very different society from the expansive society of old. Domestically it will be a society in which the old, and the very old, are well represented.[25]

Explanations: Moving Away from Families

In explaining these quite dramatic changes, we must return to the conditions of the baby boom years and the resulting youth subcultures. The demographic surge of midcentury created an environment highly favorable to the spread of radically individualistic attitudes. As younger people became more educated and assertive, social movements demanded personal liberation and fulfillment, leading many younger people to reject the traditional roles that society offered them, particularly in the context of family and parenthood. The availability of contraception, and in many countries easier access to abortion, allowed a social revolution in which sexuality could easily be separated from reproduction. For many people that separation created more favorable attitudes toward alternative forms of sexuality, especially homosexuality, as many of the most seemingly radical innovations of the socially revolutionary years of the late 1960s acquired mainstream status. Sexually libertarian attitudes that in earlier generations prevailed among the upper classes or aristocracy now became thinkable for ordinary working-class people. Although the political outbreaks of 1968 may not have directly sparked such innovations, they were associated with them in popular thought. Across Europe the term "68ism" epitomized a whole package of radical values and demands.[26]

Unprecedented prosperity had other effects, making possible the existence of generous welfare states. The growth of social welfare facilities accelerated the drift away from older family concepts, in that it became possible for individuals to survive and flourish outside the protection of those extended family networks. Unlike in premodern societies, families no longer had to plan on raising multiple children who would support their parents in their old age. The societies with the most advanced social provision were exactly those Northern European societies that led the way in the fertility decline.

Beyond such practical matters, many observers have commented on the psychological effects of belonging to families with many children and on the sense of sharing one's identity with an extended family. Large families, in that perspective, tend to value kinship, community, and shared values, and also have a commitment to posterity. That stands in sharp contrast to the individualistic values prevailing in low-fertility societies. As families shrink in size, so individuals are less likely to see themselves in those larger terms, and they lose the ideological incentive to bear children.

Multiple measures point to a systematic decline in the hitherto central importance of marriage as an institution and specifically as the enormously preferred setting for raising children. From the 1960s the number of people living together outside marriage grew in every country, as public disapproval faded. A concomitant shift involved a stunning growth in the number of births occurring outside marriage, in what used to be stigmatized as "illegitimacy." Scandinavia led the way: by the end of the century, the out-of-wedlock birthrate for Sweden was 55 percent, Norway 50 percent, Denmark 45 percent.[27]

I quote a recent study:

> In 1964, most countries in the Organisation for Economic and Co-operative Development had no more than 10 percent of their births outside of marriage. By 2014 in only five countries—Greece, Israel, Japan, South Korea and Turkey—were the proportions of births out of wedlock below 10 percent. In the large majority of more developed countries, including Germany, the United Kingdom and the United States, more than one-third of all births take place out of wedlock.

Just between 2000 and 2016, the proportion of births that occurred outside marriage in the European Union grew from 28 to over 40 percent.[28]

Prosperity and greater state support undermined the individual's need to depend on families, and at the same they reduced the demand for families to bear large numbers of children. We see this in the shrinkage of infant mortality rates, a pattern that has become so obvious and natural that we often forget how sharply this marks off present-day realities from virtually all historical societies. As we have seen, societies with very low mortality rates know they can afford to have just one or two children in the reasonable expectation that those will live to adulthood, and it is a tragedy of dreadful proportions when they do not. Around the world there is a tight correlation between the infant mortality rates of any given society (defined as a child dying before the age of 1) and the fertility rate of that community. Put crudely, a society with low infant mortality will probably produce fewer infants. The countries with the highest infant mortality rates are poor African and South Asian societies such as Afghanistan, Somalia, or Niger, with mortality rates in excess of 80 per thousand live births. Virtually all European countries—with their welfare networks and advanced medicine—are found at the opposite end of such a spectrum. France's infant mortality rate fell from 20 in the mid-1960s to just 3.1 today. Italy's rate fell from over 30 in the 1960s to its modern 3. At the bottom of the ranking are Asian societies that we have already seen to be marked by very low fertility, namely Japan and Singapore.[29]

Explanations: Women's Revolutions

Whatever route of explanation we follow, the theme of gender roles and women's aspirations is central. At every stage women were most directly affected by the new range of options and freedoms, the new array of ideas and ideologies. This new emphasis on individual choice and autonomy discouraged family formation and parenthood. Ideas and fashions come and go, but essential features of the new ideologies found an enduring foundation in social and legal developments. That was especially true in matters involving women's rights and aspirations toward gender equality. Women's legal disabilities evaporated in the face of surging feminist activism, and as we will see, laws permitting divorce, contraception, and abortion spread across the continent. Women's role in higher education continued to grow throughout the period.[30]

Following the recessions of the mid- and late 1970s, European economies moved strongly toward service industries such as banking, finance, and insurance, which offered extensive employment opportunities for office workers, and particularly for women. That change accelerated from 1980, with the rapid decline of older manufacturing plants and smokestack industries, and the industrial communities founded upon them. At the end of the century, economic growth decisively shifted toward high tech—to IT, biotech, and pharmaceuticals—with the premium such enterprises placed upon higher education. The opportunities for women to work outside the home expanded widely. Educated women earning good money were likely to postpone childbearing, if not to avoid it altogether. In the words of a recent book on the fate of the Anglican church in Britain, "For the first time, [women] were being routinely educated to the same levels as men and entering the workforce in similar numbers. It turned out that once they had the choice and the means, they proved more likely to get divorced and less likely to get married or have children. They were out of the doll's house, and never going back."[31]

Feminist ideologies promoted women's aspirations for autonomy, while the growth of a prosperous and educated female constituency in turn helped spread feminist ideas. The more prominently women featured as leading figures in political life or the mass media, the more natural such roles appeared, and the more startling or even shocking was any kind of exclusion. If the media during the baby boom years had presented encouraging images of large families, now their emphasis was on independent women, who did not necessarily need either husbands or children for self-fulfillment. Any lingering conservative hopes that feminism might have been a passing fad vanished in the face of economic reality.

Changing social ideologies conditioned the demographic change and also accelerated it: fertility rates are thus both cause and effect. Economists describe the demographic dividend that benefits a society when fertility falls, as couples have access to disposable income that would otherwise have been spent on children. At least for a few decades, the working-age population expands as the influx of women into regular employment means a larger labor force, and those women have few dependents. People who enter paid productive labor for the first time in turn become consumers, which further stimulates demand and production. Per capita incomes rise, boosting prosperity, which in turn accelerates economic and social growth, and that further undermines older social and family structures. To that extent declining fertility of itself leads to further shrinkage of the fertility rate. We are looking at a dynamic process, and a continuing one. Once the demographic change began, it became a cumulative process.[32]

This transformation is in no sense a revolutionary moment that hits a society at a particular point or a single moment. It is not an up-down choice that a society either has achieved or has not, nor is it a simple transition. It is a process spread over several decades, which might move faster or slower in particular areas.

Consequences: Living with a Revolution

Europe is a large and diverse continent, and mores and standards differ widely from place to place: no single country is typical. But with that caveat in mind, all countries to some extent share comparable trends: to much greater prosperity and level of health and education; to rapid and self-sustaining economic growth; to the emancipation of women from a near-exclusive focus on child raising; to the terminal decline of the old rural order; and in sum, to a steep and lasting fall in fertility rates. We can also point to some common consequences of the resulting low-fertility society, which to varying degrees have revolutionized European life—in politics, in culture, and most basically, in family life. Taken together these changes all reflect a steep decline in ideas of tradition and authority, of community and rootedness, of continuity and social cohesion. At the same time, they represent a widespread pattern of liberation and opening, of new opportunities. While more individualistic, the emerging society was also more atomized and fragmented. Each of these factors would in its way contribute to the religious transformation that was underway throughout these decades.

Apart from the sharply declined number of children, nontraditional families have also become common. Adults are more likely to live alone, and children are often raised by single parents. The once standard nuclear family has become almost a social outlier. We can trace the effects of demographic change through each stage of life. For one thing, children's social roles have changed radically. A society with few children is likely to view them differently, and often more protectively, than a community where children abound. Although we can certainly not draw a simple correlation here, the collapse in fertility rate coincides well with new attitudes to child protection, especially in matters of sexuality. Concerns about child sexual abuse flowered from the late 1970s, as have much more rigid attitudes about the appropriate range of behaviors in which children can properly engage. The once common theme of children exploring and playing freely outdoors has become controversial, to be replaced by forms of play approved and controlled by parents and schools.[33]

The emerging society also differed from its predecessors in a matter as fundamental as the distinction between childhood and adulthood, and that in turn contributed to falling fertility. Earlier societies had assumed that individuals would form families and begin childbearing early in life, perhaps in their early twenties. New opportunities for employment and leisure strongly encouraged both men and women to delay that process by several years, as did the popularity of higher education. It became accepted and commonplace for young adults to remain single, to enjoy the rich social facilities offered by cities, and to define their life in terms of a circle of friends, rather than family or long-term partners. The high cost of urban accommodation further encouraged young adults to remain living with their parents for years after their presence might have been thought appropriate in earlier eras. These changes served to prolong adolescence well into the twenties. That historic shift in turn reinforced the cultural pressures against early family formation and further encouraged women to leave childbearing until later—customarily, their thirties.

Since the late 1990s, these trends further accelerated with the growth of high-tech industries and social media. Although the social effects of technological change are controversial, many observers claim that younger people are so immersed in electronic communication that they find it harder to deal with personal and face-to-face interactions, and long-term relationships. That is reflected in a general decline in the amount of sexual contact that respondents consistently report in numerous surveys from technologically advanced nations in Europe and North America. Japan particularly has reported a sharp decline in sexual activity, with first experiences postponed into the thirties. International media speak of a "sex recession" or a "virginity crisis." Whatever the reasons—and the omnipresence of online pornography is also cited in this context—such trends make it unlikely that rates for marriage and family formation will return to anything like their former high levels in the foreseeable future.[34]

In the long term, perhaps the most important consequence involved the different attitudes toward aging and old age that characterized the new European world. Low-fertility societies tend to be older in their demographic profile, a trend that also benefited from medical advances and general prosperity. As people lived much longer, so the median age of societies grew steeply. Today 35 percent of Italians are aged over 55, and the comparable figure for most European nations is around a third. That compares with just 7.5 percent in fertile Nigeria, 7 percent in Kenya, and similar figures across much of Africa. The year 2019 marked a troubling milestone in Germany, where the number of people aged over 60 exceeded those under 30. Intercontinental contrasts are even greater when we consider the very old, people aged 75 or over. In a ranking of the world's nations by their median age, European nations dominate, taking all but four of the top thirty-three places. Germany, Italy, Austria, and the Baltic nations all stand near the head of the list.[35] Most Western European societies have a median age over 40, and several in the early or mid-forties: Germany's median age is 47; Italy's is around 46; Spain and the Netherlands stand at 43. The median age of the whole European Union is 44. As we have seen, the comparable figure in many African nations is closer to 16.[36]

Such trends pose grave questions for the continuation of existing social arrangements, as an ever-decreasing number of working-age people are required to support ever more elderly and dependents. Social welfare systems depend on a "biological rate of return," by which a permanently growing population can afford to pay increasing benefits, but that assumption is fatally sabotaged by consistent fertility decline. The acute aging of the continent combined with a general taste for early retirement to create a troubling imbalance between older and younger generations. By many projections the maintenance of welfare systems will simply have become impossible by mid-century, if not before.[37]

Consequences: A New Moral Order

New moral and sexual attitudes drove the move to a low-fertility society and were in turn further radicalized and institutionalized as that society emerged. Since the 1960s those changes have been manifested in multiple struggles over laws and public policies, which have been at the forefront of European public debate. Such battles have transformed political causes and allegiances, as the politics of class have given way to issues of gender, morality, and identity.

From the early 1960s, a growing number of European countries undertook significant liberalization of their laws concerning public morality, most conspicuously in sexual matters. Countries offered easier access to divorce, made contraceptive access easier, and expanded access to abortion. As so often, it is difficult to disentangle cause and effect in these areas. The new legal environment made it easier to control family size and thus to reduce fertility rates. At the same time, people living in a low-fertility society were less bound to traditional concepts of family and parenting, and wished to expand the options available to them and their juniors. Whichever direction we understand to be more important, the chronology of liberalization neatly matched the rate at which fertility was declining in particular countries. The resulting public controversies would be crucial in redrawing the lines of church power and redefining the acceptable limits of religious influence in secular life. Moral revolutions marked revolutionary shifts in religious attitudes.

Although the various legal changes were often linked together in public debate, they ranked very differently in the degree of change they demanded in social attitudes. Divorce and access to contraception were the easier cases to make, as they could both be presented as matters of individual choice that affected only the parties involved, so that the legitimate public interest was minimal. Abortion poses quite different issues if it is understood in terms not only of the rights of the woman but of the survival of her unborn child. The sequence and timing of reforms thus provides a good index of the nature of social change.

In Western Europe the post-1965 decade marked sweeping liberalization in all these areas. Change was easier in Protestant nations, and in countries like France that were officially secular, and demanded a rigid separation of church and state. But even there public morality remained surprisingly conservative. Contraceptives became freely available as late as 1965, and only in 1967 did France repeal a law restricting the dissemination of information concerning birth control.

Change was still slower in nations where the Catholic Church was stronger and could more easily mobilize electoral support. In Italy one key sign of a new era occurred in 1974, when a referendum overwhelmingly approved liberalizing divorce laws, by a majority of 59 to 41 percent. The country approved an abortion law in 1978 and in 1981 resisted a repeal attempt with an electoral majority of 68 to 32 percent. Coincidentally or not, that chronology faithfully tracks the country's fertility decline: 1976, in fact, marked the first year in which the country reached replacement level, at 2.1, a figure that had by 1981 fallen to 1.6. That is an extreme change within a very few years. Twenty percent of Italian women born in 1968—and growing up in these tumultuous years—would never bear children.[38]

Another country long regarded as a Catholic bastion was Spain, which liberalized rapidly following the restoration of political democracy in 1976. Contraceptives were legalized in 1978, homosexuality was decriminalized in the following year, and divorce became possible under a new law passed in 1981. Abortion was legalized in 1985, albeit under strict conditions. Looking at the chronology of reform, we naturally give full credit to the new democratic government, but the fact that they could achieve such progress in such a short time owes much to the ongoing demographic transition, which followed a pattern strongly reminiscent of Italy. Just in the decade following 1975, Spain's TFR declined from a high 2.75 to just 1.64.[39]

Ireland was originally much more conservative on all such issues, but the trajectory ultimately followed similar lines. Before 1980 Ireland strictly prohibited contraceptive use, and only in 1985 were contraceptives freely available without medical approval. As late as 1995, a referendum approved the legalization of divorce in that country but by a hair's breadth margin of only 0.5 percent of the vote. But moral attitudes then changed quickly. By 2018 the country held a referendum on abortion, which was approved by crushing margin of 66 to 33. As we will see, in each case the Roman Catholic Church was critical to the conservative campaigns on the various issues.[40]

Consequences: Gay Rights

In this context of shifting demographic foundations, homosexuality was a natural target for liberal reform. In a society where sexuality was vaunted as a good thing in its own right, rather than chiefly intended for reproduction, arguments against homosexual behavior lost much of their force. Particularly once a large majority of families are using contraception, that necessary linkage becomes much more tenuous, and society becomes much more accepting of nontraditional sexual relationships. Marriage itself is commonly treated as flexible and expansive, to the horror of moral traditionalists and mainstream religious institutions. In the late 1960s, gay rights movements emerged across Europe as part of the general wave of liberation enthusiasm.

Homosexuality laws were steadily liberalized in the decade or so after 1965, although the nature of change varied greatly according to the legal arrangements of particular societies. Britain and Ireland had notoriously draconian laws, whereas consensual homosexual conduct was not illegal in Italy after 1890. Although the exact nature of change varied, the consistent theme was a reduction of disabilities and a removal of condemnations based on psychiatric or medical theories. In Britain the key legal turning point occurred in 1967, while in the Netherlands, the age of consent for gay and straight relationships was equalized in 1971. Homosexual activity between men was legalized in East Germany in 1968 and in the West the following year. Spain followed in 1979.[41]

Since that time the progress of gay rights has been rapid, to the point that such ideas have become absolutely mainstreamed in western parts of the continent, where elites saw them quite as nonnegotiable as belief in racial equality. At the end of the century, the main battlefronts shifted to the idea of same-sex marriage. Initially, governments responded with forms of civil union, giving same-sex couples the legal rights associated with marriage but without the formal label. Consistently, the pioneering countries were exactly those that had been in the vanguard of the larger movement toward low fertility. In 1979 the Netherlands became the first country to grant such a status for same-sex couples, and in 1989 Denmark was the first to allow same-sex "registered partnerships." Norway and Sweden soon followed, with the Netherlands in 1997.[42]

Even that stance soon crumbled, as countries moved forcefully to unequivocal recognition of same-sex marriage. In 2001 the Netherlands approved actual same-sex marriage, together with adoption rights, with neighboring Belgium following in 2003. Many other European countries followed over the following decade. Besides the obvious pioneers, many local and regional legislatures were early adopters of reform, especially in Spain, and in 2005 the whole country accepted full-scale same-sex marriage. Significantly, the leading countries in this movement included lands that were traditionally both Catholic and Protestant. Although not necessarily uniquely influential in itself, the implementation and acceptance of same-sex marriage bespeaks the mind-boggling scale of the social and cultural trans-formation since the 1970s. The approval of adoption by same-sex couples is in some ways even more far reaching.

Usually such legal changes were effected by elected bodies, who faced conservative accusations that they were imposing elite moral ideas on a reluctant populace. In one case, though, same-sex marriage was approved following a mass referendum, and in a stunning signal of the scale of recent developments in social attitudes, that occurred in Ireland in 2015. No fewer than 62 percent of voters approved the necessary constitutional change.

Consequences: Immigration and Diversity

Beyond changes in personal and collective morality, Europe experienced a transformation of cultural and ethnic identity, which grows directly and inevitably from demographic changes.

Europe's distinctive age structure poses real problems for the long-term sustainability of that continent and its economic order. At a minimum the situation demands a steady influx of immigrants from more prolific soci-eties who are essential to undertake the jobs and pay the taxes needed so that society can function in comfort and cohesion. Such migrants could be drawn from various sources, including (at first) the poorer rural areas of now-booming countries like Italy or Spain. The other obvious pool on which to draw was in Eastern or Southeastern Europe, but the Iron Curtain separating Communist and non-Communist regions made any such effort impossible, except for the border state of Yugoslavia. Lacking the labor reserves that might have been found in countries like Poland and Romania,

Western Europe had no option but to turn beyond Europe, and especially to the colonial empires. At first, those migrants were predominantly male, but increasingly families arrived, and their age and social background ensured that they had birth rates far higher than the current European norms.

In consequence, non-European ethnic populations surged in numbers and became ever more evident as a part of the social scene. The best-known feature of this is the growth of Islamic populations in many advanced European countries since the 1960s, but Christians and other groups have also migrated from the Global South. Across Europe, Muslim populations currently vary between 5 and 8 percent in countries like Britain, Germany, Austria, Belgium, the Netherlands, and Denmark, and the proportions are far higher among children and young adults. The overall figures are probably higher in France and Sweden. The Muslim figure across the whole continent is about 5 percent. Setting aside the religious component, in 2011, 13 percent of people living in England and Wales were born outside the country. To use another measure, 11 percent of British residents in the same year traced their ancestry to Africa, South Asia, or the Caribbean. The impact of these changes is evident in the continent's major cities, where large immigrant populations have effectively supplanted older white working-class communities.[43] The new Europe is a far more diverse and globalized place than hitherto.

Older and newer populations are divided, by age, ethnicity, and often religion, and the resulting conflicts are now endemic. The sense of demographic decline—or worse—among old-stock populations fueled what political scientist Eric Kaufmann has termed a "Whiteshift," resentment that manifests in surging populist and nationalist movements. The age schism was a critical element in Britain's Brexit vote to leave the European Union in 2016, a debate that centrally involved immigration policy. Younger voters, aged 18 to 24, favored remaining in Europe by a margin of 3 to 1, while the over-65s opposed it by 2 to 1. In most nations issues of identity and ethnicity, immigration and nationality have become central to political life and have often transformed older political allegiances.[44]

As in the 1930s, fertility decline has prompted intense public debate over the emerging shape of Europe. Responding to such controversies, journalist Derek Thompson formulated a troubling but plausible theory of the "doom loop of modern liberalism." Fertility decline results from the spread of what we can generally call liberal and progressive values, especially gender equality. However, a low-fertility society demands immigration, which cannot fail to stir populist opposition. In many cases that opposition will be so substantial as to give power to highly conservative and reactionary regimes, who will reject or constrain liberal values and policies. Such a "doom loop" analysis offers a helpful approach to contemporary rhetoric about fertility and immigration.[45]

From a traditionalist or rightist standpoint, European demographic trends illustrated a decadence amounting almost to a death wish, given the influx of migrants whose values were so distinct from those of an older Europe. In this view liberalism and individualism had become excuses for simple selfishness, a refusal to consider the good of the nation or race. One person's liberation was another's empty hedonism. The consequence was collective suicide. As early as 1982, Günter Grass' novel *Headbirths* portrayed a prosperous young German couple just too engaged with career and material prosperity ever to consider children. His book's subtitle: *The Germans Are Dying Out*. From the conservative point of view, fertility decline meshed into an attractive moral narrative in which liberalism began a cycle of decline culminating in outright destruction. Social critics enthusiastically adopted demographic theories of the "low-fertility trap," a death spiral in which fertility rates fell to the point where recovery was simply not possible. In 2016 even Pope Francis warned that "the great challenge of Europe is to return to being mother Europe."[46]

Many works imagined a continent swamped or overrun by teeming masses of migrants, as conservatives freely drew analogies with the barbarian invasions of the Roman Empire. Initially such fears were strongly racial in tone, as in Raspail's novel *The Camp of the Saints*, but increasingly the nightmares became more specifically religious: Christian Europe would be conquered and then supplanted by an Islamic Eurabia. Those fears became all the more pressing during the upsurge of Islamist terrorism in the early years of this century and were given new weight by seemingly uncontrollable refugee crises like that of 2015. In 2012 French rightist Renaud Camus published his book *The Great Replacement*, which argues for the existence of a conspiracy to displace older white populations. The rhetoric of replacement entered the vocabulary of white supremacy militants worldwide. When in 2019 an extremist murdered worshipers at a New Zealand mosque, his manifesto opened with the declaration that "it's the birth rate. It's the birth rate. It's the birth rate."[47]

Conversely, Islamic enthusiasts themselves presented similar ideas not as a nightmare but as a hopeful vision, and Libyan dictator Muammar Qaddafi openly fantasized about a Muslim takeover of the continent from within, powered by high fertility rates. As I will suggest, that theory is based on dated and inaccurate demographic data about Muslims themselves, but the power of that vision is undeniable, and the associated rhetoric has fueled nativist and ultraright campaigns in many nations.[48]

In many European countries, eugenic-tinged rhetoric about family size and the number of babies has become ever more mainstream. Within the European Union, this natalist approach has found a focus in the polarizing figure of Viktor Orbán, the prime minister of Hungary since 2010. Orbán has campaigned for the defense of both Christianity and European values in the face of Islam, and speaks regularly of the fertility decline as the greatest menace facing the continent. (As we have seen, Hungary itself has a distinctly low rate.) In his view, as a means of maintaining a stable population, "immigration means surrender," and Europeans have a duty to restore a high-fertility society, with strong government encouragement and intervention. In sum, "We need Hungarian children." Loathed by liberals, Orbán's efforts to place demography at the heart of the political agenda have resonated in conservative circles.[49]

Revolution and Religion

So broad, so comprehensive have been the effects of the demographic shift that we can legitimately speak of a social revolution. In these same years, European societies also undertook another cultural leap with few historic precedents, namely a striking decline in religious behavior and faith, and a decisive move toward secularization, broadly defined. A region that had been the historic heart of Christianity became an exceedingly difficult environment for faith, and especially for religious institutions. The chronology of that transformation inseparably follows the demographic change, with all its attendant effects, and it is natural to seek some kind of connection. In fact the two phenomena were closely linked, to the point of inevitability. Religious change must be seen as one fragment of a wider social revolution and a thoroughgoing moral reconstruction, all rooted in demographics. In more ways than one, Europe led a movement into wholly new historic territory.

3

SPIRITUAL AND SECULAR

The present-day flag of the European Union shows twelve gold stars on a blue background. It was originally designed in 1955, and as the flag's creator readily avowed, it was inspired by the classic Catholic iconography of the Virgin Mary. Like older representations this followed a text in the biblical book of Revelation, with its vision of "a woman clothed with the sun, and the moon under her feet, and on her head a crown of twelve stars." In the new flag design, the central figure of Mary was removed to ensure that Protestants, Jews, and secularists would not be offended. Today few of the Europeans who know that flag so well have any sense of its origins, and European political leaders explicitly (and incorrectly) deny the Marian origins. Ironically that flag serves as an ideal symbol of a new Europe, in which a once central Christian reality has been removed so thoroughly as to be forgotten.[1]

The years of the mid-twentieth-century baby boom were a flourishing era for religion across non-Communist Europe. That situation changed dramatically from the mid-1960s, with a precipitous decline of religious practice. Just as Europe pioneered scarcely precedented patterns of low fertility, so it became the world's most secular society. The fact that the two phenomena, demographic and religious, tracked so well together does not of itself prove causation. But the more we examine the process of religious transformation, the more unavoidable becomes the demographic interpretation.[2]

A Boom in Faith

The abundance of religious buildings and other sites across Europe might give the impression that faith—above all, Christianity—was an unquestioned part of the landscape in earlier times. Actually, the situation is much more complex. Many European countries have a lengthy tradition of secularism, not to mention a lively current of anti-religious and anticlerical activism, which in extreme circumstances was expressed in anti-church violence and the murder of clergy. Institutional churches struggled with the industrial societies emerging in great cities, where "infidel" views were common. Even so, religious views remained widespread through the first half of the twentieth century, partly through a kind of "diffusive Christianity" that spread broadly Christian assumptions throughout the whole society. That was particularly evident during times of crisis such as the First World War. In several major nations, Christianity was intimately bound up with the institutional power of the state.[3]

Levels of attendance and devotion fluctuated over time, but organized Christianity and particular churches were doing very well indeed in the generation or so following the Second World War. This trend was illustrated by high levels of church attendance, by surging vocations to the priestly or monastic life, by the building of new churches, and by the growth of pilgrimage shrines. Levels of piety reached extraordinary heights in Catholic countries, with a new upsurge of Marian devotion following the pope's proclamation of the doctrine of her Assumption in 1950. That in turn provided the context for the flag of the emerging European alliance, which was publicized on the Feast of Mary's Immaculate Conception in 1955. Confrontations with Communism played their part in promoting this zeal, as did apocalyptic fears of a new world war. The euphoria surrounding the coronation of Britain's Queen Elizabeth II in 1953 gave a renewed visibility and prestige to the Church of England and to the link between church and state. The stunning success of Billy Graham's European crusades in 1954–1955 demonstrated the continuing power of enthusiastic faith in the form of evangelicalism.[4]

Religious fervor was evident even in what we today think of as very secular nations such as the Netherlands. Dutch people belonged to a particular "pillar"—whether Protestant, Catholic, or secular/social-democratic—and members differed according to the schools they attended, the media they followed, and the political parties they voted for. In a sense the pillars represented separate cultural worlds. In the 1950s Amsterdam was the setting for spectacular Marian visions, which were of course of chief interest to the Catholic pillar. In different ways what has been termed "pillarization"

(Dutch: *verzuiling*) was a critical fact in many countries, where religious affiliation (or lack of it) determined the mind-set and life chances of many ordinary people. Even wartime resistance movements were pillarized according
to faith. Across the continent avowedly Christian parties were at the heart
of postwar political reconstruction, and the building of the new European
project. Catholic labor organizations remained potent as the chief bastions
against Communist advances. In non-Communist Europe, both Catholics
and Protestants knew a complex world of interrelated Christian schools,
organizations, societies, and leagues, a whole civil society linked at least
notionally to churches. Of course there were other mighty pillars outside
the realm of religion, such as the Communist parties of France or Italy, but
faith shaped ordinary life in ways that would be inconceivable by the end
of the century.[5]

So accustomed are we to the secular and sexually liberal views of later
years that it is all but impossible for a modern audience to comprehend
the moral conservatism of the 1950s, among European Protestants as well
as Catholics. In 1955 the British royal family narrowly escaped a major
constitutional crisis when the queen's sister, Princess Margaret, agreed not
to marry a man who had been divorced and thus bowed to "the Church's
teachings that Christian marriage is indissoluble." Through the 1960s
Britain and Germany retained ferocious laws against homosexuality, and
churches were usually at the forefront of struggles against liberalization.
Catholic power over morality laws was absolute in countries like Spain
and Ireland.[6]

The Churches Decline

From the late 1960s, matters changed fundamentally. In describing the
decline of traditional religious life, we need to differentiate between two
processes that were tightly interlinked, and indeed are often treated as one
phenomenon, but which had different types of causation. The first involved
actual religious practice and observance; the second involved the political
power and influence of religious institutions.[7]

By whatever quantitative measure we use for observance, Europeans
deserted the churches en masse in these years, and unlike in the United
States, the collapse of mainstream institutions was not compensated by
an upsurge of newer denominations. Initially Protestant countries demonstrated the steepest decline, and in Britain scholars have focused on one brief
period as a key turning point in attitudes and behaviors. In his book *The
Death of Christian Britain*, Callum Brown argues that "quite suddenly in
1963, something very profound ruptured the character of the nation and its

people, sending organized Christianity on a downward spiral to the margins of social significance." He continues,

> In unprecedented numbers, the British people since the 1960s have stopped going to church, have allowed their church membership to lapse, have stopped marrying in church and have neglected to baptise their children. Meanwhile, their children, the two generations who grew to maturity in the last thirty years of the twentieth century, stopped going to Sunday school, stopped entering confirmation or communicant classes, and rarely, if ever, stepped inside a church to worship in their entire lives.

Over the next few years, "the new media, new gender roles and the moral revolution dramatically ended people's conception that they lived Christian lives." The proportion of people attending religious services has fallen by over half since the 1960s.[8]

The scale of damage was evident from the established Church of England, which notionally serves the whole population of England—53 million strong—but which currently has perhaps 700,000 regular attenders, and that number contracts annually.[9] Between 1983 and 2014, church membership fell from 40 percent to 17 percent, a drop of 58 percent. Today only 12 percent identify as Anglicans, while only 2 percent of young adults report belonging to that church, suggesting a "generational catastrophe." In 2015 an apocalyptic projection imagined the literal end of Christianity in Britain no later than 2067. British Catholics have done much better relatively but only because of the enthusiasm of successive cohorts of recent immigrants. As in much of Europe, churches have closed in alarming numbers, and repurposed former churches are an unavoidable part of the landscape in both city and country. Symbolizing shifting attitudes, from the 1970s British cathedrals began charging visitors for admission. This might have been an essential economic decision, but it sent the unfortunate message that these buildings were museums rather than living places of worship.[10]

In Germany likewise, each year the media regularly recite the latest grim statistics for the main Protestant denomination, the Evangelical Church (or EKD). Each year tells a renewed tale of falling attendance and membership, and a growing imbalance between rising numbers of funerals and declining baptisms. In the decade after 2005, Germany's Catholics closed over five hundred churches. Recalling British conditions, current studies suggest that Germany's two main Christian denominations, the EKD and the Roman Catholics, would contract from their combined membership of 45 million in 2019 to 35 million by 2025, and 23 million by 2060. Those surviving believers would of course be a much more aged group. In the Netherlands the number of church members halved between 1970 and 2014, falling from

60 to 30 percent of the population, with Catholics hardest hit. The number reporting frequent church attendance fell from 50 percent in the mid-1960s to 10 percent today, and church closures became commonplace. A fifth of all Dutch churches have now been converted to secular use. Declining zeal coincided with a dissolution of older loyalties and divisions, with "depillarization." Scandinavian countries were especially affected by such trends.[11]

The fact that people were less willing to attend church regularly was troubling enough, but the assumption was usually that they would return for major festivals and for key life events such as baptisms, marriages, or funerals. An old joke lists the three church functions as "hatched, matched, and dispatched." In that way at least, the churches would still represent the larger community in giving a religious or ritual significance to the developing life course. That assumption is no longer true. Each year the number of church baptisms or marriages continues to decline across the continent.

We have already noted the steep decline of the institution of marriage generally, as couples cohabit and bear children out of wedlock. Partly that reflects new attitudes to sexual relationships and a reluctance to accept any idea of lifetime commitment, but we also witness a rejection of any sense that church approval of family arrangements matters in any worthwhile sense. Equally unfashionable was any sense that nonmarital sexuality might in any sense be sinful. Today fewer than a quarter of British marriages involve religious ceremonies. Between 1980 and 2011, the proportion of children baptized in the Church of England fell from a third to a tenth. (In most European churches, baptism is usually given to children rather than adults.)[12]

Some of the countries hardest hit by religious decline had hitherto been seen as fortresses of Catholic piety. To oversimplify, the resulting changes can often be described through a rough-and-ready "rule of ten." In many standard indices of faith—vocations, ordinations, seminary numbers, monastic populations—the levels we find today are often around one-tenth of the scale and intensity of the high-water mark of practice in 1960. Many of Spain's dioceses have reported no seminary admissions for some years, as the numbers of newly ordained priests have collapsed. Even in Ireland seven of the country's eight seminaries have closed. German vocations have all but vanished. In 2016 the once pivotal Archdiocese of Munich had just one new seminarian. Scarcely less important in European history is the Austrian Archdiocese of Vienna, which in 2012 announced plans to consolidate its parishes from 660 to 150 over the next decade. The reasons cited, typically, were an acute shortage of priests and the decline of regular churchgoing.[13]

Monastic houses have been particularly hard hit—again, all the more tellingly given their soaring popularity in the 1950s. From the mid-1960s, the number of new entries declined suddenly and steeply, and the typical profile of a monk or nun became increasingly associated with advanced old age. Between 1965 and 1995, the number of nuns in Western European nations roughly halved, and the fall has continued since then. To take a characteristic example of male religious, in 1958 the Augustinian Order in the Netherlands had 380 friars. By 2015 the number was 39, and the youngest friar was aged 70. In the present century, church authorities have had no alternative but to undertake mass closures. In Spain over the past decade, houses have been closing at the rate of a hundred a year. In 2018 Pope Francis lamented the "hemorrhaging" of priests and nuns. "God only knows," he said, "how many seminaries, churches, monasteries and convents will be closed in the next few years."[14]

France represents these problems in acute form. Less than half the population even notionally identifies as Catholic, and their actual levels of participation are weak. By 2012 35 percent of the population reported "no religion," a number that rose to 63 percent among young people. The country scores slightly better than the "rule of ten," with the number of newly ordained priests dropping from almost six hundred in 1960 to around a hundred annually today, but that decline still represents a crisis. The average age of French priests is a daunting 70, and each year marks the deaths of elderly priests who can never be replaced. That makes it exceedingly difficult to serve an ecclesiastical structure created for a totally different religious environment. Many of France's thirty-six thousand parishes cannot be served by regular full-time priests and thus face mergers with other units, which often lie some distance away. A fifth of the county's fifteen thousand historic churches face outright closure. In many countries church authorities have imported priests from the teeming seminaries of Africa or Asia. These might be excellent clergy in their own right, but their use promotes popular detachment from a church that seems so disconnected from local communities and their concerns. Indeed, that trend gives European believers a sense that they are being served by a missionary church. In Italy foreign-born clergy serve 40 percent of parishes.[15]

Faith's Long, Withdrawing Roar

The precipitous decline of institutional faith across much of Europe has attracted much commentary and also inspired some excellent social science research. The problem is that the results of this work are often confusing, as equally valid surveys produce results that seem wildly contradictory. Briefly, they show a great many self-defined Christians, most of whom do not practice and scarcely believe in significant parts of the worldview.

The Pew Research Center has in recent years done some significant studies, which at first sight offer a paradoxical finding. Looking at Western European nations, a survey published in 2018 found that some 70 percent of the population identified as Christian, with numbers reaching 80 percent in such long-familiar centers of piety as Austria, Ireland, and Italy, and even 41 percent in the Netherlands. But before churches could take comfort in these numbers, the same survey also showed a very low level of actual church attendance on any regular scale, defined as attending monthly or more often. (Those figures take no account of the eternal problem of people overclaiming the amount of their church attendance.) Those reporting as "church attending Christians" represented just 10 to 15 percent of the population of most of Northern Europe and Scandinavia, 18 percent in Britain and France. The largest proportions of churchgoing Christians were in Ireland, Italy, and Portugal, but not even in those lands did the attending faithful come close to majority status. Given recent developments it will be interesting to see how long that Irish figure remains stable.[16]

Europe is a large and diverse continent, and conditions vary a great deal from place to place. Some nations still report high church attendance and participation, and over 40 percent of Poles report attending church weekly. Even so, much of Central and Eastern Europe looks very "Western" in its religious picture. Hungary, the Czech Republic, Bulgaria, and the Baltic nations have low attendance rates comparable to Scandinavia or the Netherlands.[17]

Applying another criterion for measuring religious attitudes, Western European nations rank low on a global survey of respondents who agree that religion plays a very important part in their lives. Such religious-oriented individuals constitute just 10 percent of the populations of Britain, Germany, France, and Sweden, and most Western European nations fall below 20 percent. Those figures are not much higher if they are applied just to self-described Christians, rather than to the population as a whole. Another survey published in 2015 offered a picture of religiosity around the world that meshes nicely with findings from many other polls. Questioners simply asked people whether they felt religious (however they defined the term), and the results varied enormously. All the top twenty-five nations were located in Africa, the Middle East, or Southeast Asia, and each of these reported religious sentiments with response rates of 95 percent or higher. At the other extreme were twenty-three nations drawn mainly from Europe (fourteen nations) but with some Asian names, including China and Japan. Predictable members of the list included the Netherlands and Great Britain, together with Sweden, Norway, Estonia, and the Czech Republic.[18]

By far the commonest European pattern is that of the nonpracticing Christians, those who nominally cite Christian identity but have nothing to do with institutional life. That category accounts for almost half of all Western Europeans, for whom religion played little part in their lives. The mystery, perhaps, is why so many continue to cite Christian affiliation at all, as we are long past the era when a denial of orthodox faith involved any social stigma and still less any negative real-world consequences. One factor is the growth of Islam, which has persuaded some Europeans to proclaim a Christian identity as a marker that distinguishes them from their Muslim neighbors. Such an identity statement need have no actual substance in religious practice.

Nons and Nones

No less telling is the dramatic rise in respondents who are wholly religiously unaffiliated—those who deny any religious link whatever, rather than just being spiritually lukewarm or inactive. A striking 2016 study showed only a third of Dutch people claiming any faith at all, with Christianity still the largest component, at 25 percent. That number was exactly paralleled by the quarter of the population who were outright atheists. Even the number who reported belief in any higher power, rather than a specific concept of God, is falling steadily. By 2017, 52 percent of British people reported having no religion, and the rate for people under 24 was 70 percent. The most significant growth was among those who accepted the label of "confident atheists." Those figures were rather worse than the larger European norm, but the picture of European detachment from religion is common. Across the region the proportion of the religiously unaffiliated is an impressive 24 percent, outnumbering churchgoing Christians. Besides the Netherlands, the unaffiliated figure is highest in Belgium, Norway, and Sweden, at over 35 percent. The lowest figures were for Ireland, Portugal, and Austria, at 15 percent. Throughout the region the great majority of these unaffiliated—the Nones—had been baptized and raised Christian. Overwhelmingly those unaffiliated agreed with the statement that science made religion unnecessary for them. (I will discuss the concept of the Nones further in chapter 5.)[19]

Straightforward atheism has also become a common creed, markedly so in some societies. In a recent survey, the proportion flatly asserting no belief in God was at its height in the Czech Republic (66 percent) and Sweden (60 percent), with high levels of disbelief in Belgium, the Netherlands, Norway, and Estonia. This trend is particularly pronounced in large cities.

Berlin vaunts its role as the atheist capital of Europe, and 60 percent of residents claim no religion.[20]

The drift away from religion is so advanced, and progressing so swiftly, that some scientific surveys project the extinction of faith of all kinds from several nations by the end of the present century. A study reported to the American Physical Society in 2011 predicted that by the end of the present century, nine nations would be entirely free of religion. Six of these were European, namely Austria, the Czech Republic, Finland, Ireland, the Netherlands, and Switzerland. Very striking here was the inclusion of nations like Austria and Ireland, where levels of faith are presently holding up relatively well. Actually the study suggested that other nations might well be following a like trajectory, but their official statistics did not permit the kind of analysis that would permit such conclusions. Not included in the list, therefore, was Great Britain, which commonly appears alongside the Netherlands in listings of the world's most secular societies. (The other three nations on the APS listing were all anglophone members of the former British Empire, namely Australia, New Zealand, and Canada.) Of course, any such long-term projections are tenuous, but the listing of countries is suggestive.[21]

Fertility and the Secular

As I have remarked, the chronology of the religious decline so exactly follows the fertility shift that a linkage of some kind is probable, even if the chain of causation is not clear. Did a shift in attitudes to faith contribute to reducing fertility, or did a decline in fertility undermine religious loyalties? Or, as seems most likely, did the two trends march together side by side?[22]

In the first chapter, I suggested a rough model of the interaction between demographic change and the fate of religion. The experience of the 1950s gives a sense of this relationship, as we observe the intimate relationship between large families and thriving religious communities. Regardless of denomination, much of church life in that era revolved around activities involving children, including church schools and the various rites of passage. That model depended on voluntary contributions of time and effort from parents, chiefly mothers, who might not be in full-time employment. In a world with much more limited mobility than today, those families likely had ties to institutions spanning multiple generations. Especially in small towns and villages, this made churches fundamental to the structures of community, and to be excluded from the place of worship was to be shut off from the community. In Italy passionate local loyalty is often termed *campanilismo*, literally devotion to the church bell tower that is inevitably at the heart of the community and its life; we note that the focus is the church building, rather than any religious doctrine. While teenagers and young adults might drift away from religious practice, they were likely to return when they had young families of their own, to whom they hoped to pass on values and a sense of community. When adults returned to church life, they judged religious institutions by the quality of their programs for the young.[23]

In contrast we look at the very different society of the later twentieth century, as so many factors conspired to undermine those forces that had hitherto sustained religious loyalties. As women moved into the workplace, many found themselves without the time and commitment to fulfill narrowly defined maternal roles, so that family size shrank. The number of children fell, and populations aged. Through the early 1960s, the proportion of Italians aged 14 or under was always over a quarter, but by the end of the century, it was usually below 14 percent. Meanwhile, the country's median age grew from 32 in 1965 to over 40 at the end of the century and 47 today. Removing the family ties to institutional faith reduced participation and attendance, and contributed to the decline of the "mass church" model. As people postponed marriage and the establishment of families, that further contributed to the decline of organized faith, as fewer people entered the family life that so often persuades people to join religious bodies and to return to churches or institutions they abandoned in their early years.[24] Only when we take children out of the picture do we see how fundamental large families are to traditional religious practice.[25]

Changes in women's role transformed what had for centuries been a fundamental part of life in the Catholic and Orthodox worlds, which was the existence of nuns. Apart from their pivotal role in education, Catholic nuns were essential to the provision of medical services, to the point that nurses' uniforms worldwide ultimately derive from the distinctive garb worn by nuns in the nineteenth century. Yet orders of nuns went into a tailspin from the mid-1960s, as convents emptied out and new vocations all but ceased. To understand this we return once more to the demographic changes of the time. In the 1950s the main option available to women in many societies was marriage and motherhood, leaving the convent life as a rare alternative, and one with significant prestige. From the 1960s the range of opportunities expanded enormously, causing many thousands of women who would otherwise have joined convents to find secular careers and professions, usually after attending colleges or universities. Together with the shrinking numbers of children, the near vanishing of nuns constituted a revolution in the Catholic Church.[26]

In other ways too, changing patterns of education helped undermine clerical authority. Traditionally the educated status of clergy contributed to their prestige and to the acceptance of their leadership, especially when their experience might have involved study in great cities or universities. In so many senses, clergy genuinely were a class set apart. In a modern setting, any such assumption is gravely undermined by the vast proliferation of higher education among laypeople—especially among women—which offers a frontal challenge to clericalism.

At the same time, rural depopulation and urban expansion both contributed to the decline of religious institutions. The exodus from rural areas disrupted what had been very high-fertility communities, which had organized their social life around churches and their bells. In such villages and small towns, small population size created a stronger sense of community, which fostered participation in ongoing religious activities. Those conditions changed fundamentally in the more anonymous circumstances of cities and suburbs.

The Decline of Death

One fundamental change in life experience has in recent times become so obvious that we scarcely notice it, and that involves awareness of death.

Over the past century, life expectancy has grown in all advanced countries (with Russia as a notorious outlier). If we list the world's nations by life expectancy, we observe a pattern we have seen before in so many other contexts, with the poorer countries of Africa and South Asia as the shortest lived and the greatest longevity in Europe and East Asia. In those latter regions, revolutions in medicine and hygiene mean that we are simply far less likely to witness frequent funerals or deathbeds than were our predecessors in earlier eras, particularly deaths involving babies or small children, or of women who die in childbirth. Indeed, the plunge in maternal mortality rates has been almost as spectacular as that in infant mortality. Changes in fertility have also played a vital role in changing consciousness of death and the transience of life. Among other things, it means that any given person today has far fewer siblings or close relatives, all the uncles, aunts, and cousins that would once have proliferated and who would have died at relatively early ages. Putting those trends together, it is vastly less likely that a European in the 2020s will during the course of a given year know intimates who will die, and who will require the services and consolations of religion. And overwhelmingly deaths are a matter for the old and the very old. Even when deaths occur, they are less visible because they almost certainly take place outside the family home, usually in hospitals.[27]

This quite literal life-and-death shift of attitudes had multiple effects. I have already noted how new social attitudes encouraged women to postpone childbearing, often into their late thirties or beyond. Such a decision would have seemed reckless or foolhardy to earlier generations, who had justifiable doubts about whether anyone could rely on surviving into those years and, moreover, in good health. A woman who became a mother at age 35 or 40 stood a high chance of failing to see that child reach adulthood and leaving a child orphaned or motherless. Against that background, beginning parenthood earlier—probably in the late teens—was a rational decision. It also made high fertility rates almost certain. Awareness of death prompts the initiation of life.

The transition away from early mortality had sweeping consequences for religion and religious behavior. Awareness of the death of others is likely to make survivors more conscious of their own mortality, as an event that could happen to them in the near future. Although this is no iron rule, we can reasonably expect such conditions to make people think more about concepts like survival after death and about the supernatural realm in general. The prospect of death gave concern not just to the very old but to teenagers and young adults; how could it not? Poet Philip Larkin defined religion as "That vast moth-eaten musical brocade / Created to pretend we never die."[28]

But death faded as an omnipresent reality. We can trace the impact on baptisms, which became far less common in the late twentieth century. For one thing, there were far fewer children to be baptized and thus to bond families to the church. But changes of attitude also played their part. Prior to the twentieth century, high infant mortality made it quite likely that a new baby would die within the first months or years of life, so that it was imperative to offer baptism as soon as possible. Reinforcing that idea was a common belief that baptism averted the peril of hellfire. As the century progressed, the supernatural theme declined to a vanishing point, while better medicine largely removed any need for early church intervention. Instead of a near-universal rite of passage, the ritual came to be a conscious decision by those with a particular commitment to the church.

A society that by our standards is immersed in death and dying also offers many functions for religious professionals and clergy, in some faiths more than others. In Catholic societies especially, clergy were traditionally expected to attend the deathbed, but other denominations also gave ministers a prominent role in comforting the dead and consoling survivors. At least in popular religious culture, believers felt that proper assistance at the moment of death could make the difference between eternal salvation and damnation. For centuries the "good death" represented a vast theme in popular religious literature and sermons. Between them, weddings, baptisms, and funerals represented a very sizable part of what clergy did, and when we remove the element of "dispatched" from the package, we not only excise a major share of clergy time but a significant element of their whole raison d'être. An increasingly indifferent public no longer saw any necessity to involve the church at any point in their lives or family arrangements. The modern "decline of death" contributed powerfully to that trend.

Specifically within Catholicism, theological and liturgical usage reinforced these changes. For centuries popular religious belief put huge weight on the Last Rites, and the assumption that those rituals were a key element in the forgiveness of sins and the transition to a blessed immortality. The church might not have asserted or supported those beliefs formally, but they were widely accepted. It thus represented a massive shift in the 1970s when the church explicitly drew the distinction between the more general anointing of the sick and the long-familiar Extreme Unction, which was popularly portrayed as a death ritual. That contributed powerfully to ending the priest's indispensable role at the deathbed.

Death's role in stimulating religious behavior may explain an otherwise curious element in the longer-term story of fertility decline. As we have seen, much of Europe experienced a major fertility drop after the First World War, although there was nothing like the modern secular shift. One reason for that was the strong presence of death and death rituals as a consequence of the First World War, in an era when so much time was spent building and dedicating monuments to the war dead and holding services of remembrance. Clergy of most denominations acquired a whole new function that added to their social significance and esteem. In terms of ideology and belief, an overwhelming interest in the supernatural and the afterlife is indicated by the buoyant popularity of Spiritualism and other mystical movements, which reached their apex in these years.[29]

A society's degree of awareness of death—or its ignorance—is a powerful variable in determining its religious orientation. By this standard late twentieth-century Europe represented a startling new world, and a far more secular one.

Revolutions in Morality

Besides mortality, questions of morality also forced change. Changes in sexual morality above all were powerful drivers in the movement away from religion in this same era and in the decline of religious organizations. As we saw in the previous chapter, the fertility shift was inextricably linked with revolutionary changes in sexual morality, both in public attitudes and in the legislative environment. For religious institutions, that provoked a vicious cycle. The harder the churches fought to resist those changes, the more they undermined their own prestige and power. The more defeats the churches suffered, the more public morality shifted away from what the churches regarded as an appropriate moral consensus. Endemic morality battles and culture wars proved devastating for the churches' political power.

Earlier I mentioned the claim that the year 1963 marked a historic turning point in the British disengagement with religion. Although no single year can take the credit or blame for tectonic shifts in culture or social history, that particular year is widely cited in other British contexts. It is taken as marking the onset of the sexual revolution—wryly described as "the year that sex was invented"—and new freedom in the mass media. It is likewise claimed as the beginning of the youth revolution, symbolized by the triumphant success of the Beatles. In Britain, as in much of Western Europe, baby boom births peaked in 1963 and 1964, before beginning their steep fall. Religious change coincided neatly with moral, cultural, and demographic shifts.[30]

In the larger Catholic world, the year 1968 was a vital pivot. As we have seen, in that year Pope Paul VI issued the encyclical *Humanae Vitae*, which restated traditional bans on artificial contraception. This was at a time when the Catholic faithful were assumed to be devoted to the teachings of the church and the papacy, and indeed many Catholics did follow the teachings. But a steadily increasing number did not, initially in the developed countries, and then worldwide. Not only did the underlying social currents prove too strong for religious authority, but the act of dissidence in that sphere encouraged believers to ignore or even contest church teachings in other matters, as would emerge in later political controversies. The outcome was a growing sense that religion was a privatized or individual concern, and certainly in matters as vital as the fate of one's family and children. Issues of sexuality, gender, and family took precedence over religious commands—a vital precedent.

That shift in turn led to another historic change in church structures, namely the steep decline in confessions from the mid-1960s onward. As a practice, regular personal confession to a priest had been a strict church norm for centuries, yet many European and North American believers simply abandoned it within a decade or two, leaving frequent confession as the preserve of the elderly and very traditional minded. Explanations for this change are various, but one popular interpretation is that many laypeople lost respect for the church's authority to enforce or regulate sexual norms and behavior, matters that had provided so much of the substance of confessions in years gone by. The contraception crisis greatly added to the feeling that this was none of the clergy's business. By the early twenty-first century, regular confession had become so slight a part of the European Catholic world that scholars studying Catholic practice no longer include it on their questionnaires.[31] The near-overnight fading of confession represented a grave diminution of priestly authority. It resulted not from activism by liberal reformers but rather from tectonic shifts in the attitudes and behaviors of grassroots believers.

Across the non-Communist continent, the degree of change between (say) 1965 and 1985 was almost inconceivable, whether we are considering attitudes to contraception, divorce, abortion, homosexuality, or pornography. In the 1990s the collapse of Communism spread Western European standards eastward. In a startling irony, the hammer and sickle emblem shifted from being the heroic sign of global Communist aspirations to becoming something like a logo for particularly daring Internet pornography.

Fighting against Revolution

In non-Communist Europe the sexual revolution was enacted in the teeth of opposition from organized churches. In Italy, Spain, and other Catholic nations, the successive referenda and legislative debates that marked the progress of new attitudes reflected defeats for the power of the organized church and for devout lay groups. When the church today expresses its own seemingly implacable opposition to innovations like same-sex marriage, it is presenting views that are most closely associated with the very old and the ultra-conservative. As progressive social attitudes are associated with one's level of educational attainment, that further reinforces the ugly stereotype of the religious conservative as ignorant or uneducated. The clergy on whom the burden of argument must fall are not only exclusively male but, in most cases, well above the retirement age common in most of Europe. Even apart from hints of sexual deviance, the age and gender of priests seems to confirm every accusation that the church is hopelessly patriarchal, hidebound, and out of touch with contemporary realities. This is after all a society where women are so visible in the worlds of politics, business, and media. As an institution the church becomes indefensible.[32]

Again, these political conflicts involved a cumulative process. The more political capital the church invested in these struggles, the more it presented itself as hostile to the expressed views of younger members of society, and especially of women, who in turn were more likely to oppose church power. Repeated defeats in turn suggested the weakened state of an institution increasingly associated with older citizens and reduced religious influence in other public matters.

Although issues of morality and sexuality remain divisive, the battles for progressive views are largely ended among younger citizens. That is especially true in the area of homosexuality, in Western Europe at least. Even among the continent's thriving far-right parties and sects, issues of race and religion are absolutely paramount, to the near-total exclusion of matters of sexual identity. One recent survey indicates that, in most countries of Western Europe, the proportion of young adults (aged 18 to 34) that opposes same-sex marriage now varies between 10 and 15 percent, and even that number is shrinking steadily.[33]

An Extreme Case: Belgium

Belgium offers a notable illustration of these processes at work. Historically Belgium was a center of Catholic spiritual and cultural life, and the country's Catholic loyalties were reinforced by the heroic actions of church leaders in resisting German occupation during the First World War. In the later twentieth century, that Catholic identity came close to obliteration, as the country shared the general demographic decline. The TFR fell below replacement in the early 1970s and reached a trough of 1.51 in 1985. At 1.7, the rate today is below that of Denmark or the Netherlands, and rates for contraceptive usage are little below those of Protestant Northern Europe.[34]

By all the standard measures, the Belgian church is in deep trouble. Sunday Mass attendance is below 10 percent, and today, fewer than half of parents have their children baptized as Catholics. Vocations have fallen to almost literally nothing: in 2007 only two priestly ordinations occurred in the whole country. Only 55 percent of Belgians even identify as Christian, a level comparable to Scandinavia. In 2016 the Brussels Archdiocese announced sweeping plans to concentrate religious services in a small number of flagship churches, radically consolidating parishes. That would involve the closure of a majority of the city's churches, over a hundred in all. As was remarked in 2015, "In today's Belgium, religious observance is mainly the preserve of the elderly, or of the Muslim minority."[35]

Even by European standards, Belgium stands at the vanguard of secular and liberal/progressive approaches to legislation, as distinctive Catholic moral positions have become ever less influential. In 1990 Belgium legalized abortion, and in 2003 it became the second country in the world (after the Netherlands) to approve same-sex marriage. In 2002 the country approved euthanasia, and in 2014 extended that policy to allow the euthanasia of children. Those last measures occurred despite the opposition of even very liberal clerics who had been sympathetic to earlier reforms in sexual matters. Observers sometimes warn that particular reforms represent a "slippery slope," leading to something worse or more extreme, but from a Catholic perspective, it is difficult to see how much further a secularization of law might proceed. Belgium already stands at the bottom of that metaphorical slope.

An Exceptional Case: Poland

Although most of the trends we are discussing here apply generally across much of the continent, some East-West distinctions do remain.[36] Same-sex marriage still remains a marker, with rates of disapproval running above 50 percent even among young adults (aged 18 to 34) in most of the former Eastern Bloc and even in the otherwise secular Baltics. Almost certainly this represents a delay of a few years in a homogenization with Western Europe, but it does remind us of the complicated and diverse nature of European social patterns. Given the very different positions that the respective halves of Europe occupied just a generation ago, we should perhaps be taken aback that they have converged as much as they have.

One European country in particular demands special attention because at first sight, it represents such a glaring contradiction to wider patterns. In demographic terms Poland fits the larger story of Catholic Europe very well, with a steep decline in fertility from the early 1980s onward. The Polish TFR stood at 3.0 in 1960, fell below replacement in the late 1980s, and today is closely comparable to Italy or Spain. The country's economy has boomed over the past generation, with a huge expansion of the service sector and high tech, and GDP per capita has expanded fivefold since the late 1980s. By all rights, we should expect the country's religious development to echo that of other Catholic nations, whereas in fact it has seemingly followed a precisely opposite direction. By all the usual measures, this is among the most religious nations in Europe: 41 percent of Poles attend church weekly, as opposed to just 19 percent reporting "seldom or never." The Catholic Church remains strong and popular with extraordinary levels of vocations, and Polish priests have become a sought-after "export" to other nations facing clergy shortages. Poland represents a puzzling and counterintuitive model of a society that is at once low fertility and high faith—actually, at the extreme end of both trends.[37]

This exception must be explained in terms of the highly distinctive circumstances of Polish history. Since the eighteenth century, as Polish nationality was suppressed, national and cultural identity were both strongly identified with Catholicism and the church. That was true in other nations, notably Ireland, but the tradition received a mighty boost in recent times with the combined events of the papacy of the Polish national icon Pope

John Paul II and the overthrow of Communism. In consequence, Catholicism continued to permeate Polish national consciousness in ways that had long since stopped being true of other formerly oppressed nations. This served to counteract—or at least postpone—any possible drives toward secularization arising from social or demographic factors.

It remains to be seen how long such influences might remain effective. Analogies with Ireland suggest that a generation or so of prosperity and sexual transformations will indeed undermine what appear to be even the deepest-rooted religious loyalties. Although this may represent only an early stage in the process, sexual scandals and abuse cases have recently begun to assail the prestige of the Polish church. The church also faces negative consequences from its close alliance with the conservative regimes that have dominated Polish politics over the past decade. The church has won political rewards from that affiliation, but it has also suffered much criticism, especially from the activities of far-right militants who espouse extreme Christian nationalism. Poland has for some years been engaged in bitter culture wars, in which church authorities have often been identified with worldly political causes. The long-term consequences of such a struggle remain to be seen. Most probably the Polish exception is not a contradiction of the demographic interpretation but rather an example of a delayed decline.[38]

Alternative Explanations

Few commentators dispute the general trend of religious decline in these decades, although alternative explanations are sometimes advanced. Catholics debate the impact of the extensive reforms undertaken within that church following the second Vatican Council, which met from 1958 through 1963 and which exercised its greatest influence over the following decade or so. According to conservatives Catholic loyalties were strained to breaking point by the liberal reforms as they affected ordinary parish life, while the recurring spectacle of clerical dissidence further undermined church prestige. Dutch and Belgian clergy were at the forefront of liberal activism, and as we have seen, church decline in both countries has been very marked. Moreover, the chronology does indeed mesh with the decline as we observe it in parts of Catholic Europe.[39]

But affairs within the Catholic Church had next to no impact on the Protestant nations, where religious decline was already well underway by the mid-1960s. Instead of provoking the moral revolution and the resulting religious decline, it is much more probable that the battles within the church in the 1960s and 1970s were a consequence of those social changes, rather than a cause. In issues like the debates over contraception, dissident and

liberal clergy were responding to a fast-changing mood among their parish-
ioners, at a time when gender roles and expectations were in flux and when
attitudes to sexuality were already moving away steadily from prescribed
church norms. The church could not hold back a surging tide.

Abuse Scandals

Nor should we invoke as an explanation the various scandals involving child
sexual abuse by clergy, or at least without major qualifications. In modern
times clergy abuse scandals first came to light on a significant scale in the
United States in the 1980s, before reaching the status of an "epidemic" in
the 1990s. Such cases subsequently came to light in Europe, especially since
the start of the present century. Scandals have affected many religious communities in various nations, especially the Catholic Church, but also Anglicans, and the effects on the prestige and influence of these churches have
been disastrous. Abuse cases, whether fictional or based on real cases, have
become a popular genre in the cinema and television of several nations. In
Ireland, at least, many observers have cited the inflammatory impact of these
controversies in discrediting church stances in moral debates and indeed in
influencing key referenda. Even in this once notoriously pious land, bitterly
anticlerical sentiments are now commonplace.[40]

Having said that, the chronology of abuse scandals suggests next to no
connection with church decline in most countries, as the great majority of
cases occurred long after the contraction was well underway. If the abuse
crisis had its impact in Ireland, that occurred decades after the church was
already in free fall in nations like Spain and Belgium.

Again too, we should question the sequence of influences in deciding
what causes what. How far did the abuse scandals drive disaffection from
the churches, as opposed to resulting from it? Of course most such scandals
have revealed authentic misconduct, and to that extent, the resulting revelations have been necessary and appropriate. Yet without the underlying
drift away from the churches in previous years, it is unthinkable that these
instances would have been investigated, that the media would have had the
courage to take on the powerful churches, or that they would have received
mass public support. In Catholic societies in particular, such revelations simply could not have happened before the 1970s, because of the overwhelming respect and prestige that those churches and their clergy held among
believers. For many years before that time, anticlerical and anti-religious
activists had regularly circulated stories of clerical misdeeds, usually sexual
in nature, and Catholics more or less unanimously ignored them as partisan rants. On a practical level, any filmmaker of an earlier generation who

might have proposed a project depicting sexual abuse by clergy would have faced implacable opposition from believers both clerical and lay, and the near-certain prospect of effective boycotts would have made any such effort commercially suicidal. Only after the shift in religious attitudes in the last quarter of the century did conditions change to permit a new receptivity to charges and the possibility of airing them.

Among other developments, new attitudes to sexuality cast a different light on the practice of celibacy and encouraged perceptions that it must conceal deviant or hypocritical behavior. In particular, the new awareness of homosexuality, and a sense of its prevalence, made people more willing to believe that supposedly celibate clergy might well be sexually active in various covert ways, including pedophilia. (It is scarcely necessary to add that this is not to suggest any actual linkage between homosexuality and sexual misconduct with children.) When the abuse scandals surfaced, ordinary people heard what they were already prepared to believe, and perhaps what they expected.

The disaffection and anticlericalism that have become evident in recent years were thus part of the causation of such scandals, rather than a consequence. As I have already noted, one aspect of the larger demographic change was a new emphasis on the value and protection of children, and the media framing of these scandals brilliantly exploited those concerns, setting sinister authoritarian clerics against the young and vulnerable. That gave powerful rhetorical ammunition to activists in successive public debates and referenda over morality. As progressive critics might ask, by what right did the church dare challenge the behavior of consenting adults in sexual matters, when it tolerated the grave crimes of clergy against the innocent? When abuse scandals did emerge, they provided a justification for believers to leave the church, perhaps severing ties altogether. It remains an open question whether those defectors would have left at some point anyway and found their moment in such egregious crises.

To return to the Polish example noted earlier, the country's church has through the years faced isolated charges of clerical abuse, but the sense of a systematic problem or crisis only emerged in the late 2010s. As reports of abuse mounted, they achieved national audiences through films and media presentations, often release through unofficial media like YouTube.[41] Mounting attacks on the church in sexual matters segued naturally into denunciations of its political attitudes and alliances with conservative politics. As in Ireland, Belgium, and other countries, this suggests that the scandals are a symptom of institutional decline, rather than its cause.

Secularization?

I have spoken of religious decline, measured in terms of the sharply diminished influence of churches and of popular detachment from institutional faith. Both those trends are usually described as part of the process of secularization, a concept long familiar to sociologists and social theorists, although it has been much debated and attacked through the years. In the late twentieth century the upsurge of faith in many unsuspected corners of the world threw grave doubt on claims about any inevitable movement toward the secular, while European scholars were taken aback by what initially seemed to be a strong rebound in the churches of formerly Communist Eastern Europe. Globally the resurgence of political Islam made religion and religious conflict central to any understanding of world affairs. Secularization theory also faced a spectacular counterexample in the highly advanced but strongly religious United States. Having said that, the secularization idea generally does work well as a template for understanding changes in contemporary Europe, and I will be using this model repeatedly throughout the present book. But we do need to appreciate some of the limitations in what the theory claims, especially in a matter as critical as the definition of religion or religious behavior.[42]

The secularization thesis suggests that religious institutions were generally formed in premodern settings, which is where they find their natural home, both socially and intellectually. Traditional institutional faith also assumes a world in which religious professionals boast superior access to education or learning and are moreover connected to the larger world in ways not available to most ordinary believers. Circumstances change when new economic arrangements disrupt older communities and advance urbanization and industrialization.[43] Modernity promotes individualism, privatization, and the dominance of a scientific worldview that renders obsolete religious claims to provide healings or miracles. As modernity advances, so religion withdraws. Scholars speak of the removal of religious meaning through a process of desacralization or disenchantment. In practical terms the modern welfare state provides the social services and education once supplied by religious-based charities or movements, so that citizens know they can comfortably rely on government-provided assistance in time of crisis. Modernization also implies the division of activities into separate spheres, for instance, of science and the economy, and religion just becomes another of those realms, with no necessary privileged authority over any other aspect of life. Secularization entails the loss of cultural authority by religious institutions, which also forfeit social power and political influence.[44]

To that extent Europe has incontestably been undergoing a kind of secularization, and many would cite the continent's recent experience as a textbook example of that theory in action. This is so significant because, as we will see, something like the European process has subsequently swept over much of the world, so that conditions that we presently see in Belgium or Germany might be expected to be reproduced much farther afield.

Believing and Belonging

But as commonly presented, the secularization idea intermingles two themes that do not necessarily belong together, namely the institutional and the intellectual. That necessary distinction is illustrated by the work of Grace Davie, whose 1994 work on modern British religious history was subtitled *Believing without Belonging*. That phrase has become popular in the scholarly literature. While fully admitting the massive popular detachment from religious structures—from belonging and participation—Davie argued that religious belief remained widespread. Strictly secularist or irreligious views did and do exist, but they are most advanced among cultural and political elites, rather than ordinary people. Davie further suggested that the Christian presence still remains potent through social memory, and that Europe's cultural Christians are "content to let both churches and churchgoers enact a memory on their behalf," secure in the knowledge that Christianity is there if and when they need it. People thus have no problem in defining themselves as Christians, however little that is reflected in actual behavior. Davie's distinction is very important—although we must recall that it applies particularly to countries where churches are intimately allied to states and thus have something of the character of public utilities to provide services as needed, rather than as in the United States, where believers see churches as voluntary associations demanding their support and participation. It also remains an open question how long "believing" can endure without the institutional support and communal reinforcement provided by belonging.[45]

That distinction is so important for what it suggests about secularization, which generally measures a drop in *belonging* but is so often misinterpreted as an evaporation of actual belief. To understand this we might imagine a country where, in recent times, religious institutions have effectively collapsed. Levels of attendance and participation are negligible. At the same time, surveys repeatedly suggest strong religious interests among the population. Overwhelming majorities profess to believe in God, say that religion is important to them, and every day they pray or read sacred texts. At the same time, most would be horrified if religious institutions or clergy claimed a significant role in policy making. Is that society an example of secularization? Many theorists would say, emphatically, yes. As the theory predicts, people express religious interests according to principles of individualism and privatization. And although religious belief is high presently, it is unlikely to remain so without institutional structures. Other observers disagree strongly, as it seems absurd to describe a society as "secular" when it is so evidently oriented toward religious belief and a supernatural worldview. If religious movements or institutions are not apparent presently, the potential audience exists for some such upsurge in future. Both sides in such an argument are correct to some degree, and the problem lies in an oversimple use of terms like *secular* and *secularization*. We have to know what we are measuring.

Such a hypothetical example is highly relevant to modern-day Europe. On the one hand, we unquestionably witness the decline or near collapse of religious structures, whether we measure that by the esteem in which they are held, the political power they wield, or the adherents they can attract to their services. That change assuredly involves a profound change of values. But that is distinct from challenging or rejecting religious belief, insofar as that means accepting a worldview founded on the workings of the supernatural and perhaps even interpreting that through the orthodoxies of one of the great religions. Believing withstands modernity.

The distinction between institutions and beliefs is essential to understanding the currently popular concept of the "Nones," who report rejecting religious affiliations; but that is quite different from assuming that they are denying religious or supernatural belief as such. It is perfectly possible to believe without belonging (and indeed, to belong without believing). We will return to that issue in chapter 5, in the context of the United States.[46]

Belief in Europe

The decline of supernatural belief undoubtedly has occurred in much of the West, and faith continues to recede. As a character in one of Tom Stoppard's plays aptly remarked, "There is presumably a calendar date—a moment—when the onus of proof passed from the atheist to the believer, when, quite suddenly, secretly, the noes had it." Arguably, that date is now past, in most of Western Europe at least. But any narrative of the loss of religious faith must be kept separate from the decline of institutions, and evidence for such faith is evident even in the most apparently secularized parts of Europe.[47]

Even as the institutions fade, belief in God—at least in some form—proves remarkably stubborn. I earlier cited a survey showing high levels of atheist sentiment in some thirty-four European countries, but that same poll also gave believers some grounds for cheer. Belief in God—either unquestioning or with some qualifications—was expressed by overwhelming majorities across Eastern Europe and the Balkans. At the same time such a position was held by a majority of respondents in all but six of the nations sampled, even in such seemingly secular lands as Germany, France, and Britain. In another recent survey in Western Europe, an impressive 26 percent of respondents reject any belief in God, even in the vague form of some kind of higher power. But that number is close to the 27 percent who profess a belief not only in God but specifically as the deity is presented in the Bible. To that extent atheism and orthodox Christianity march hand in hand statistically. The largest contingent in that study was the 38 percent who believe not in a biblical God but in a higher power, however conceived.[48] That higher power belief is very widespread and is held by over half of nonpracticing Christians and even a third of churchgoers. In some form, the divine exercises a powerful appeal for millions who might never darken the doors of a place of worship.

We should also note that it is simply impossible to compare such figures for belief with earlier times, because the sophisticated opinion surveys that exist today were wholly unavailable a century ago (say), never mind for more remote historical periods. We cannot compare like with like, as we can—however cautiously—when we measure actual behavior or participation. When we read, for instance, that in modern France, 11 percent of respondents accept God's existence absolutely while 45 percent are less certain and 37 percent are atheists, we may feel intuitively that levels of belief have declined sharply over the past 100 or 150 years, but we cannot even attempt to prove it. Modern nonspecialists generally underestimate just how common rationalist, materialist, and anti-religious views were in earlier eras. Conceivably, believers in earlier eras had just as many doubts as their modern counterparts, even if most did not express them so publicly.[49]

Spiritual and Religious

However extensive its effects on institutions, secularization does not mark the obliteration of religion as such, or the death of God, since a notion of higher powers appears to be hardwired into our consciousness. Arguably this religious instinct is now manifested in forms of noninstitutional spirituality that are more personal, autonomous, nondogmatic, and nonjudgmental. The most successful appeal to precisely the sectors of the potential audience most detached from institutional faiths, especially among women. Broadly New Age movements have been successful across Europe, and they have attracted a large scholarly literature. As ideas of religious community fray, private and individual practices remain and even flourish, to the point that some scholars speak of resacralization or reenchantment as a powerful trend in the modern world. We can use many words to describe that process, but secularization of itself scarcely fits.[50]

When we measure religious practice in any society, we naturally look at the behaviors normally associated with institutions, so in a Christian setting that would chiefly mean attendance at weekly Sunday services. But such an emphasis diverts our attention from other important and widespread forms of expression. The very years that have witnessed the most alarming decline of Europe's churches have also been a remarkably successful period for some traditional religious forms, above all for pilgrimage. Pilgrim shrines flourish across Europe, some drawing millions of followers each year, and new pilgrim destinations have emerged to meet the demand. Moreover, these places offer strikingly traditional or even medieval attractions, with their Marian focus, the veneration of mysterious Black Virgins, and ubiquitous healing miracles.[51]

Several European centers draw pilgrims on a scale that we might better associate with Latin America, and since the 1970s those numbers have grown substantially. Lourdes, which drew about a million visitors each year in the 1950s, now records closer to six million annually. Each year Poland's Jasna Góra, in Częstochowa, attracts four or five million who come to see a miraculous picture of the Virgin, while four million believers visit the site of Mary's apparition at Portugal's Fátima. Just since the late 1980s, pilgrimage has enjoyed a breathtaking revival at Santiago de Compostela, which now attracts some half a million pilgrims in a regular year, rising to a million in special holy years. Shrine-rich Italy offers Rome and Assisi, Padua and Turin. Even in Europe's supposedly secular heart, on the German-Dutch frontier, Mary's shrine at Kevelaer draws eight hundred thousand visitors a year. Since the fall of Communism, pilgrimage has likewise revived in the Orthodox world. The believer seeking spiritual direction can once more resort to several historic landmarks of Russian faith, including Optina Pustyn, which in its day welcomed Tolstoy and Dostoevsky. Over and above these Christian sites, New Age movements have their own sacred landscapes and pilgrim sites.

However hostile they might be to hierarchies, however unwilling to attend weekly services, a great many Europeans continue to show a potent interest in religious and spiritual affairs. An interest in spirituality remains high across the continent, and it requires little imagination to see how easily

these interests and enthusiasms could be mobilized by new and emerging religious movements. If low-fertility societies are malarial swamps for
institutional religion, they might be quite hospitable to diverse forms of
spirituality.

Newcomers

Also, even slight acquaintance with major European cities suggests how
very unsecular they are and how religious institutions of various kinds
are flourishing. These include an abundance of mosques and other Islamic
sites. By no means all those reported Muslims are necessarily devout, but
many do indeed practice their religion at far higher rates than their old-
stock neighbors. Nor do those comments take account of Christian immigrants, whose European churches range in scale from what Americans term
"storefront operations" to vast megachurches. Depending on the locality,
these churches might serve people from Asia, Latin America, or Africa, but
Africans are most in evidence—Nigerians in Britain or Italy, Congolese in
France or Belgium. Most are charismatic and Pentecostal in character and
are as far removed from secular worldviews as it is possible to imagine. One
wide-ranging study of Christianity in contemporary London describes *The
Desecularisation of the City*.[52]
    At first sight these diverse institutions—Muslim, Christian, and
others—might seem marginal to the larger religious story, an inconvenient
exception to the secularization narrative, but that is not the case. Exactly
the same social and demographic forces that drove religious decline among
old-stock residents also created the need for mass immigration and with it
the populations who are responsible for the new spiritual upsurge. Societies
with low TFRs and aging populations may tend toward the secular, but they
cannot long survive without importing immigrants, who are younger, fertile, and more actively religious. Whatever their religious orientation might
have been in their home countries, those new settlers turn to churches or
mosques to seek the community and the practical assistance they so desperately need in making their global moves.[53] To that extent, secularization is a
self-limiting process. Sociologist of religion Andrew Greeley justly remarked
that "religion is always declining, and always reviving."[54]
    We commonly draw a dichotomy between secular and religious, so that
an individual or a society has to be in one camp rather than another. The
demographic changes we are witnessing, though, subvert traditional ideas
of institutional and hierarchical religion, expressed in respect for clerical
power and regular religious practice. Yet the changes do not undermine
much religious behavior and spiritual attitudes. This suggests that much

"traditional" and "institutional" religion is grounded in particular demographic settings, and when the settings change fundamentally, so do those structures. And as we will see, those comments apply across the spectrum of religions worldwide.

4

THE REVOLUTION GOES GLOBAL

n 1968, at the height of concern about a population explosion, the distinguished demographer Philip M. Hauser tried to project what the world would look like fifty years hence. In the then-distant year of 2018, he suggested, global population would rise from its present level of 3.5 billion to 9.7 billion. That estimate was considerably too high, by about 2 billion, and in reality we are unlikely to reach that near-10 billion level much before the 2050s, if ever. But the reason for that error is illuminating. Like most observers at the time, Hauser observed common trends of high fertility in the "Third World"—in the three continents of Africa, Asia, and Latin America—and saw no reason to question why those patterns should change. In reality different regions would pursue very different directions, socially, economically, and demographically, and some would hew much closer to the European reality we have identified. That would be especially true in Latin America and large sections of Asia, where Hauser had foreseen the sharpest population growth. Hence those two billion missing humans.[1]

For decades scholars had gazed with puzzlement at European social patterns and birth rates, stressing that these were an exceptional case. Scarcely noticed even by many experts, very comparable realities were in fact spreading around world at breakneck pace. As fertility rates plummeted, so did religiosity and adherence to institutional religion. In those senses at least, "Europe" became something like global normality.

An Emerging World

Demographers had long been accustomed to what are commonly known as Third World population patterns. In a typical country in those regions in the 1960s, ordinary people expressed little confidence in the state's chance to take care of them in old age, while more children meant extra hands to work in a family farm or enterprise. Large families were thus very desirable, and fertility rates were usually high, running at 6 or 7 per woman, far above replacement rate. As medical facilities improved somewhat and infant mortality rates declined, that resulted in major population growth, which in turn sparked the Western concern about overpopulation. A few non-Western countries lowered their population growth rates quite dramatically as they became prosperous, notably Japan, but others largely did not. The term "Third World" acquired disastrous connotations of extreme and inevitable poverty, which were seemingly inevitably linked to race and to nonwhiteness. Increasingly, observers spoke of the "Global South," which still differentiated those poor and fecund nations from the prosperous and (generally) low-fertility Northern world.[2]

In the late twentieth century, the world's economic and political arrangements moved far beyond the simple dualities of Rich North and Poor South. In 1981 Antoine van Agtmael created the optimistic term "emerging markets" to characterize rising nations such as China and Brazil, and that emergence has been impressive. Since 2000, experts have been keenly interested in identifying rising and emerging economies that promise to match or overtake the familiar Euro-American leaders by 2050 or so. Alongside the traditional developed world are now a series of rising nations, grouped under catchy acronyms. The original list named the BRICs (Brazil, Russia, India, China) but other (overlapping) contenders include the MINTS (Malaysia, Indonesia, Nigeria, Turkey, South Africa), the KIMs (South Korea, Indonesia, Mexico), and the still more diffuse Next Eleven. In all, a dozen or so "inbetweener" names feature regularly as rising global contenders. In the 1970s and 1980s, the world's economic powerhouses comprised the so-called Group of Seven, or G7, which included the four largest European economies in addition to the United States, Canada, and Japan. Since 1999 the equivalent elite club has been the G20, in which Euro-American nations share the table with such countries as China but also key nations in Africa, Asia, and Latin America.[3]

Falling Fertility

From the 1980s onward, fertility rates both in the more advanced and the "emerging" sections of the Global South plummeted, at a rate even sharper than that of Europe. In the early 1970s, over a hundred countries representing some 43 percent of the world's population still had sky-high fertility rates of 5 or more per woman. Major changes became apparent at the end of the century in developing nations like Brazil, Mexico, and India, and subsequently a historic move toward sub-replacement fertility has occurred in many nations. Given what we know of the world today, it is astonishing that in 1950 *no* countries were in this sub-replacement category. But at some point in the 2010s, the world reached a significant tipping point when half the global population lived in countries with sub-replacement fertility. Of those people, a quarter live in societies where the fertility rate is between 1.8 and 2.1, but three-quarters are in still lower categories, of below 1.8—a figure that not long ago would have been characterized as Scandinavian. Twenty years ago, demographers used the term "intermediate fertility" to describe countries with TFRs between 2.2 and 5. Today, anything over 3.5 would definitely fall into the category of high rather than middling. Our standards have changed so much, and so fast.[4]

Between 1950 and the mid-1980s, world population was expanding at a predictable rate of roughly 20 percent each decade, but in the 2010s the figure was below 11 percent and falling steadily. We see the consequences of this decline in a significant scaling back of projections for the world's future population. Planetary population stood at 1 billion around 1800, 3 billion by 1959, and 7 billion by 2011. During the twentieth century alone, global population quadrupled. Those increases are inconceivably vast, but how much further might they develop? In 1968 the United Nations Population Division created near panic by predicting that global population in 2050 would be 12 billion, but estimates have fallen ever since, and the best current projection is around 9 billion, with some degree of flexibility. The United Nations further projects that by midcentury, the global fertility rate will be around 2.0, at sub-replacement, or perhaps even lower, so that overall population will begin to decline.[5] If not entirely global, the demographic transition will have affected most of the world.

Largely this is a consequence of economic trends similar to those of Europe. As industry and services grew as a consequence of globalization, so new employment opportunities opened, particularly for women workers. Women's educational opportunities expanded greatly, while contraceptive use also expanded. Throughout the process governments often played a vital part, and in the wider quest for development and modernization, even repressive or authoritarian regimes acted to expand women's education and contraceptive access. In some instances government-sponsored family-planning programs were highly interventionist, and even coercive. More generally the fertility drop was a matter of changes at the grass roots, as ordinary and often uneducated women acquired agency and opened opportunities for themselves. Urbanization played its role, as people moved from villages to cities, and those cities expanded vastly. Globally the share of the world's people living in the countryside fell from 86 percent in 1900 to 53 percent at the end of the century, and it actually fell below half around 2007. Largely, urban populations tend to be much less fecund than their rural kinfolk. Inner cities especially are uncongenial settings for raising families, all the more so where property prices are so extravagantly high.[6]

Around the world too, the popularity of mass media cannot be underestimated, especially television, with the growth of access via satellite and cable channels. Just in the past decade, smartphones and social media have further revolutionized means of communication and information sharing. By 2019 half the world's population had Internet access. Throughout, the dominance of American and European programming has raised global awareness of the high standards of living characteristic of those regions and thereby increased social aspirations. The media have also portrayed the central role of active and emancipated women. If the media were not explicitly propagandizing for women's emancipation and for smaller families, that was a natural consequence of their activities. Media also propagated Western attitudes toward alternate forms of sexuality and from a strongly gay-friendly stance.

The steepest fertility declines came in two regions, namely the Pacific Rim and Latin America.[7] In both, we witness trends we have already encountered in Europe, both in terms of new attitudes toward family and the individual, and radically altered forms of religious expression.

Asian Miracles

Looking today at the futuristic skylines of cities like Singapore or Hong Kong, it is easy to forget how recently they gained that prosperity and separated themselves from other non-Western nations that have progressed much more slowly. Measured by GDP per capita, South Korea in the 1960s was a poorer country than Egypt or Ghana. Matters then changed rapidly, as several nations developed ferociously successful export-led economies and joined the club of high-income nations. The pioneers were the Four Tigers of South Korea, Hong Kong, Singapore, and Taiwan. That drive to growth in turn spilled over into other countries on the Pacific Rim, so that with varying degrees of plausibility, we speak of the Tiger Cubs—Indonesia, Malaysia, the Philippines, Thailand, and Vietnam. Progress there has been uneven, and the late 1990s witnessed a grueling economic downturn, but conditions soon improved. In the new century, the colossal growth of China further accelerated growth in East and Southeast Asia.[8]

Pacific Rim societies shared economic trends very much like we have seen in Europe, as mature economic growth produced a decisive shift to service industries and high tech. As women's social roles were transformed and their access to education expanded, so the Tigers' fertility rates collapsed. Meanwhile the industrial boom drove a mass urban migration and expansion and a consequent emptying of rural areas. As fertility rates fell, so the demographic dividend further accelerated development.

Some countries experienced quite spectacular fertility declines. Taiwan's TFR, which approached 6.0 in 1960, fell to replacement by 1984 and by 2010 actually dipped below 1.0, briefly giving it the world's lowest rate. People married later, women bore their first child at more advanced ages, and more people remained single. The resulting plunge in fertility occurred despite government subsidies and other incentives to encourage families to have children. Nor was Taiwan unique. South Korea's fertility rate in the 1960s was about 6.0, while today it is below 1.0.[9]

Of the world's 224 nations, Taiwan and South Korea both stand among the bottom six, all with TFRs well below 1.5, with that of the city-state of Singapore the very lowest, at 0.83. Japan also ranks among this low-fertility list, although a little higher. In 2004 such figures persuaded demographers to invent a whole new category below "low fertility," and these East Asian lands became exemplars of the "lowest low," with rock-bottom TFRs below 1.3. If sustained, such numbers presaged a population *implosion*. Such crude figures speak volumes for the role of women, for social expectations about women's role and their autonomy, and for attitudes toward sexuality. As we have observed in Japan, low-fertility societies have aged or aging populations. The median age of Taiwan's population is 41; South Korea's is 42.[10]

The advanced character of these prosperous Tigers is scarcely surprising, but similar social patterns have subsequently emerged in the Tiger Cub nations. For much of the twentieth century, Thailand was cited as a classic example of Third World population characteristics, with the growth that implied. The country probably had 6.5 million people in 1900, rising to 20 million by 1950 and 60 million by 1996. But total fertility rates were falling, from around 7.0 in the 1960s to 1.52 by 2017. The country's population today is 70 million, with annual population growth at just 0.3 percent, and some projections see this contracting steadily in coming decades. Thailand's median age is a venerable 38, roughly equivalent to that of the

United States or Norway. Economically, the country has long since ceased to be the peasant society of the older stereotypes, as over half the population is now urban.[11]

Similar stories emerge from other nations that would have occupied center stage in older social science textbooks about the looming menace of overpopulation. Although it is nowhere near as advanced or as economically developed as Taiwan, Vietnam's TFR today is 1.81, down from 6.35 in 1960.[12] Across the region youth bulges have largely vanished.

Fertility declines in other nations are doubly important because of the possible impact on the world's religious map. Indonesia, notably, is by far the world's largest Islamic nation, home to a seventh of the world's Muslims. (We will discuss Indonesia further in chapter 7.) Like its neighbors, Indonesia's fertility rate has plunged in recent decades and now stands exactly at the replacement rate, at 2.11. There is no reason to doubt that recent declines will continue. Similar comments apply to the neighboring nation of the Philippines, which already has one of the world's largest Catholic populations, and that conspicuous role in the Christian world will grow still further by midcentury. In the past century, the country was a textbook example of runaway growth. The Philippine population swelled from perhaps 9 million in 1914 to 100 million today, and that number is projected to grow to 150 million by 2050. Mainly that growth results from high fertility rates. In 1960 the average Filipina woman could expect to have seven children during the course of her life, and as recently as 1983 the rate was still a Third World 5.1. Since the 1980s, though, the fertility rate has plummeted, to 3.1 today, and most projections suggest a continuing decline, which will soon fall below replacement. Demographically the country is moving fast toward European conditions, although with a lag of several decades.[13]

South Asia also produced its demographic shocks. Popular Western images of the Third World commonly drew on Indian horror stories, notably of the poverty of Calcutta (Kolkata) as perceived through heroic tales of the humanitarian work of Mother Teresa. Uncontrollable population growth dominated such narratives, provoking desperate attempts to fight further growth. Just as China was introducing its rigid one-child policy, so India experimented with scarcely less radical interventions. Between 1975 and 1977, India's ruling Congress Party proclaimed an emergency regime that suspended many democratic forms. One aspect of this was a desperately unpopular top-down program of forced sterilizations and vasectomies, which affected eight million Indians. The scheme ended ignominiously in 1977, and nothing like it has been tried subsequently. Most Western nonspecialists probably still assume that that older picture of runaway population growth remains broadly true, but it assuredly does not. India's TFR fell from around 6.0 in 1960 to just 2.4 in 2018—above replacement rate but still falling sharply. Put another way, India's fertility rates today are quite comparable to what American or European rates were back at the time of the Population Bomb panic of the 1960s. (We will look more closely at India's demographic trends in chapter 8.) In neighboring Sri Lanka, fertility rates fell from 5.5 in 1960 to replacement in 2016 and 2.0 today.[14]

Returning to the 1968 projection with which we began this chapter, such booming Asian nations account for the largest share of those expected-but-missing two billion people who should have been walking the earth by 2018.

Religious Crises

Traditional Western images of East Asia generally included potent stereo-types of religious attitudes and behavior, to set aside the images of excru-ciating overpopulation. Besides a romanticization of "Eastern spirituality," we sometimes find common themes of fanaticism and credulity. But just as the demographic stereotypes have broken down, so have assumptions about religiosity. If much of Europe seems post-Christian, then other sections of the globe can with equal justice be characterized as (for instance) post-Buddhist. If beliefs linger, then in many areas at least, practice has declined or even collapsed, as has the sense of automatic obedience to institutional hierarchies.

Any comparison with Europe faces serious limitations in terms of the definition of religion in East and Southeast Asian societies, so that by defi-nition, any drift away from that system must be assessed on its own terms. The very concept of "religion," or of "a religion," is distinctively European and Christian—or arguably, Judeo-Christian—and can only with difficulty be applied elsewhere. That Western package stresses such core themes as exclusive belief and adherence to doctrines, institutional membership, and the possibility of conversion, and few of these concepts work well in an Asian setting. By Western Christian standards, Asian societies might appear highly religious, but much of their belief system is inextricably linked with ideas that in the West would be more usually described as philosophy, social ethics, aesthetics, psychology, or superstition. Western scholars have often tried to confront these differences by invoking notions of "high" and "low" religion, which rarely work in an Asian context. More broadly, ideas that Westerners label as religious would in an Asian context be part of culture; that would be especially true of Chinese-derived ideas and movements such as Confucianism. Taken together this explains why East Asians can declare their religious affiliations in terms that baffle Westerners, for whom faiths are an either/or proposition: you cannot be a Christian and a Muslim simultaneously. Yet you can at once frequent Buddhist and Daoist rituals or attend both Shinto and Buddhist shrines.

Certainly many Asian societies have religious institutions, which historically have enjoyed immense power and prestige, not to mention wealth. Arguably the Buddhist order of monks, the *sangha*, is the oldest institution of any kind in continuous operation anywhere on the planet. Even so, a great deal of religious behavior is carried out by individuals and families, either in the context of their homes or of shrines, and that has always been true. To that extent it already fits the definition we have already encountered of individual and privatized behavior. If secularization were to occur in such a context, how would we recognize or measure it?

But even granting those differences, rapid fertility decline has produced evidence of religious transformations that recall or parallel European trends. In Asia too we see an impact on religious forms and practices.[15]

Japanese Crisis

Changes have been most marked in Japan, which has the longest record of advanced economic development, and (as we have seen) of fertility decline. Scholars often use the country as a type site for discussions and analyses of the long-term effects of extreme low fertility, of the scarcity of children, and of the steady growth of an elderly population. Not since the mid-1970s has the country known replacement fertility. Not surprisingly then, following from European analogies, Japan's levels of religious practice are in free fall, with no obvious signs of recovery.[16]

Japanese people freely alternate between religious traditions. They use Shinto rituals and clergy on some occasions and Buddhist on others, with no sense of incongruity. The actual level of identification with any particular faith is weak, and different surveys will show the proportion of Japanese who identify with Buddhism at anywhere between 40 and 75 percent. By some estimates 71 percent of Japanese are Buddhists, and 84 percent follow Shinto, not counting tiny handfuls adhering to other faiths.[17] The total of course far exceeds 100 percent. Everything depends on how the question is phrased and who is asking it. Some people are very committed to Buddhist traditions or movements, while others only resort to that faith for rituals involving funerals—hence the dismissive label of "funeral Buddhism," or "death Buddhism." Young Japanese people visiting the West are advised to declare themselves Buddhist, as a reliable way to win the sympathy of local people, but that rarely reflects any deep personal commitment.

However ill focused or baffling that mixture of faiths might seem to Westerners, it has historically caused few problems in Japan, nor prevented that country having an extremely rich tradition of religious behavior, manifested in art, literature, and popular movements. As in the West, revivals and religious movements have often bubbled to the surface, and mainstream institutions have enjoyed varying degrees of success in appropriating them to their own interests. On the darker side, during the Second World War, no combatant nation was as fervent as Japan in constantly and systematically invoking religious justifications and in presenting its cause in spiritual terms. The nation was explicitly fighting a holy war. Dismantling that religious framework was a primary goal of the postwar occupation.[18]

In contrast, modern-day Japan looks radically secular, with a strong European cast. A typical survey shows just 10 percent of Japanese professing that religion is very important to them, the same level as in France, Germany, or the United Kingdom. By some measures it is the world's most secular society.[19]

Many of the factors we have already encountered in a European context apply with special force in Japan, including the low number of children, weak family ties to religious institutions, and rural depopulation. Some special themes also apply, especially what I have termed the "decline of death" and the diminished likelihood that one will be involved with multiple or recurrent commemorations of death. That poses a special burden for a faith like Buddhism that is so invested in funeral rituals. When Japan's Buddhists bemoan the sad state of their faith, they often highlight the shift away from religious burials, a trend that has given so much business to a flourishing secular funeral industry. "Death Buddhism" has fared badly in the new environment. So have the healing movements that in various forms have often surfaced as influential forces in Japanese spirituality. They have failed to compete with one of the world's most advanced medical systems, in a setting in which health care is both free and readily available.

Japanese Buddhists in particular lament the parlous state of their faith. Even among those who identify as Buddhist, the degree of involvement in formal religious activities has plummeted in recent decades, so that few Japanese Buddhists ever have contact with a temple. Buddhist priests are well aware that they are largely of the older generation, offering little appeal to the young, although some younger clerics try to repackage their message in trendy contemporary forms. (At every stage of this story, analogies to Europe's Catholics are obvious.) The country simply no longer has the cohorts of young men who might have flocked to the monasteries. In 2014 one Shin Buddhist organization prepared a helpful and much-needed text for its members, a "Guide to Dissolve Temples."[20]

The country has some eighty thousand Shinto temples and shrines, which are distributed to service what was once a thriving rural population.

Through the years that rural society has all but evaporated. Since 1950 the urban share of the country's population has risen from 53 to 93 percent. That has left some of the most glorious shrines and temples isolated in abandoned landscapes, far removed from where people actually live. With its very aged population and total absence of the young, this rural landscape fits the *Children of Men* scenario. Already a quarter of those shrines are not served by a priest, and by some estimates, around 40 percent of temples and shrines will cease to function by 2040.[21] Wherever possible local businesses and governments have tried to attract visitors to the old centers but with little hope of seeking a spiritual revival. Instead, these are purely commercial ventures, encouraging what Europeans call heritage tourism. Many temples survive as social centers for local communities, relying on the income produced by cafes or stores. Again, it is difficult not to think of conditions in Europe's Christian monasteries.

In religious terms Japan, like Europe, exemplifies new and radically revised approaches to tradition and authority, to community and rootedness, to continuity and social cohesion. Obviously the religious retreat is not absolute, and a few shrines do flourish, while particular holidays still focus communal loyalty. Also, as in Europe, decline in mass adherence or participation is compensated by the rise of smaller and more activist groups and movements, especially those that define themselves within the Buddhist framework. But these do not draw on mass audiences. Also, in contrast to Europe, Japan has virtually no significant immigrant communities who might have revived fading local institutions. In its religious life, Japan offers a grim picture, if not a near-death experience.

South Korea

If the Japanese experience seems extreme, we already see signs that existing religions are facing mounting difficulties elsewhere, and in countries that we conventionally think of in terms of religious enthusiasm. If some religious traditions are conspicuously booming, we should stress the fairly short period in which these countries have moved to ultralow fertility, to join the ranks of the "lowest low."

Even some of those seemingly powerful religious movements have acute weaknesses. We look at South Korea, with its "lowest low" fertility rates. At the same time, the country has for some decades been regarded as a near miracle in the story of global Christianity. Since the 1960s Christian churches of all kinds have boomed, and the country is host to some of the world's largest evangelical and Pentecostal congregations. It is difficult to miss an institution like the Yoido Full Gospel Church, founded in 1958, and which presently has some eight hundred thousand members. In the words of one journalistic report, "In many South Korean cities, there are more churches than convenience stores."[22] The nighttime streetscape of Seoul is distinctive for its abundance of neon crosses, each marking a church, usually Protestant in orientation. Although South Korea does not have an outright Christian majority, Christian numbers have expanded rapidly in recent decades. Globally the country sponsors the largest number of missionaries, exceeded only by the United States. How can we reconcile such a picture with any claims of religious decline? Surely you cannot at the same time have a religious boom amounting to something like a national revival, and a religious crisis.

But the story is more complex. Traditionally Buddhism was at the heart of Korean religion, and this was critical to its broader national culture, but the faith has declined sharply during the present century. Just in the decade after 2005, the proportion of South Koreans professing themselves Buddhists fell from 23 to 16 percent. The number of young people seeking ordination as monks and nuns has also plummeted, to the alarm of Buddhist authorities. As in the Christian West, Buddhist Korea has seen a serious graying of its clergy. In other ways too, this trend parallels the comparable decline of Christian monastic orders in the West. In earlier times young people would find opportunities in the monastic life that they could not obtain in the secular world, especially education. That was a particular issue for girls and women. The situation changed with the growth of public education and more generally with the expansion of professions and secular careers. Just as those trends discouraged traditional high-fertility family structures, they drew people away from organized faith, and there is no sign that conditions will ever revert to older norms. Reinforcing those larger trends, well-publicized scandals about monkish misdeeds have further contributed to discrediting the clerical profession.[23]

We might imagine that this is part of a larger shift from Buddhism to Christianity, and this is the way the story is presented in the West. Yet Christian leaders too are scarcely less nervous about their own prospects, and like Buddhists, they are very conscious of a failure to attract young believers.[24] Even in the apparently thriving megachurches, clergy regularly offer pessimistic predictions of their fate as refuges for the aged. Many of the largest churches have been struck by grave scandals, mainly involving financial rather than sexual misdeeds, but these have still proved damaging.

Most troubling for believers of all shades is the mushroom growth of those professing no religion whatever, a category that in the United States we have come to call the "Nones" (and whom we will discuss in the next chapter). The same census that revealed the shrinkage of Buddhism also

indicated that just between 2005 and 2015, the number of Koreans admitting no religion whatever had grown from 47 to 56 percent. Most observers expect a similar increase by the time of the next count, in 2025. Such
numbers cast a different light on claims of enduring Christian triumphs in
that nation. They also confirm the likely religious trajectory of a lowest-low-
fertility society.[25]

Thailand

Similar declines affect other countries in the region, to varying degrees, with
Buddhism as the faith tradition most immediately endangered by social and
demographic change. Thailand offers a prime example. We have already
noted the sharp demographic plunge here, in a land in which Buddhism
is strongly entrenched and officially established. Unlike Korea or Japan,
where new demographic patterns are well established, there is no comparable growth of irreligion or Nones.

But Buddhist authorities are profoundly concerned about accumulating
signs of trouble in the national faith. For several years now, Thai Buddhist
authorities have expressed increasing alarm about attendance at wats (or
temples), while the quantity and quality of recruits to the monastic order
have likewise fallen. An acute shortage of Thai monks has led abbots of
depleted monasteries to the once unthinkable solution of importing newcomers from the neighboring nation of poorer and much more fertile Myanmar. Although some Buddhist movements are flourishing, they have done so
by adapting to the very different new society, with its more individualistic
and less communal orientation. The great example is the Dhammakaya,
which offers a kind of prosperity gospel. This example suggests a pattern
that we often find around the world, in which the decline of mass popular
involvement in religion is supplanted by the activism of a smaller core of
more committed and activist believers.[26]

Earlier I suggested that Europe's clergy abuse scandals should be seen
as a consequence, rather than a cause, of popular detachment from traditional religions. Many non-European societies demonstrate a similar
linkage, and by no means within a Christian context. In each case educated laypeople—especially women—are no longer willing to tolerate hypocritical abuses by hierarchies who claim the right to impose their sexual
morality and approved family structures on lay believers. Such resistance
is only possible when demographic changes have already alienated those
former faithful from the traditional structures. When scandals do erupt,
they further discredit institutions and drive former church members out

of the religious tradition together, either to some rival church or else to wholly nonreligious positions.

In Thailand and other Buddhist nations, the past decade has witnessed grave and systematic scandals involving religious leaders and institutions. Many institutions have been accused of a roster of crimes that includes embezzlement, drug dealing, and sexual misconduct. Some of the monks and temples accused have been among the country's most visible and influential. Even the Dhammakaya temple has been implicated in money laundering. As in any society or faith tradition, misbehavior and criminality are nothing new, but what has changed is the willingness of media to present these stories openly. As in Europe a preexisting decline in deferential faith creates the conditions in which wrong behavior can be exposed and acknowledged and for such accounts to be reported and believed.[27]

Moral Revolutions

Religious changes are particularly difficult to track in Asian societies with Chinese spiritual foundations, where institutional structures are far weaker than in Buddhist societies. Both Taiwan and Singapore are extremely low-fertility societies, and as we might expect, both demonstrate dramatically reduced religious interest or enthusiasm. That is especially true in Singapore, which is a city-state and exemplifies the strongly secular character that we would expect of any major metropolis. Nor, in either case, has a decline in traditional religion been compensated by the rise of some new faith, comparable to the Christian expansion in South Korea.

Quite apart from explicit accounts of religious decline, we also find examples of moral shifts that would once have been considered unacceptable and even blasphemous, and which are rooted in changes in family structure. Again as in Europe, changing attitudes are indicated by views on homosexuality and same-sex marriage. Most Asian countries retain laws against homosexuality that by Euro-American standards appear extremely strict or draconian. These laws are rooted in the various religious traditions of particular societies, which reinforce and are supported by popular codes and mores. In Chinese societies the normal interpretation of Confucian values places an overwhelming emphasis on family and procreation, which is supported by traditional Chinese religions. Scholarly readings of Confucian traditions suggest much more liberal attitudes, but these have limited effect on everyday attitudes and policy positions.[28]

But the continued existence of such laws conceals far-reaching changes below the surface. Singapore's laws on homosexuality remain harsh, even prohibiting sexual activity in private, but the laws are laxly enforced. In practice same-sex relationships are common and undisguised, especially among educated urban dwellers and professionals. The city even has an exuberantly popular gay pride parade. The issue is not so much whether laws will change as how soon.

Taiwan offers perhaps the clearest example of transformation in the face of social and demographic revolution. As we have seen, the country has one of the world's lowest fertility rates, with the attendant social effects. As the birth rate fell and family structures changed, so older moral restrictions based on both Confucian and Christian norms evaporated (although Christian numbers have never been large, conservative Christians were influential in the ruling elite of the Nationalist Party). In the present century, the country has emerged as a thriving gay center and a cutting-edge society in terms of LGBT rights. Its vast annual gay pride event is characterized as the second largest in Asia. That is somewhat misleading, as the other contender for that title is in Tel Aviv, in Israel, a country that few think of as "Asian." (The other celebrated Asian event is in Seoul, South Korea.) Remarkably for any part of Asia, Taiwan has also implemented same-sex marriage. The idea had been under debate since 2003, and a Constitutional Court decision in 2017 removed legal obstacles. In 2019 Taiwan became the first Asian country to offer full legal recognition.[29]

A Chinese Mystery

With its vast population, the economic superpower of China naturally commands a unique position in any consideration of Asian affairs. In so many respects, China is one of the world's most important nations—in economic terms but also on account of its vast population, almost a fifth of all humanity. For many reasons, though, it is extraordinarily difficult to incorporate into the specific story that I am addressing here of the relationship between fertility and religious behavior. At first sight China is indeed a country with extremely low fertility and comparably minimal religious activity. But the country's peculiar political history makes it extraordinarily difficult to draw further conclusions.[30]

One problem concerns sources of information. Through the years Chinese governments have varied greatly as to their openness to investigation and criticism, but the country remains under stringent official control, which is often deeply repressive. That makes it hard to carry out conventional survey efforts, and people are reluctant to respond frankly. An answer that is noncontroversial today might in future prove deeply embarrassing. That caution is particularly true in religious life, which through the years has been shaped by the shifting whims of governments, which at various times have sought either to annihilate religious faith or to grant it great latitude.

In terms of demography as much as religion, in no sense is China a normal society. Its modern economic development had many parallels to that of neighboring Dragons and Tigers, with a historic population move from the countryside to the cities and the breakneck expansion of industries and services of all kinds, which drew tens of millions of women into employment. How could such turmoil fail to have its demographic effects? But for half a century, the country's fertility was conditioned not by shifts in popular behavior or attitudes but was rather determined by official fiat from the central government. The limit had been set at two children until 1979 when the regime decreed its one-child policy, which endured until 2016.[31] Had the regime not acted as it did, China today would probably have at least 2 billion people, rather than the actual figure of 1.4 billion. But the policy had unforeseen consequences, especially in the skewing of sex ratios in a society with a strong preference for male offspring. When the government relaxed its restriction on family size in 2015, that imbalance of sexes combined with economic and social changes to make it difficult to revert to anything like normal demographic patterns. It will take decades to assess the outcomes of the radical Chinese experiment with demographic engineering.

Based on the evidence, we can say that Chinese fertility rates are among the world's lowest. Through the opening years of the century, the TFR ran at around 1.5 and today stands at only 1.6. We would expect such a statistic to be associated with a very secular orientation, but our evidence is mixed. One recent survey found that only 3 percent of Chinese regard religion as very important in their lives, a number that suggests the near-extinction of religion. On the other hand, plausible estimates of the country's Christian and Muslim populations suggest far higher degrees of religious involvement and activism than this would imply, quite apart from the impressive and visible revival of native Chinese traditions such as Daoism. This is not to suggest that China is a seething cauldron of incipient religious revival but rather that available statistics are deceptive.[32]

If not actually admitting defeat on Chinese conditions, researchers on religion need to concede the severe limitations that must shape any possible analysis. That is unfortunate, as the picture that emerges appears to fit consistently with the rest of this enormous region.

Transition in Latin America

Older visions of overpopulation commonly drew on conditions in Latin America as much as Asia, but here too matters have been changing almost too fast for most observers to keep pace. As in East Asia, economic and demographic transformations have proceeded in tandem, with clear religious consequences.

Through the twentieth century, Latin America had notched some of the world's highest fertility rates, and particular countries experienced astonishing population growth of six- or eight- or even tenfold over the course of the century. During the century, Brazil's population swelled from 18 million to over 170 million; Mexico's from 14 million to 100 million; Peru's from 3 million to 27 million. At the end of the century, fertility rates slowed suddenly, and in several countries fell below replacement. Even in the case of those mushrooming nations just mentioned, the rate of growth stabilized markedly around 2000, so that the further huge increases foretold by some experts failed to materialize. In the 1960s Brazil's fertility rate hovered around 6 children per woman, but that figure reached replacement in 2005 and today stands at 1.75. Chile's present rate is similar, while Uruguay's is around 1.8. At 2.2, Argentina's is still above replacement, but the rate is falling fast. We are witnessing a social revolution in progress, and a gender revolution.[33]

Economic development is a key driver of demographic change, and the sporadic and patchy nature of growth has produced sharply differentiated patterns of fertility. In Mexico, the country's TFR in the early 1970s was still approaching 7.0, but it then fell to 3.0 by 1995, and by 2018 it stood at just 2.1. But if we break that figure down by states and regions, sharply different patterns emerge. The highest rates still persist in the country's rural and poorly developed southwest, in states like Chiapas and Oaxaca, although even there, fertility today runs above 2.4—in historic terms, a very low level. The closer we come to the United States, in the most advanced regions that profited most from free trade pacts, globalization, and intensive tourism, the more European the fertility picture appears. Half of Mexico's thirty-one states are already below replacement, and eight have European-looking rates below 1.9.[34]

Religious Transformations

Such figures make nonsense of conventional assumptions about Third World fertility rates. Equally discredited is the image of those societies being bastions of simplistic peasant faith—a belittling vision always rooted in Western condescension. In fact religious decline has been a marked feature of Latin American countries in recent decades. This undermines the long-dominant narrative of a faithful Catholic society being revolutionized by an upsurge of Protestant and Pentecostal fervor. While there is much truth to such accounts, a great deal more is happening.[35]

The region presents a complex picture, with seemingly strong evidence of continuing passion for religion. Over 480 million Latin Americans are officially described as Catholic, making South America the world's most Catholic continent. Notionally at least, Brazil and Mexico stand alongside the Philippines at the head of a list of the world's largest Catholic populations. However, many of those notional Catholics participate little in church life, and their faith is at best nominal. The best available survey of religion in the region is a Pew Research Center study published in 2014, which found that 69 percent of the Latin American population identifies as Catholic as against 19 percent Protestant.[36] Those Protestant numbers rise significantly in particular regions, to over a quarter in Brazil. Brazil is home to some spectacularly successful Pentecostal megachurches, which Catholic clergy seek to imitate in order to hold on to believers. New evangelical churches are also booming in the other Latin nations, to the point that Protestants claim to be living through a new Reformation.

But this world is changing. Some observers, in fact, even speak of secularization. In the 2014 Pew survey, Catholics and Protestants accounted for 88 percent of people in the region, but that still leaves room for a large and swelling number who followed no religion. Eight percent of Brazilians now say they follow no religion, and the proportion of unaffiliated—of Nones—is much higher among the under-20s. The proportion of unaffiliated is at its highest in such highly developed countries as Chile (16 percent) and Argentina (11 percent), as well as several smaller states of Central America and the Caribbean (El Salvador, Honduras, the Dominican Republic), where the rate runs between 10 and 18 percent. In Chile, the number of Nones has expanded substantially in recent years, and today the figure is at least 25 percent, substantially larger than the well-publicized and highly active Protestant population. As so often in such classifications, Uruguay emerges as the region's most secular and European-looking country, with almost 40 percent having no religious affiliation.[37]

A similar impression emerges from a 2018 survey that asked people around the world how important religion was to them. The lowest rates were of course found in Western Europe, at 10 to 20 percent of respondents, with Russia and Japan comparable. The United States figure was over 50 percent. But some of the world's lowest rates on the "very important" scale were found in Argentina, Chile, and Uruguay, and even the Mexican figure was well below that of the United States.[38]

Legal Change

In other ways too, many Latin American societies are in the midst of social revolutions familiar from Europe. As we have seen, one of the best indexes of shifting moral attitudes is the legal acceptance of same-sex marriage.

The spread of that institution beyond Europe correlates well with other measures of secularization and with very low fertility rates. Where such a measure has been proposed in a Christian context, it has been in the face of stern opposition from both the Catholic Church and from evangelical or Pentecostal churches, who are well organized politically. Even so, such seemingly daunting opposition has not succeeded in preventing the spread of same-sex marriage through most of Latin America's most significant and influential nations. Uruguay passed a national civil union law in 2009 and established full marriage rights in 2013. Brazil approved same-sex unions in 2004, with gay marriages following in 2013, subject to some local discretion. Argentina legalized same-sex marriage in 2010. Mexico has for some years approved the practice according to local jurisdictions, and the states with the more progressive views in this matter are of course the regions with lowest fertility.[39]

Here as elsewhere, it is not that the churches are expelled from the political arena, but rather that ordinary people do not believe that church views on issues of morality and sexuality should be applied through law. This represents a massive move toward the kind of processes I outlined earlier, of a differentiation that consigns religion to its own particular sphere and a privatization of faith. That entails an emphasis on individual rights and obligations. From this perspective religious attitudes belong strictly within a prescribed realm, with ever less application to regulation over self and family. Also illustrating this is the broad adoption of contraceptive use, which played so large a role in fertility reduction from the 1970s onward. Across the continent—as in the Philippines—that revolution occurred despite the strenuous but largely futile campaigning of Catholic authorities. As we have seen in Europe, the act of dissidence in this particular area encouraged a drift to a great privatization of religion and a willingness to disobey authority in other areas.

Colombia offers a good illustration of recent changes. Traditionally this was a textbook model of a very high fertility/high faith society, and during the twentieth century, the country's population exploded from below 4 million to 40 million—notable even by the standards of Latin America in those years. But the country's TFR fell from 6.8 in 1960 to replacement level in 2001 and 1.85 by 2016. Today its population growth rate places it alongside countries like Ireland or Switzerland.[40]

Changes in fertility have had potent consequences for issues of morality and of religious authority. In recent years Colombia has adopted quite progressive policies in matters of gender and sexuality, stunningly so for what was long a deeply conservative Catholic country, with an equally moralistic evangelical minority. Even so, the country legalized same-sex marriage in 2016 and moved expeditiously toward full equality for its LGBT population. Just how rapidly those progressive views were advancing has become a source of acute concern to conservative Catholics and especially evangelicals. In 2016 such galvanized religious opposition led to the paper-thin defeat of a historic peace agreement that would have ended the country's long-running guerrilla warfare and brought a much-desired peace. Even so, the country's secular direction in terms of gender and sexual morality is clear.[41]

Abortion laws offer a more mixed picture. Uruguay permits abortions through the first trimester, while Brazil grants terminations to safeguard the life of the mother or in cases of rape. For all its secular orientation on other matters, Chile stands out as a conservative bastion, with a strict abortion law. Otherwise, though, we witness a major trend toward liberalizing morality laws, on issues that both Protestant and Catholic churches hold dear. Over the coming decade, we will see liberal reforms on all these issues triumphing in several more countries, with the churches doing little more than fighting rearguard actions.

Scandals

Across the continent the frequency of scandals in recent years—largely over the past decade—illustrates a fundamental change in public mood and a radical new willingness to challenge clerical structures. Catholic clergy abuse scandals on the familiar Western model have flared in several of the nations that I have touched on, including Brazil, Mexico, and others. By far the most devastating and systematic have occurred in Chile, where as we have already seen, nonreligious views were already commonplace. Although the details of these cases lie beyond the scope of this book, one key scandal involved a charismatic priest named Fernando Karadima, who was publicly accused of abuse in 2010. Over the decades Karadima had mentored many other priests, some of whom had reached high rank in the hierarchy, and accusations suggested a conspiratorial network of abusers at the heart of the nation's church. The scandal tainted the pope, Francis I, who had promoted some of the accused offenders. In terms of its impact on church prestige, and the loyalties of the faithful, the Chilean story has been quite comparable to that of Ireland.[42]

Beyond the news media, tales of clergy abuse have become almost a freestanding genre in Latin American cinema, and that has undoubtedly contributed further to discrediting organized faith. Just to take Chile, one of the most esteemed films from that country in recent years is *The Club* (2015), which has as its setting a remote seaside house that serves as a refuge for disgraced clergy, whose sins are mainly sexual in nature. That same year brought another devastating Chilean study of a serially abusive cleric in *Karadima's Forest*. The Mexican *Perfect Obedience* (2014) likewise describes predatory priests, in a tale inspired by the true-life career of Marcial Maciel, the high-profile founder of the worldwide Legion of Christ movement. Such cultural landmarks demonstrate a shift in popular attitudes to the church, and they further contribute to the decline of authority structures.

As in Europe, nobody is seriously predicting the destruction of the Catholic Church or the end of Christianity, and evangelical churches continue to flourish. So do spiritual practices that appeal to individuals and families and that can be pursued without any commitment to formal adherence to any institution whatever or subscription to any particular code of morals. As an institution pilgrimage remains as flourishing as ever, and that is especially true in countries like Mexico and Colombia where churches have suffered grave setbacks. Each year up to ten million attend the pilgrimage of Our Lady of Guadalupe in Mexico City, and comparable throngs visit Brazil's Basilica of Our Lady Aparecida. Far from declining, numbers have actually risen in the past decade. But all this happens against a background of a widespread questioning of the most basic assumptions about the role of the church—of any church—in society. That critique has its roots in larger changes in society and in the structure of the family.

At so many points, the recent history of both East Asia and Latin America seems to offer a convincing illustration of secularization theory in action, as demography interacts intimately with both modernity and secularity. The theory appears to be well established, and its predictive powers are reliable. That is, at least, until we look at the one very important country that, at least in its surface, makes nonsense of any such claims. How have recent social changes played out in the United States?

5

THE UNITED STATES

The United States has long been a source of real concern to scholars of religion. The country is wealthy and very advanced technologically, and in so many ways it parallels other highly developed societies in Western Europe or East Asia. In religious terms, however, the country has long appeared a dramatic exception, a wild card. If indeed modernization produces secularization, and that process can be measured by GDP per capita or levels of female education, then why do such formulas evidently not work in the United States? If (as we are told) wealthy and educated people inevitably abandon religion, how can we explain the geographical spread and social makeup of many of America's most successful megachurches? Apart from being a rich society, it is also by many measures one of the world's most religious. As a typical study headlined in 2010, "Religiosity Highest in World's Poorest Nations: United States Is among the Rich Countries That Buck the Trend." European visitors are stunned to see the proliferation not just of places of worship but of very new structures erected within the past few years. The vast car parks required by thriving congregations seemingly offer a conspicuous sign of pervasive faith comparable to the church spires of the Middle Ages.[1]

Intimately related to that spiritual vigor, the country for many years had a fertility rate notably higher than what we might expect of an economically advanced nation. By all rights the United States should for some decades now have been a low-faith and low-fertility society, instead of the diametric opposite. Looking around the world, we can point to and explain some specific local exceptions to broad social trends, but in this case we are dealing with the economic and cultural heart of the advanced world. How can this paradox be resolved?[2]

Having said this, the United States has in very recent times moved decisively toward what scholars regard as a normal trajectory. Finally the U.S. fertility rate is dropping well below replacement, and as we would expect, that change is accompanied by growing signs of secularization. If these trends continue, then the United States will be experiencing something like the European demographic revolution, albeit after a pronounced delay. If that is correct, then we are in the early stages of an authentic religious and cultural revolution, or rather a network of interlinked transformations.

Between Two Worlds?

That American anomaly has for some thirty years intrigued scholars. Among many examples, the excellent British sociologist Grace Davie cited it when challenging the familiar idea that European secular values would inexorably spread worldwide, alongside social and economic development. She used U.S. evidence to argue that worldwide, religion was flourishing, and it was secular Europe that constituted the exceptional case. Esteemed social theorist Joel Kotkin likewise used distinctive U.S. demographic and religious data to produce an optimistic vision of the country's near future. Writing as recently as 2010, he argued that U.S. fertility rates still stood at or above replacement, so that the country appeared to have avoided the social snares facing Europe. I have often made such arguments in my own writings and presentations, and as with Kotkin and Davie, those ideas were correct when they were written. In terms of faith and religious practice, the United States long seemed to perch incongruously between (fairly) faithless Europe and deeply pious Africa.[3] It was a nation standing between two worlds.[4]

Standard accounts of recent U.S. trends note that the country had a high TFR in the boomer years—3.65 in 1960—but that then fell sharply in the mid-1970s, to just 1.77 in 1975 and 1.74 in 1976. Numbers then remained low through the mid-1980s. So far, so European. But unlike Europe, numbers then rebounded in the late 1980s, to around 2.0 or a little over from 1990 onward, and it was still at a replacement 2.1 as late as 2010. From this perspective the United States flirted with European patterns in the mid-1970s but then thoroughly rejected that European approach. In the opening years of the century, commentators were analyzing the yawning demographic chasm that separated old Europe and young America, and speculating how this might create insoluble political and cultural tensions. Repeatedly, this surging United States exceeded population targets, for instance reaching the figure of 300 million several years ahead of schedule.[5]

The Great Fertility Decline

But later changes have been marked, with the years 2008–2010 marking a crucial era of transition to sub-replacement conditions. In 2011 the TFR fell to 1.9, and by 2016 the rate matched the low of the mid-1970s. At 1.73, the U.S. figure for 2018 placed the United States alongside Denmark or Brazil in the league table of fertility rates, and well below Norway and Sweden. When that low figure was reported, some commentators responded with concern about the consequences of a shrinking population, especially in economic terms. Others, meanwhile, expressed skepticism about the reported decline. They protested, legitimately, that the simple rate was a crude measure, and that American women might be postponing bearing children, rather than forsaking parenthood altogether. Even so, as we have seen, delaying motherhood past 35 or so does make it much less likely that a woman will bear multiple children.[6]

The United States genuinely does appear to have moved to a low-fertility scenario, and many different statistics confirm that picture. Very much the same picture emerges from general fertility rates, which are calculated from the number of babies born to females aged between 15 and 44. The U.S. figure peaked at over 120 in the late 1950s and then plummeted to the mid-60s by 1975–1976. That number rose to 70 by the end of the century, but by 2017 reached a very low (and Scandinavian-looking) 60. Put another way, that is close to half what the rate would have been sixty years ago. The annual rate of population growth reached 2 percent at the height of the baby boom and was still 1.4 percent in 1994, but by 2016 it cratered to 0.7 percent. That was the lowest rate of increase since the worst Depression years of the mid-1930s. Even in a catalog of superlatives, the collapse in teenage childbearing has been startling. In the late 1950s, the birth rate per thousand females aged 15 to 19 was usually in the 90s, and it was still in the 40s in the years leading up to the crash of 2008. By 2019 the figure was just 17, reflecting both greater access to contraception, and higher educational aspirations.[7]

In 2007 the U.S. TFR of 2.1 compared with a European Union figure below 1.6. By 2018 U.S. and EU figures were fast converging, toward a shared figure of 1.7.[8] The low current figures occurred despite relatively good economic conditions, which would normally have been expected to encourage optimism and to drive family formation. Instead of demonstrating a fundamental or eternal U.S. demographic difference, such figures rather suggest that it was the high-fertility years of 1985–2010 that were exceptional, and that in the long term the country has indeed been Europeanizing. The question today should not be, "Why is the country having a mysterious baby bust?" but rather, "What took you so long to get here?"

Any attempt at explaining that trajectory must stress the role of economic conditions. The fertility revival of the 1980s coincides closely with a remarkable economic boom, the longest in the nation's history, which lasted from 1983 through 2007, with only a brief recession in 1992. The 1990s were an era of prosperity and optimism, and the early years of the present century were marked by an outpouring of cheap credit and easy money, which led to an effervescent property boom. Millions of people found themselves able to buy houses or condos that would once have seemed unattainable, and that provided a strong incentive to start families. As a raw number, births reached an all-time peak precisely in 2007, at 4.3 million.[9]

The apocalyptic crash of 2007–2008 fundamentally darkened the national mood, ending the housing boom and initiating the worst and most prolonged recession since the 1930s. Millions lost their newly purchased homes. Birth rates plummeted, and the actual number of annual births soon fell below 4 million. The demographic damage was all the greater among immigrant and particularly Latino communities, who had set such hopes on the earlier boom and were now set back so badly. In most societies immigrant populations tend to have high birth rates when they first arrive in a new country, but over time these rates fall to approach those of old-stock populations: we see this for instance with Muslim migrants in Europe. But in the U.S. case, the impact on Latino populations was far more sudden, and just in the post-2007 decade, the fertility rate for Latino women fell from roughly 3.0 to 2.0. An economic crash precipitated a demographic bust, and in matters of fertility, the effects may be irreversible. By 2018 the overall number of births was the lowest it had been since 1986.[10]

No account of changes in fertility can omit that economic dimension, but by the same token, that cannot be the whole story. As we have seen, economic booms in other societies have tended to reduce rather than stimulate fertility, and the effects of the pre-2007 boom in Europe or the Pacific Rim were not vaguely comparable to those in the United States. As I will suggest later, the United States has many cultural and social aspects that set it apart from other advanced societies, and those do justify a theory of American exceptionalism. But for present purposes, the main point is that America's recent fertility boom now appears to have ended decisively, leaving the country looking much more "normal" in international terms. At long last, it seems, the European Revolution—the Second Demographic Transition—has arrived.

Secular America?

The implications of that fertility decline are many and various, and they increasingly concern marketers and businesspeople, military planners, and government agencies. Above all they raise grave concerns about the provision of pensions and services to the elderly, in an aging society. But what about religion? Can we now predict that the United States is destined to follow Europe, Japan, and so many other nations along the path to secularization, or at least to a collapse of institutional religion? In those terms also, will the United States cease to position itself between two worlds and become instead a "normal" advanced country? The answer to those questions is profoundly important for American society, for its moral debates, and for its political alignments.

Since the turn of the century, a number of surveys and social science studies have claimed to see such a secular drift. This is reflected in shrinking numbers reporting church membership, and particularly of those identifying with religious traditions of any kind. In each case the evidence for such claims has to be treated with caution and is open to a good deal of interpretation. Contrary to some reports, U.S. churches and synagogues are not facing imminent apocalypse. But enough signs are present to suggest a real religious decline in the near future, and the speed of recent change has been striking.

Until recently the evidence for American religiosity was strong and consistent. In 2012, 80 percent of Americans declared that they never doubted the existence of God. The "never-doubter" category is impressive for its categorical nature, suggesting as it does a degree of unquestioning faith that would be striking in any society in the modern age. The number of never-doubters has indeed contracted somewhat since the 1980s—especially among young adults—but that is still an impressive portrait of faith. Still in 2012, 76 percent of Americans said prayer was very important in their life, a number unchanged since 1987. Fifty-eight percent of Americans said religion was very important in their lives, compared to around 20 percent in Germany, Spain, or Britain. Although scholars debate the value of these figures, reported rates of attendance at places of worship remain astronomical by European standards.[11]

But signs of decline are evident. The proportion of Americans who said that religion was very important in their lives has been falling steadily since 2007, along with such gauges as the numbers who pray daily. Between 2000 and 2019, the proportion of Americans who report attending religious services weekly fell from 41 percent to 29 percent. The proportion of never-attenders has grown from 14 to 26 percent, and among younger respondents aged 18 to 34, the share is a sizable and growing 36 percent. The proportion of Americans who identify as Christian dropped likewise, and just in the short period between 2007 and 2019, it fell from 78 to 65 percent. Most observers are projecting that surveys in coming years will show a still further decline, almost certainly to below 60 percent by 2025. Nor has this shortfall been met by significant growth in other faith traditions. Contrary to the impression of the United States as a melting pot of faiths, the proportion of Americans who follow non-Christian religions is relatively small, and strikingly so by the standards of many nations in Europe or the Middle East—perhaps 6 percent of the population all told, if we include Jews, Muslims, Buddhists, Hindus, and Sikhs. The fate of American religion depends on the Christian story.[12]

Recent studies of institutional membership have been still more dramatic. A Gallup survey published in 2019 found that since 1999, religious membership had plunged from roughly 70 percent of the population to 50 percent, and the rate of decline was significantly larger among particular groups. The story had a political edge, with a much higher fall among Democrats than Republicans. Most disturbing of all for the religious institutions was the steep fall in membership among Latinos, who represent such a key component of the nation's ethnic future. Echoing that figure, already in 2014, 18 percent of U.S. Latinos reported themselves as Nones, having no religious affiliation, and that figure is assuredly higher today.[13] By midcentury over a quarter of Americans will be Latino. This is potentially a grim picture for churches.

Signs of decline are clearer when viewed in the long term. For some decades scholars debating secularization offered different explanations for the apparent U.S. exceptionalism. Some argued that the strength of U.S. religion actively contradicted or disproved the underlying theory, while others objected that the United States was indeed experiencing trends comparable to Europe, albeit on a slower and more gradual scale, spread over several decades. Recent trends clearly favor the latter approach, as stated powerfully by scholars David Voas and Mark Chaves. As Chaves remarks,

> The US decline has been so gradual that until recently scientists haven't had enough data to be sure the trend was real. The US has long been considered an exception to the modern claim that religion is declining, but if you look at the trajectory, and the generational dynamic that is producing the trajectory, we may not be an exception after all.[14]

Claims about declining faith have sparked protests from a number of observers, who make some valid methodological points that apply to social surveys generally. Some of those objections sound purely technical, but they do matter. A quarter century ago, pollsters could rely on a predictable share of respondents picking up their phones and agreeing to answer questions. The whole economy of communications has since then been utterly transformed by the rise of cellphones and the coming of caller ID. Chances of finding representative samples have declined accordingly. In the specific context of religion, critics protested that in focusing on institutional membership, studies miss key changes in the evolving structure of American religion. Although formal membership was so fundamental to traditional institutions, it is far less so to some more modern congregations, such as megachurches and other overtly nondenominational bodies. It is quite possible to be highly religious while still reporting being a nonmember of any congregation or denomination. And while studies note the continuing shrinkage of membership in major denominations like the Southern Baptists, a large proportion of American congregations are independent and freestanding, commonly evangelical and Pentecostal in their coloring. Some of those churches have sizable congregations, which are not recorded by any central denominational headquarters or other data collection center.[15]

All these points must be taken seriously, and debates on such matters will continue. But the cumulative impression of decline is unavoidable.

Nones: Myth and Reality

In many surveys, particularly those stemming from the highly reputable Pew Research Center, a steadily growing number of respondents report their religious affiliation as None. That category undeniably includes many Americans who do fit the characterization of secular and secularized, and the growth of this population neatly coincides with the fertility decline. It is hard to interpret the story of the Nones except in terms of a general secular drift and of the contraction of institutional faith. But we still fall short of proclaiming the death of faith as such, still less of God.

Although the "None" terminology dates back to the 1960s, a Pew study published in 2012 drew intense media attention to what appeared to be a rising social trend. Not only were the Nones abundant, but their numbers had grown sharply, from 8 percent in 1990 to 15 percent in 2007 and to 20 percent by 2012. Another Pew report in 2013 found that "Religious 'nones'—a shorthand we use to refer to people who self-identify as atheists or agnostics, as well as those who say their religion is 'nothing in particular'—now make up roughly 23% of the U.S. adult population." Today the figure is 26 percent. Among America's three largest constituencies, Nones have now edged ahead of both Catholics and evangelical Protestants, and their lead is growing. Before too long, perhaps as early as the 2030s, America's Nones will presumably outnumber its self-described Christians. Making this prospect more likely, the proportion of Nones reported in each successive survey is significantly larger among young adults and millennials, indicating that the share of Nones is destined to swell in coming decades. One study in 2016 found that almost 40 percent of those aged 18 to 29 were unaffiliated, and even among those aged 30 to 49, the figure was 29 percent. The Nones, then, have grown in precisely the years of the demographic realignment and the fall in fertility rates. That neatly fits the model of a low-fertility and low-faith society.[16]

If in fact we understand these people to be of "no religion"—defined as atheists or agnostics—then the United States is evidently moving to European patterns at a headlong rate. To put it crudely, America's religious future appears to be None. Such a reading has featured often in recent headlines, commonly because it reflects the outcome desired by progressive or liberal commentators. Secularist Michael Shermer claims that "a 2013 Harris Poll of 2,250 American adults, for example, found that 23 percent of all Americans have forsaken religion altogether." Even well-informed Christian journalist Peggy Wehmeyer remarks that "Americans are abandoning the faith in droves. For the first time, religious 'nones,' those who claim no religion at all, top a survey of American religious identity." In 2016 the widely read magazine *National Geographic* presented a major report on "The World's Newest Major Religion: No Religion; As secularism grows, atheists and agnostics are trying to expand and diversify their ranks." As the title suggests, the story implied that "Nones" were identical to atheists or agnostics.[17]

But this is very questionable and brings us back to the question raised in chapter 3 about the meaning of secularization. It all depends on what we mean by "religion" and by having a religion. When we say that people "stopped believing," the natural follow-up question is, believing in what? In the whole supernatural worldview or just in the ideas and beliefs presented by familiar religious institutions? This also raises the fundamental issue of belonging and believing. The surveys to which I have referred measure shifts in *belonging*, which subsequent reports then misinterpret as a fall in *believing*. Beyond argument the Nones must feature prominently in any realistic discussion of the U.S. religious scene. But we need to read the evidence cautiously.

Nones: Continuing to Believe

In fact the available evidence contradicts the suggestion that the Nones are identical to atheists or agnostics. Taken together, American atheists and agnostics made up 5 percent of the population in 2009, as against 9 percent today. Viewed over the span of modern U.S. history, that represents a solid increase but not a revolution. The real growth was among those denying any religious affiliation, here described as "nothing in particular."[18]

Yet by any reasonable standard, American Nones are a surprisingly religious community. In 2012 a third of the unaffiliated said that religion was very important or somewhat important in their life:

> Two-thirds of them say they believe in God (68%). More than half say they often feel a deep connection with nature and the earth (58%), while more than a third classify themselves as "spiritual" but not "religious" (37%), and one-in-five (21%) say they pray every day.

Those proportions are of course higher for the sizable majority of Nones who are "nothing in particular," rather than avowedly atheist or agnostic. Many Nones fit the profile of a person who believes in God and might well pray regularly but rejects a religious affiliation. Given the religious breakdown of the larger population, most of the Nones come from Christian backgrounds, so that the religion that they choose not to admit to belonging to is Christianity.[19]

A venerable joke declares that everyone in the U.S. South is a Baptist. Baptists are Baptist, of course. Catholics are really Baptist, and atheists are Baptist, because the God they don't believe in is the Baptist God. A variant makes the same point about Lutherans in Minnesota, and other regional examples assuredly exist. The joke makes an excellent point about the default or residual quality of the religious belief system that underlies a formal denial of faith or denomination. Nonreligious attitudes certainly have grown in the past two decades or so, but much of the None phenomenon actually involves a changing approach to self-identification, rather than an outright desertion of religion. It actually recalls the European evidence we encountered about the large number of Europeans who define as Christian, but whose actual level of religious practice is strictly limited.

Nones: Ceasing to Belong

What is different about the United States is that the Nones are not formally identifying even as Christian, and that fact—that denial of belonging—requires explanation. To understand the American situation, we can usefully compare studies undertaken in the 1980s or 1990s, which likewise indicated a reluctance to commit to specific denominations or doctrinal assertions. In 1993 scholars Barry Kosmin and Seymour Lachman suggested that 86 percent of Americans were Christian, with Catholics by far the largest proportion, at 26 percent, and Baptists (almost 20 percent) the largest Protestant group. (And even at that point, Nones constituted over 8 percent of the whole.) Each denomination was listed according to size, but any estimates of actual numbers were severely skewed by the large number—over 14 percent of the whole—who claimed to be just "Protestant" or "Christian." Many such people identified with the Christian faith in general but were not prepared to be aligned with particular denominations. In some cases that might reflect indecision or a wooly kind of religious sentiment, but such a response might equally imply a principled reluctance to endorse divisions within the faith.[20]

As the new century began, social and political changes were altering people's willingness to profess even a loose alignment with denominations or with religion in general. The reaction that produced the Nones is directed not against faith but against institutions and how they behave. As the Pew study noted in 2012, "Overwhelmingly, [the Nones] think that religious organizations are too concerned with money and power, too focused on rules and too involved in politics." Meanwhile, many Protestants, particularly evangelicals, were troubled or disgusted by the appropriation of religious rhetoric by conservative and Religious Right politicians, who seemingly made "evangelical" or even "Christian" a synonym for Republican causes of the most reactionary kind. That distaste reached new heights with the Trump victory in 2016, when evangelical politics were widely criticized as a thin disguise for white racial self-interest—for advocacy of "White Christian America." Catholics meanwhile were alienated by the seemingly endless cycle of clergy abuse scandals, which entered a new and still more alarming phase after 2002. Beyond the general air of scandal, individual dioceses and parishes were hit hard by recurrent stories of particular priests being implicated or removed, and institutions being forced to pay vast settlements, with dioceses forced into bankruptcy.[21]

The rise of the Nones coincides closely with these twin trends, and the predictable consequence would be to discourage individuals from admitting to generic labels with which they had been comfortable only a few years previously. A person who in 1993 might have affirmed his or her identity as Protestant or Christian might now choose the "None" label, regardless of any change in actual belief or practice. In these years the proportion of Americans who admitted to being Catholic dropped by 5 or 6 percent, and most of those presumably migrated to the "None" camp. Reported levels of religious affiliation declined quite steeply, regardless of any necessary change in supernatural belief. When a 2018 study asked "nothing in particulars" why they rejected religious affiliation, 47 percent disliked the positions churches took on social or political issues, and 31 percent disliked religious leaders. Only 21 percent denied a belief in God. I suspect that as future surveys track the numbers of Nones, we will see a steep upswing during and following that traumatic election year of 2016. How could we not?[22]

Those political grievances contribute to the partisan divergence among the Nones, who are much more likely to find themselves in the Democratic camp, rather than the Republican. Between 1990 and 2016, the proportion of white Democrats who claimed no religious affiliation grew from 8 to 33 percent. That study I noted earlier of falling church membership suggested that since 1999, membership of religious bodies had fallen by 8 percentage points among Republicans but 23 points among Democrats.[23]

Of itself rejecting religious affiliation does not mean forfeiting a religious worldview or indeed abandoning any substantial amount of the belief system of any particular faith. To that extent it is wildly inaccurate to see the Nones as (in Shermer's phrase) "forsaking religion altogether." But the Nones are a real phenomenon, and arguably the existence of the category in itself contributes to genuine religious decline. For one thing, in a highly religious society, considerable community pressure persuades many people to state notional adherence to a prevailing religion as a kind of default position, from which it takes real motivation and willpower to dissent. We think of Catholics in American big cities in the 1950s or Baptists in much of the South (think back to that joke about everyone in the South being Baptist). The fact that people in significant numbers are now prepared to admit "nothing in particular" demonstrates a serious weakening of that community solidarity, as well as of the strength of institutions.

Arguably too, the growth of such publicly confessed indifference helps shape the statistics on which we base our knowledge of religious activity and participation, in making people more prepared to admit publicly that they never attend religious services. In that case the decline of attendance we have witnessed in recent years might be a dual phenomenon. While some people really have stopped attending churches, others have just become willing to state publicly that they do not attend, instead of pretending piety, as they have in the past. We can legitimately wonder how far the recorded drop in attendance figures represents an actual change in behavior, rather than greater honesty among respondents. We might be observing a change less in either *believing* or *belonging* than in *admitting*. Generally too, the more attention that Nones receive, the more acceptable that position becomes, particularly among the young. In a historic departure from precedent, in his 2009 inaugural speech, the new president Obama described the United States as a nation of "Christians and Muslims, Jews and Hindus—and nonbelievers."[24]

At the same time, media framing of None as meaning no religion, rather than just no affiliation, raises the profile of active atheism or agnosticism, and places those approaches in the cultural mainstream. Against such a background, politicians or media outlets feel far less pressure to make even residual acknowledgments of religious opinions and constituencies, making it much easier to adopt avowedly secular stances. The question also arises: How long is it possible not to belong to a faith before it affects one's basic belief in that system?

The Nones, presently, have not abandoned religion as such. But they do herald a powerful movement toward the secular.

Where Have All the Cultists Gone?

As evidence of looming secularization, we might also point to one curious religious trend that is subject to multiple interpretations, and this is the precipitous decline of the fringe religious movements that are conventionally called "cults." (Religion scholars dislike the name as judgmental, but it will serve at present.) I freely admit that the evidence for such a change is subjective, without the solid survey evidence associated with the Nones, but nevertheless, we are witnessing a real historical change.[25]

Throughout the nation's history, the United States has been richly productive of small, controversial religious movements with ideas regarded as eccentric. The great majority have been broadly Christian in content, although some have been esoteric or New Age, and others have imported Asian ideas. So persistent have such groups been that they even enjoyed a fresh upsurge in the worst years of the Depression of the 1930s, when so many mainstream religious institutions faced crisis. Such groups have been controversial because of the challenge they pose to conventional orthodoxy, but also because some tend to be authoritarian and exploitative of their members. Repeatedly through the centuries, campaigns against such movements have become so widespread as to constitute national cult scares or panics, which the news media publicize enthusiastically and which often lead to calls for legislative action. The most celebrated of these outbreaks occurred between the late 1960s and early 1980s, the era of such groups as the Hare Krishna movement, the "Moonies" (Unification Church), the Peoples Temple, or the Children of God, but also a host of others. The last of the classic panics involved the Waco siege and massacre of 1993.

But matters today are utterly different. Over the past quarter century, no such waves of concern and investigation have occurred on any but the most local level, and most nonspecialists would find it all but impossible to name any currently active "cult" or unconventional religious movement.

When mass media use cult themes, as films have done so regularly over the past decade, the subjects are usually drawn from that earlier efflorescence, from the Peoples Temple or the Branch Davidians. In 2018 the widely viewed Netflix documentary series *Wild Wild Country* harked back to the Rajneeshi sect of the early 1980s.

In the context of U.S. history, that lack of awareness of a strictly contemporary religious fringe is an extremely unusual situation, if not quite unprecedented. It is all the odder because one might have expected the Internet to have provided a fertile environment for the proliferation of extreme or unconventional religious themes. The same technological changes—Internet and social media—mean that national media would find it much easier to pick up on local stories and panics if they were occurring and bring them to national attention.

In order to explain the change, I would suggest that earlier waves of enthusiasm on the religious margins actually reflected the widespread passion that animated mainstream faith but that could not be contained within orthodox boundaries. In that sense the widespread spiritual unrest of the 1970s was the penumbra of a set of revival and charismatic movements that ultimately transformed mainstream religious life—evangelical and charismatic, but also Catholic and Jewish. If the country genuinely were moving toward rapid secularization, then one of the first symptoms we would expect would be a general reduction of interest in spiritual or religious matters across large sections of society, of the kind that was so richly productive of fringe groups in earlier years. We would no longer find the broad but ill-focused concern that manifested itself in the supernatural boom of the 1970s. Without a solid core of spiritual activism and inquiry, there would be no foundation for the extremism that produced so many prospective members for the cults. In consequence we would witness a precipitous decline in activism and enthusiasm on the spiritual fringe, which is exactly what has taken place. Cults and insurgent religious movements, in that sense, would be canaries in a coal mine, and their disappearance deserves attention.[26]

However much conservative religious critics might dislike this association, the cult boom was in some ways a gauge of the nation's thriving spiritual vigor, and the loss of fringe sects is a disturbing sign of secular trends in progress.

Explanations

As in Europe, American fertility rates track together with the retreat of institutional religion, and many of the same factors are certainly at work.

The oddity is not what occurred but its chronology. Special factors were at work in the United States that help account for the several-decade delay in the secular shift—even if they do not offer a perfect explanation of that phenomenon.

In so many ways, American developments since the 1970s have closely paralleled the trends we have already witnessed in Europe and that in fact have often been more advanced in the United States. The social revolution of the late 1960s was rooted at least as firmly in the United States as in Europe, to the extent that Europeans borrowed many styles and movements that originated across the Atlantic.

Gender issues have been decisive throughout. From the 1970s changes in the economy massively increased women's participation in the workforce, reducing the wish or capacity to bear large numbers of children. Women's involvement in higher education has also grown impressively in the same era. Family structures have weakened and become less rigid. By 2013, the proportion of American babies born outside marriage was over 40 percent. Although the United States has always been a heavily urbanized nation, much recent economic growth has been heavily concentrated in key urban complexes, and as we have seen, fertility rates fall steeply in the most urban areas. This is a key variable in determining women's age at motherhood, which in turn affects the total number of children she will bear. Within the United States, the disparities between rural and urban areas have become very substantial, with particular differences between the low-fertility coastal areas and the high-fertility South and Great Plains. A typical first-time mother in San Francisco or New York is ten years older than her counterpart in the country's heartland—roughly, the difference between 31 and 21. As we have seen in Europe, the United States demonstrates a solid and consistent correlation between family size and religious affiliation, and later family formation contributes to religious decline.[27]

As new family structures spread, so societies become more tolerant of alternative sexual arrangements. In the U.S. context, public attitudes to homosexuality have liberalized unimaginably compared to even twenty years ago. Unlike in other countries, it is difficult to use progress toward same-sex marriage as an index of popular values, as so many of the key changes in this area occurred through the actions of unelected courts, rather than through legislatures or referenda, but the overall trajectory is very similar to that of Europe. After the first state (Massachusetts) legalized the practice in 2004, a further decade was required before it acquired national status in 2015.[28] We have already remarked that the spread of liberal attitudes about gender and sexuality—again, especially among the young—sparked popular revulsion against those churches that used religious language in culture war struggles. Meanwhile, new attitudes to children and concerns about aggressive male sexuality contributed to public outrage over clergy abuse scandals. Such controversies were as much an indicator of underlying attitudes as a driver of change, but both helped spawn the growth of the Nones.

Why the American Exception?

The parallels with Europe are obvious, and we can see abundant reasons why the United States that boomed economically from the 1980s onward should in theory have led the way to secularization, instead of the reverse. Looking at the actual chronology of religious change, we might initially imagine that the United States was a latecomer to the world of industrialization, urbanization, and electronic media, as opposed to being a pathbreaking pioneer. Why the delay?

Several explanations can be offered for the disparity between the United States and the rest of the world. Crucially, any attempts at transatlantic comparisons are bedeviled by the vast size of the United States relative to Europe and its extreme internal diversity. In consequence it should better be considered as a subcontinent, rather than a nation on European lines. In multiple ways the resulting diversity has contributed to the nation's religiosity and the power of its religious institutions. In the modern context, it has seriously delayed—if not actually prevented—the secular onslaught.

Unlike other leading nations, the United States has always been polycentric and has never had a single overwhelming capital city that served as the center of political power, economic might, and media influence. In consequence, the country has been decentralized, allowing local cultures to flourish, a diversity reflected (for instance) in the lack of a standard approved accent in speaking. Decentralization has vast implications for media operations, publishing, and news services. For one thing the lack of centralized broadcasting on European or Japanese lines meant that radio and television have always been open to religious activists of all shades, who from the 1950s onward used them effectively. Evangelical broadcasters in particular were a key force driving the religious upsurge that occurred in the 1970s and 1980s, in the same years that European churches were entering crisis. It was quite possible to live one's whole life consuming nothing but religious broadcasts, offered on multiple channels, alternating perhaps with unflinchingly conservative opinion on secular issues. Taken together, that activity supplied an enviable foundation for social and political mobilization, through the Reagan years and beyond. In Britain or France, in contrast, media until recently operated under tight central control, and usually reflected metropolitan opinions and values, which acquired the status of national orthodoxies and which permitted few dissenting voices. That was especially true in matters of gender and sexuality. From that perspective anything like the American religious media world was a distant dream or, for many, a nightmare.

Geographical size also implies physical movement and relocation, and those factors too have contributed to the strength of religious institutions. By the standards of other advanced nations, Americans have always moved frequently and by great distances, often remaining in particular places for short periods and being far removed from their original homes and families. In such mobile circumstances, people have always sought institutions where they could find instant community, people of like mind with whom to socialize, and where they could find different kinds of support. Historically, this has meant churches and other religious institutions.

Immigrant Faith

Steady waves of international migrants have created further demand for religious communities and contributed to the enduring strength of religious institutions on U.S. shores. The United States has a large population of foreign born, presently some 13.7 percent of the national population, or 45 million people. As in Europe, immigration represents a powerful factor in demographic trends, and recent immigrants are likely to have higher fertility rates than old-stock residents. Without those immigrants the country's fertility rate would have been far lower than was actually the case, and perhaps as low as Germany or Spain.[29]

In the United States, immigration has had a distinctive religious quality. The overwhelming majority of those migrants have been Christian, in accord with the dominant faith of the country, and they have strengthened that tradition. That is an obvious contrast with the European situation, where so many of the migrants were Muslim and established alternative religious communities. Repeatedly those migrants to the United States have revived stagnant or fading congregations—often, in part, because of their far higher fertility. The revival of U.S. fertility rates after 1975—and the strengthening of religious loyalties—coincided with the enormous wave of migration resulting from the 1965 Immigration Act. Throughout its history, the country has always been open to the efforts of immigrant religious entrepreneurs, who have regularly played a disproportionate role in stirring religious activism.

That immigrant factor was critical for Catholic numbers. If we look at long-term surveys of American faith, one reliable constant for many years was the Catholic population, which stood at a solid 25 percent, fluctuating only a point or two either way. That remained true through all the ideological struggles of the 1970s and 1980s, and through the early phases of the abuse crisis, right up to 2010. But that fact should surprise us. From the mid-1960s, the U.S. Catholic Church suffered all the internal woes and conflicts that we have traced in Europe, with a crisis of vocations and a collapsing number of nuns and religious. Yet as American-born Catholics detached from the church, or forsook it outright, their numbers were constantly replaced and even augmented by immigrants. This same era of Catholic crisis also marked the enormous immigration wave, with all the Catholic newcomers: Latinos, of course, but also Africans and East and South Asians. By no means all Latinos are Catholics, faithful or otherwise, and Protestant evangelicalism is growing fast in that population. Even so, those immigrants provided an enormous boost for Catholic numbers. If we subtract the immigrant presence, the state of old-stock congregations would have been bleak indeed, approaching the decline of mainline Protestants. Immigration served to mask underlying decline and did so very effectively.[30]

The fact that the Catholic proportion of the population since the 1980s remained steady as long as it did, rather than plunging, is actually one of the most remarkable stories in modern American religion. As I have remarked, current trends in church membership raise grave questions about how long that Latino buttress will survive.

Faith and Security

That immigrant presence can be only a part of any explanation. To take an obvious comparison, the proportion of immigrants in the overall population is substantially higher in Canada than the United States, although Canada regularly features in lists of the world's most secular societies. At the same time, within the United States, domestic old-stock populations have also remained true to older religious traditions, at levels far higher than in Europe. Across much of the South and Midwest, for example, those older populations—white and black—have not only maintained high levels of religious participation but have been open to recurrent waves of Christian revivalism and political organization.

Obviously, we should be suspicious about any reductionist account that sees religious behavior in only material terms: culture matters, and so do ideas and beliefs. But at the same time, social and economic factors do play their part in shaping religious responses, and part of the American difference here involves the concept of existential security, which I described in the opening chapter. According to this theory, societies with limited state power or welfare facilities leave citizens far more to their own devices in terms of achieving security and well-being, for which they depend on families and communities. Such societies tend to have larger families and depend more on religion and religious institutions. Insecure societies tend toward high fertility and high faith. As societies develop more formal mechanisms for welfare, education, and health, so the dependence on families and communities fades, and so does religion. The better ordinary people are served through state-based services, the greater their sense of security, and the less need they have to depend on religious congregations. That is a crude statement of the theory, but it does identify the key elements.[31]

The American state is extremely powerful in many ways, but until quite recently the country's social safety net was weak by the standards of most advanced nations, and that was especially true in medical matters. American provision for medical care was far less generous or sweeping than anything prevailing in Europe, Canada, or Japan, quite apart from huge differences in welfare benefits generally. The United States also deviated from European norms in its infant mortality figures, which as I have already noted, correlate to fertility. Despite its advanced science and medicine, the U.S. rate in 2017 was 5.8, as against an average of 3.4 for comparable countries. In Europe the closest parallel to the U.S. rates would be found in the Balkan states or in the poorer nations of the East.[32]

People who lack confidence in the state's ability to look after them are more likely to focus on their families and to have larger families. Also, of necessity, many Americans have had to depend on neighbors, and above all on religious institutions, which play a large role in the provision of social and family services. That remained true in the years between (say) 1965 and 2010, the era when Europe was undergoing its twin transformations in faith and fertility. In the U.S. context, changes in welfare provision in that era actually tended to make the system less rather than more generous, as occurred during the presidency of Bill Clinton. That trend was only reversed by the substantial expansion of medical provisions under the Obama administration. From that perspective it is less surprising that Americans would remain more closely bound to their religious congregations through years that, on a national level, appeared to witness such relentless expansion.

None of these various factors in itself necessarily accounts for the apparent delay in a European-style drift away from both religion and high fertility in the United States. But taken together they help us understand what otherwise remains a puzzling difference.

Red and Blue Americas

The matter of America's size, and its consequent diversity, also affects the pace of change within the country, which has advanced much further and more rapidly in some regions than others. That differential rate of change has contributed to some familiar national divisions and conflicts.[33]

While low fertility and low faith advance in tandem, the process has to be analyzed on a local and regional scale. Accordingly, anything we say about U.S. social patterns, or any kind of European convergence, has to be broken down by region and subgroup. In 2017, when the U.S. national TFR was 1.77, the actual rate ranged widely between regions and individual states. New England stood at the very low end of fertility, with Massachusetts, Rhode Island, Vermont, and New Hampshire all around 1.52, Connecticut and Maine a little higher. At the other extreme were the Dakotas, Utah, and Nebraska, all near replacement rate. A similar divergence emerges in infant mortality rates, which we have already seen track closely with fertility, and the highest figures are found in the South and Midwest.[34]

In different areas of the country, changes in fertility have been intimately linked to religious patterns and to cultural attitudes. Repeated surveys have confirmed a familiar geographical pattern in which religious attitudes and behaviors are very common and standard in Midwestern states, while the West Coast and New England tend to be far more secular. In Washington State, for instance—the "None Zone"—Nones constitute almost a third of the population. That religious division further correlates to political behavior. That is particularly likely in the U.S. context, where so much of the substance of politics revolves around issues of religion and morality, with gender and sexuality at the core of so much controversy. In the 2016 presidential election, those who attended religious services weekly favored Donald Trump over Hillary Clinton by a margin of 53 to 29 percent.[35]

Broadly, states and regions with higher fertility rates tend to retain older religious patterns and in their politics, veer toward the Red side of the partisan divide. Low-faith and low-fertility areas are significantly Bluer. This point was evident in the 2004 presidential election, when fertility rates offered an accurate predictor of which states would vote Republican (Bush) or Democrat (Kerry). High-fertility states went conservative and Republican; low-fertility went liberal and Democrat. The odd state out was Michigan, a high-fertility region that nevertheless opted for Kerry. What made the critical difference here was the state's high degree of union membership and activism.[36]

Of course, social patterns in themselves cannot predict electoral outcomes, which among other things depend on party structures, electoral laws, and disparities between groups in voter registration. But the connection between fertility and political outcomes demands attention. Presently a map of U.S. states by fertility unnervingly echoes political divisions, and more especially stances in the culture wars. Using only fertility data, an observer who knew nothing of American political geography would correctly deduce that the country's liberal heartlands must be based in the Northeast (New England, New York, Pennsylvania) and the West Coast, the "Left Coast" (California, Oregon, Washington), with an outlier in Colorado. In 2017 all those regions had TFRs at or below 1.71. To put that in global context, that rate would be comparable to those of Belgium, Denmark, or the Baltic states, all countries well known for low fertility. Conservative bastions, on the other hand, would include a solid heartland bloc (Nebraska, Kansas, Iowa, the Dakotas, Utah, Texas, Arkansas, and Oklahoma). In the middle of the fertility table are several states that we would expect (correctly) to be electoral swing states, such as Arizona, North Carolina, Georgia, or Michigan.[37]

Our imaginary observer would make errors, such as presuming that low-fertility Florida must be part of the ultraliberal bloc, whereas in fact it is a hard-fought swing state. Yet Florida's electoral outcomes have long been distorted by severe laws that disfranchised felons, in effect removing large sections of left-leaning African American and Latino populations from the voter rolls. On the other side of the divide, we might also expect high-fertility Hawaii to be loyally conservative and Republican, which it certainly is not. But again, special local circumstances apply here, in the state's distinctive ethnic structure.

Generally, a map of fertility rates remains a remarkably reliable predictor of political alignments.

The End of Red America?

It is intriguing to speculate on the impact of what seems likely to be the further decline in fertility rates in coming years. Over the past decade, the trend in rates has been sharply downward, and it is highly probable that this will continue. If indeed low-fertility societies like New England tend to be liberal and deep Blue, then can we assume that this would also be the coloring of a near-future America that has shifted toward a comparable demographic reality? If Nebraska (say) acquires the demographic and religious coloring of Oregon, does it likewise assume a deep Blue political coloring? In those hypothetical circumstances, then demography would consign the

Red side—and the Republican Party—to historical oblivion and probably within just a decade or two.

While recent history should make us nervous about making any political predictions, a long-term perspective suggests that the partisan future is nothing like so predetermined. Historically the two major parties have regularly shifted the content of their messages and the basis of their electoral appeal, and they will presumably do so again. There was a time when hard-bitten segregationists found their natural home in the Democratic Party, while educated feminists gravitated to the Republicans. It is very probable that in future, we will see a major shift in the ideological substance of Red politics, when so many issues that were once sharply divisive have been settled so decisively as liberal victories. Issues of gay rights and same-sex marriage are the obvious example, but many religious-related issues that were once reliable hot-button conservative causes have likewise faded from view. Examples include school prayer and the teaching of evolution.

If religious loyalties do fade in society at large, then issues and causes growing out of those ideologies will likewise disappear from partisan agendas. In another decade we can easily imagine the persistence or even revival of a powerful Republican Party, and indeed a Red America, but defined according to issues quite different from what we would assume today.

A Quiet Revolution?

So integral has religion been to American life and thought throughout its history that any prospect of secularization—however we define the term—is explosive. It also seems improbable when we see how deeply embedded religious thought and assumptions are among so many Americans, in so many different classes and races, and especially in particular geographical settings. This shows no sign of transforming overnight. At the same time, it is useful to consider one troubling precedent, namely what occurred in the Canadian province of Québec half a century ago, during its Quiet Revolution. Within just a decade or two, a province legendary for its deep and pervasive piety became one of the world's most radically secular societies, where Catholic practice in particular was mainly the preserve of immigrants from Africa, Asia, and the Caribbean.[38]

Taken singly any of the reported indicators of religious decline in the United States might be explained away, but the accumulated weight of evidence now paints a convincing picture, all the more so when placed alongside the undeniable fact of steep and continuing fertility decline. As I have remarked, this may or may not constitute secularization in the traditional model. If a None believes in God and prays frequently, then terms like "secular" must be used sparingly. The Nones correspond closely to the religious pattern that we saw in modern Europe, in which many people criticize ecclesiastical structure and hierarchy while maintaining a strong and even passionate spiritual or supernatural orientation. But in an American context, any such movement away from formal churches and institutions would be noteworthy and, for many, traumatic.[39]

As to timing, analogies with Europe suggest that once such a process gets underway, it can proceed very rapidly indeed. Matters might develop differently on U.S. soil, but we should contemplate the possibility that in religious terms, the 2020s will be for the United States what the 1970s were for Western Europe.

PART II

6

AFRICA

When the twentieth century began, the lands that would become the nation of Kenya had a tiny population of 1.5 million, although precise estimates are difficult to come by. That number then grew spectacularly, amply justifying the familiar language of "explosion." National population reached 10 million by 1966, 30 million by the end of the century, and (probably) 50 million today. Such a story meshes well with the patterns we have already seen in countries of Asia or Latin America, but with the key difference that Kenya is still well above replacement rate. Although Kenya's TFR has fallen from a high of around 7.0 in the mid-1960s, the rate is still over 2.9. By 2050 Kenya could have 95 million people. The country has a marked youth bulge, with one of the world's youngest populations. Some 40 percent of Kenyans are below the age of 15, with another 20 percent aged between 15 and 24. Together those figures present a sharp contrast to what we have witnessed in other continents, but the most striking point is where they stand on an African continuum. Despite Kenya's present and continuing growth, that fertility rate is by some margin one of the *lowest* in sub-Saharan Africa.[1]

As many other non-African countries have moved decisively to a low-fertility model—as they have become Sterilia—older demographic patterns are far from extinct. The world of Fertilia is much in evidence in Africa, in parts of South Asia, and across large sections of the region known as MENA, the Middle East and North Africa. In most of those countries—with a few notable exceptions—high fertility is combined with intense religiosity, and with political and religious conflict. In most cases those conflicts involve a substantial religious element, which defines the ideology of combatants. If signs of change are beginning to appear in such nations, they are doing so gradually and sporadically.[2]

The political turmoil in such regions naturally disturbs governments and security experts, but these patterns also have other long-term consequences. High-fertility societies remain very religious, and that religious identity plays a critical role in global faith and in global conflict. As populations swell in Africa above all, so they include ever-larger shares of the believers whose religions are best established there, which above all means Islam and Christianity. Demography has redrawn the world's religious maps and will continue to do so at least for decades to come. In matters of faith as much as fertility, the contrast between Africa and the rest of the world becomes ever sharper.

Africa's Population Boom

Over the past century, the growth of the African population has been one of the most significant facts of global demography. A hundred years ago, economically advanced and urbanized Europe confronted a lightly populated and largely nonurban Africa, but matters have since changed utterly. Africa's total population grew from just 110 million in 1900 to a billion by 2015, and with a likely increase to 2.5 billion by 2050. (Older population estimates are of course subject to much uncertainty.) Africans made up 7 percent of the human race in 1900, compared to over a quarter projected for 2050. Although any longer-term projections are multiply dubious, some estimates predict that by 2100 a third of all humans then alive will be African. The rate of increase is all the larger if we focus on just black or sub-Saharan Africa. By 2050 a list of the twenty countries with the largest populations will include no fewer than six black African nations: Nigeria, the Democratic Republic of the Congo (DRC), Ethiopia, Tanzania, Uganda, and Kenya. Taken together, according to this projection, those countries alone will have over 1.1 billion citizens. Apart from Russia no European names will still feature on such a list of the most populous nations.[3]

Africans justly complain that Western experts tend to treat the continent as a homogeneous whole, rather than recognizing the enormous disparities and distinctions found within its sprawling reality. Having said this, most African regions do share certain realities that set them apart from the rest of the world, and demography is a prime example. Across the continent the main force driving recent growth is high fertility rates, which have more than compensated for the effects of wars, epidemic diseases, and infant mortality. The role of fertility is obvious from the fast-growing population of the DRC. A country that had just 12 million people in 1950 has 85 million today, and that number should approach 200 million by 2050. The surge has occurred despite a perfect storm of disasters that have devastated the country and its population. These include huge losses to AIDS, as well as perhaps five million deaths in the horrific wars that raged between 1996 and 2003.[4]

No less striking has been the stubborn maintenance of those "highest-high" fertility rates right up to the present day. True, rates have declined from a continental average of 6.5 in the 1970s to 4.4 today, but that 4.4 is still very high. In a 2017 ranking of the world's 224 nations by total fertility rates, African nations secured forty-three out of the top fifty slots. With the exception of Egypt, all those high-fertility African nations were in sub-Saharan or Saharan regions. Three of these nations, Niger, Mali, and Angola, still retain TFRs in excess of 6.0, with a dozen more between 5.0 and 6.0. Among the continent's most important nations, Nigeria has a TFR of 5.07, with Uganda at 5.71, Ethiopia at 4.99, and the DRC at 4.39. In this framework Kenya places only at number 56 in this league table, well behind most other African lands. Among the sub-Saharan nations, the lowest TFR is that of South Africa, which stands at number 91. Outside Africa, the other very high-fertility nations were Middle Eastern and South Asian, and part of that famous Arc of Crisis; we will discuss these in the next chapter.[5]

As I have noted earlier, infant mortality rates correlate well with those fertility rates and help to explain them. If we list the world's nations in terms of their infant mortality rates, African nations occupy the vast majority of the leading forty-five names, those with rates of 40 or more deaths per thousand live births. By way of comparison, most European nations have rates of 5 or less. A 2011 study noted that of the ten million children who died each year before age 5, half were located in sub-Saharan Africa.[6] The need to produce children to replace those who were lost means that African women have very low rates of contraceptive use, far lower than in Latin America.

Uganda offers a revealing case study. The lands that became Uganda had around 2 million people in 1900, rising to 5 million in 1950 and 20 million by 1996. To put that figure in a U.S. context, Uganda covers a slightly smaller land area than Oregon, with its 4.2 million people, but Uganda's present population is 44 million. When I was initially working on these matters twenty years ago, I expressed skepticism about estimates made at the time that Uganda's population might rise to 80 million by 2050. In fact I was too conservative, and present projections are closer to 100 million. The country's infant mortality rate is a parlous 56 per thousand births.[7]

Earlier I described the strikingly elderly age profiles of societies in Europe and East Asia. Africa, in contrast, is astonishingly youthful. In a list of nations ranked by the median age of the population, African countries occupy all but four of the forty lowest rungs—all societies with a median of 20 years or less.[8] By this standard the world's very youngest nations are Uganda, Niger, and Mali, all with median ages below 16. As a continent the median age of Africa's people is just 19.5.

These demographic trends are reflected in the enormous growth of cities. Africa is currently passing through a vast process of urbanization, in fact, the largest of its kind in human history. Before the 1960s sub-Saharan Africa lacked major urban complexes, except in South Africa. As late as 1980, less than 30 percent of Africans lived in cities, compared to a projected figure of 50 percent by 2050. In Nigeria the Lagos metropolitan area has grown from 400,000 in the 1950s to at least 18 million today. Like all such numbers, any estimates include a major element of guesswork because of the large number of residents living in shantytowns, which lie substantially outside government control or awareness. Just how high urban numbers could rise is multiply controversial, but some knowledgeable experts project that Lagos by 2050 could have an inconceivably vast population of over 85 million. Comparable growth has affected communities like Kinshasa (present population 12 million), Brazzaville (14 million), Luanda (7 million), and Dar es Salaam (6 million). In Kenya Nairobi's population has grown from barely 5,000 in 1900 to 100,000 in the early 1950s and over 5 million today in the larger metropolitan region. By 2050 Nairobi could have 14 million people.[9]

Some presently obscure centers will feature prominently on future maps of the world's largest cities. One stunning example comes from the poor West African land of Burkina Faso, formerly Upper Volta, which is little known to nonspecialist Westerners. In 1900 the country probably had 2.5 million people, as against 20 million today, and that number is projected to rise to over 43 million by 2050. As of 2017 the country's TFR was 5.71. In 1900 the country was wholly nonurban. Its capital, Ouagadougou ("Ouaga"), barely existed and had at most a few thousand residents. Today it has over 2 million, and by midcentury Ouaga should be home to 7 million. Similar stories could be told of Niamey in Niger and Blantyre in Malawi. Over the coming thirty years, perhaps 80 percent of Africa's new residents will live in cities.[10]

Reasons for Growth

These demographic patterns are closely linked to problems of poverty and of weak states. Overwhelmingly, African nations dominate a listing of the world's poorest nations. In 2016 African states made up twenty-two of the twenty-eight nations with GDP per capita of less than $1,000. That includes such populous nations as the DRC and Ethiopia, with Tanzania just over the $1,000 figure. If experts can quibble at length about the exact worth of GDP statistics, many other gauges offer a similar evaluation.[11]

While acknowledging such grim statistics, that does not necessarily mean accepting the familiar stereotype of Africa as hopelessly mired in deprivation and chaos. Some countries have indeed made massive economic progress during the present century. In the mid-2010s, several countries in sub-Saharan Africa were growing economically at rates approaching East Asia, and some nations also have rich natural resources. Ethiopia is notable among what some observers were calling the African Lions, an optimistic echo of the Asian Tigers. Through the past decade, the country was regularly hitting annual growth rates in excess of 10 percent. Partly this regional progress is a consequence of the insatiable global demand for minerals and natural resources, especially from China, but services and manufacturing are also growing. Substantial professional and middle classes exist in many African nations.[12]

The problem is that such new wealth is often poorly distributed. This is partly due to systematic corruption and misgovernment, which has made little progress in building up the continent's woefully inadequate infrastructure. Such failures are especially evident in Nigeria, conditions that are often summarized by the term *kleptocracy*, government by thieves. Although Kenya's GDP per capita has risen substantially in the present century, it is still only $1,800 per person, compared to $40,000 in an advanced European nation like France or the UK, and $50,000 in the Netherlands. Also, the enormous youth bulge in African nations means that it is never possible even for sizable economic growth to provide anything like the number of jobs that would be needed to bring a majority of the population into a new economy and social order. That lack of employment opportunities especially affects women, who are less likely to be drawn out of the home and family setting into the workplace. That contributes to the maintenance of traditional concepts of gender and a central emphasis on motherhood in defining women's roles.[13]

Economic weakness, reinforced by government failures, does not permit societies to move to anything like the sense of security, stability, and predictability that we find in the European model. Even in peaceful regions, stable and honest government is a distant dream. Wise city dwellers know better than to count on power supplies being regularly available, and they constantly face the hazard of violent crime. Newer values of radical individualism have made strictly limited inroads on traditional societies, with their strong sense of community, communalism, mutual reliance, and deference to authority. Out of stern practical necessity, African societies still value large families, and a widespread tolerance of polygamy contributes to high fertility.

Bastions of Faith

Three religious systems dominate modern Africa, namely primal traditional religions, Islam, and Christianity. During the twentieth century, the numbers following traditional systems have fallen steeply, although aspects of those systems assuredly survive in the faiths to which people have converted. Over the whole century, perhaps half of Africans abandoned primal religions to espouse Christianity or Islam, and Christian converts probably outnumbered Muslims by 3 or 4 to 1. The growth of both religions would be a dramatic enough story in its own right, but the booming continental population gives it a special weight on a global scale.

At every stage, the continent's modern religious history must be understood in the context of the demographic trends I have described. As we have seen, the link between fertility and religion is not a simple matter of causation, but rather the two factors are inextricably linked. African Christians and Muslims alike follow religious patterns that mark them as very different from those of Europe—or from many other parts of the Global South. Regardless of language or region, surveys repeatedly show extraordinarily high levels of religious practice and belief, with many showing a belief in God at or near 100 percent. Demographic needs ensure that challenges to traditional codes of gender roles and sexual morality are few and respect for religious authority is high. For both Christians and Muslims, family, religion, and community stand and fall together. That picture does not apply equally to the whole continent, and there are some signs of change, but presently most of Africa remains as "notoriously religious" as it ever was.[14]

I have already described the 2015 survey that asked respondents whether they felt religious. At the top of the list were three African countries—Ethiopia, Malawi, and Niger, all at 99 percent—and all the top twenty-five nations were located in Africa, the Middle East, or Southeast Asia. Each of these twenty-five reported religious sentiments with response rates of 95 percent or higher. At the other extreme were twenty-three nations drawn mainly from Europe (fourteen nations) but with several Asian names. When asked about the role religion played in their lives, Africa produced some of the highest numbers reporting "very important": 98 percent in Ethiopia, 88 percent in Nigeria, 86 percent in Uganda.[15]

Social and demographic trends shape attitudes to religion and also determine the particular forms that it takes. In so many areas, religion supplies many functions that secular society evidently cannot, above all in matters of health, medicine, and medical provision.

As we have seen, the demographic transition means a decisive move away from high death rates as well as high fertility, but African circumstances mean continued vulnerability to sickness and early death. Poverty in an African context naturally means exposure to diseases and conditions long consigned to the past in Europe, aggravated by polluted water and environmental hazards, and the hot climate poses special additional risks. Ill health is pervasive, and medical facilities are strictly limited. Taken together this creates quite overwhelming openness to anyone offering healing of body and mind, and that has strong religious consequences. In saying this I am certainly not trying to offer any kind of reductionist explanation of religious change or growth. Rather, social and demographic circumstances shape the attitudes of believers, actual or potential, and thus determine the messages offered by religious institutions.

While traditional primal religions offered their spiritual resources for healing, the greatest beneficiaries have been Christian churches of all shades. Indeed, the great expansion of native African churches coincided with the influenza epidemic of 1918, and the most successful subsequent waves of mass growth have been healing related. A belief in miracles is deeply embedded in African cultures, as is an openness to claims of prophetic revelation. In most societies belief in supernatural forces and forms of witchcraft is commonplace, despite efforts by mainstream religious institutions to limit or reject such ideas. Many successful churches offer their services in spiritual warfare, besides healing and exorcism.[16]

Without the promise of healing and miracle, the growth of African Christianity is incomprehensible. Traditionally Islam too benefited from a belief in the healing powers of its sacred objects and texts. In West Africa, thriving Sufi orders attracted support through their charismatic leaders, who were associated with miraculous powers. That element of Islam has been challenged severely in recent years with the upsurge of new and more fundamentalist forms of faith, but historically it constituted a major part of the religion's appeal.

Across the continent it is impossible to miss the huge enthusiasm for religious participation and a zeal for religious behavior of all kinds. Religious behavior pervades ordinary life: witness the slogans and Bible verses that are so common on taxis or stores, or the willingness of people waiting in queues to join in hymns with little notice. That enthusiasm transcends faiths or denominations. We see it in the vast crowds drawn to Christian revivals or miracle crusades. Believers are willing, even eager, to join in events that to a European or American seem intolerably demanding, such as all-night meetings of prayer and praise. Even Muslims have adopted related forms of gathering in order to meet the interfaith competition.

Striking too is the persistence of such high religiosity in the face of rapid social transformation. Signs of faith are ubiquitous in Africa's booming cities, and the continent's farflung migrant communities carry their faith with them. On the Christian side of the equation, individual African migrants have joined mainstream churches in North America or Europe, but distinctively African churches are also commonplace around the world. In each case local believers are impressed or startled by the obvious commitment and religious passion of the newcomers—usually, but not always, in a positive way.

The World's Religious Map

Once a religion has become established in a particular social landscape, demography plays the critical role in its further expansion. This is evident in Africa, which will increasingly play a central role in the global picture of Christian numbers and to a somewhat lesser extent, of Islam.

In 1900 Africa had 10 million Christians, or 10 percent of the population. That proportion has since grown powerfully due to conversion, rising to almost half the continental population today. But the surge in the overall population of sub-Saharan Africa has vastly increased the absolute number of Christians, which now stands around half a billion and which will reach a billion by 2050.[17] By that point Africa will have by far the world's largest Christian population, and the numbers are still more awe-inspiring when we take account of African migrants living in other continents, especially in Europe. By 2050 a list of the ten countries worldwide with the largest Christian populations will include several African members, including Nigeria, Ethiopia, the DRC, and Uganda. Between 1900 and 2050, the African share of global Christian population will have grown from perhaps a couple of percent to over a third.

To take Kenya again, the Christian proportion of the population has unquestionably swelled since the mid-twentieth century, to reach a modern figure of perhaps 80 or 85 percent. But the increase in raw numbers is still more impressive, growing from perhaps 4 million in the mid-1960s to over 40 million today and conceivably to 75 million by the middle of this century.

Any number of African countries tell a similar story, the main variable being the relative strength of Christianity and Islam. In 1900 the lands that became Nigeria had around 16 million inhabitants, of whom a tiny fraction were Christian—perhaps 180,000. That same area now contains almost 200 million people, a figure that could exceed 400 million by 2050. Even if Christians make not a single new convert in that land but merely retain their current share of population, then between 2020 and 2050, the number of Nigerian Christians will grow from around 90 million to over 180 million. At that point Nigeria will be one of the most significant centers of Christianity worldwide, and high on the list of adherents of multiple traditions and denominations—of Catholics, Anglicans, and other "mainline" groupings, plus multiple churches of local African origin. Put another way, between 1900 and 2050, Christian numbers would have grown by at least a thousandfold, and that is overwhelmingly a demographic outcome.

To return to Uganda, Christianity was quite new in the country in 1900 but has since become the dominant religion. Perhaps 40 percent of Ugandans are Catholic, 32 percent Anglican, and 13 percent other Protestant. Muslims make up 13 percent. If for the sake of argument, we assume that the balance of faiths has held more or less steady, this means that the number of Ugandan Christians has grown from 3 or 4 million in 1950 to 37 million today, with a possible expansion to over 80 million by 2050. In 1900, likewise, Ethiopia had around 12 million people, rising to 40 million by 1980 and around 100 million today. By 2050 the figure could be 180 million. If we assume that Christians represent around half the total, then the number of Ethiopian Christians will have grown from 6 million in 1900 to over 90 million in 2050, and again, that assumes no conversion or evangelism.[18]

The Roman Catholic experience demonstrates the impact of such changes, a point of singular importance since this remains by far the largest religious institution in existence. In 1900 that church could muster just a couple of million followers in the whole of Africa. By 2015 that number topped 200 million, and some observers even argue that is an undercount. Within a decade from now, Catholic numbers in Africa will exceed those in Europe, although any comparison needs to recognize that those European numbers will include a good number of African migrants. By 2040 Africa's Catholic population could constitute a quarter of the total, or a staggering 460 million believers. In 2015 a group of Africa's leading clerics and primates contributed to a book about the continent's new realities, under the illuminating title of *Christ's New Homeland*.[19]

Islam in Africa

Near-identical demographic factors explain the growth of African Islam in these same years. As an absolute number, there are vastly more African

Muslims than there were in the mid-twentieth century. In the mid-1940s, Africa as a whole probably had 40 million Muslims, as against half a billion today. Just looking at the sub-Saharan regions, the Muslim population reached 250 million by 2015 but is projected to rise to 670 million by 2050. That is a rate of increase even steeper than the Christian figure.[20]

The Muslim share of Nigeria's population grew from 26 percent in 1900 to 45 percent today, which in absolute terms represented an increase from 4 million to 90 million and quite possibly to 180 million by 2050. Among many other countries, we might look at the small nation of Burkina Faso. In 1900 it probably had fewer than a million Muslims, less than half the population. That proportion has grown subsequently, to 60 percent today, but the absolute numbers indicate a much more dramatic change. Burkina Faso today has 12 million Muslims, a figure that will likely rise to 25 million by 2050. By that point its capital city of Ouagadougou will be a Muslim metropolis, presumably with the full panoply of religious institutions, mosques, and schools that we would expect in such a center.

However impressive such changes might be, their impact on the global stage is relatively smaller than that of African Christianity, because Islam worldwide has grown steadily in many other parts of the world outside Africa. Even so, African countries do play a larger role in the larger Muslim picture. Nigeria in 1900 constituted less than 2 percent of the world Muslim population, compared to over 5 percent today. From being a thinly populated outlier on the edges of the Muslim world, Nigeria is increasingly a key player in that realm.

Global Schisms

In other ways too, the growth of African numbers poses much less of a challenge to Islam worldwide than the comparable expansion of Christian numbers does to that faith. In the Islamic case, African Muslims largely share the conservative values that would be commonplace elsewhere in centers of that faith, whether in South Asia or the Middle East. In all such societies, the emphasis on traditional gender structures and female roles is intimately tied up with religion and bolstered by religious sanctions. Such high-fertility societies are deeply invested in notions of family honor and the defense of female chastity. If we imagine a world in which Africa became ever more decisively the core of Islamic numbers, that would not of itself herald a major change in the nature of the faith.

The Christian story in such matters is vastly different. Like Islam, booming African Christianity has shared the conservative mores and sexual values of the larger society, but that has often set them at odds with Christians elsewhere in the world. The resulting conflicts and schisms raise worrying questions for the unity of Christianity at large and for individual churches and denominations.

Raw numbers alone do not determine the role that any geographical area plays in a religious organization or institution, and they never have. Even so, the rise of Christian strength in Africa especially—together with some other areas of the Global South—has coincided with the accelerating secularization that we have already traced in older centers of the faith, above all in Europe. The rise of Christian communities in Nigeria or Uganda coincides with the precipitous decline in nations like Germany and Britain. Even so, those older churches still retain a large share of institutional wealth, and of soft power generally, especially access to media. The potential for conflict within churches is present, and it has erupted over those key themes of sexual morality that increasingly serve as cultural markers between high- and low-fertility societies.[21]

These issues of family and fertility also shape how different parts of the world interact with each other. As we have seen, attitudes to fertility are intimately bound up with sexual mores and with gender attitudes. For Western societies, especially in Europe, gay rights and women's rights are an integral part of the human rights package, much to the bafflement of other societies that have not gone through the full demographic transition. In turn, those moral conflicts are regularly framed in religious terms. Notoriously they divide Christian denominations like the global Anglican Communion, which has been rent so viciously by gay rights controversies. For twenty years Anglicanism has been divided between, on the one hand, liberal Britain and North America, and on the other, such conservative churches as Nigeria, Kenya, and Rwanda. In the United States, the conflict has generated open schism, as (mainly white) conservative Episcopalians have placed themselves under the ecclesiastical control of primates and senior clergy from Africa—a situation that would have seemed unthinkable a couple of generations ago.

Although in subtler form, similar confrontations have occurred among the world's Methodists and European Lutherans, with gay issues always to the fore. Even the Roman Catholic Church has faced tensions, although nothing yet vaguely approaching the Anglican scenario. In 2015 a Synod on the Family held in Rome showed the strength of a conservative caucus of African prelates, who resisted even mild reforms in Church attitudes to sexuality, marriage, or celibacy. If African numbers grow as they are projected to do—and if that strength is reflected in greater strength in the College of Cardinals—then we can expect an ever-growing African influence in the character of the church as a whole.[22]

Youth and Conflict

In culture and church politics, demographic-driven religious change has sparked conflict and dissension that has been bloodless in nature. Much more immediately dangerous are the religious conflicts that have blighted so many parts of modern Africa. Time and again religion has been strongly associated with violence and warfare, with tensions between Christians and Muslims a perennial theme. This has been evident in intercommunal struggles marked by pogroms and ethnic purges, most notoriously in Nigeria but also in many other countries. Religion provides the rationale for guerrilla and terrorist movements, some of which have affiliated with larger global causes. Among Islamist groups the most notorious include Nigeria's Boko Haram, the Somali al-Shabab, and the West African movement al-Qaeda in the Islamic Maghreb (AQIM). Among the countries we have encountered in this chapter, Kenya has suffered both from interreligious conflicts and brutal terrorism, while Burkina Faso has been the repeated target of jihadi extremism. Nigeria has witnessed bitter fighting between Christians and Muslims in provinces where the two faiths live in close proximity. Religion thus appears to be a source for hatred and destruction, recalling the battles that rent Europe during the Thirty Years' War of the seventeenth century.[23]

In fact the wave of contemporary religious struggles has to be understood through the intertwined effects of religion and demography, of faith and fertility. It is not so much that religion is driving conflict but that conflicts that do occur often—not invariably—find expression in religious forms.[24]

Before blaming religion as such for the turmoil—any religion—we should stress that demographic factors of themselves show a clear and consistent linkage to disorder and violence. High fertility commonly means a society with a large proportion of the young and very young. In any society teenagers and young adults aged between about 15 and 24—particularly young males—are a source of turbulence and are at the highest risk of involvement in crime. How states cope with such a situation depends on the strength of state institutions and mechanisms, and their economic resources. Although some countries can provide adequate employment for teeming legions of teenagers and young adults, that is rarely true of societies in early stages of modernization and industrialization. Young people thus find themselves angry and frustrated, in search of scapegoats, and open to the messages of radicalism, secular or religious. The lower a country's median age, the greater the prospects for instability. With all allowances for local conditions, we can even offer likely figures that correlate closely with instability. This would include a society where the proportion of people aged between 15 and 24 is around 20 percent and where the median age of the population is 22 or less.[25]

This linkage becomes evident from a list of the countries with the highest fertility rates, with TFRs of 5.0 or higher, countries with pronounced youth bulges. Few such societies have escaped internal warfare in recent years, often on a horrendous scale, although only in some cases was violence explicitly associated with religion. In some cases—Nigeria, Chad, Somalia—the religious component is inescapable, as combatants adopted the symbols and rhetoric of their rival faiths. But the list would also include Burundi, long the scene of brutal violence between tribal groupings, and ethnic purges that on occasion have approached genocidal proportions, yet lacking any religious element. Another very high-fertility society is South Sudan, which was founded in 2011 as a result of seemingly interminable warfare between Christians and Muslims in the former nation of Sudan. But even after that secession, domestic conflicts have continued to rage, making it one of the world's most egregiously failed states, and that violence has occurred entirely between Christians. Other nations on this grim list would include the DRC, the setting for untold violence and slaughter, and again, with no discernible religious agenda. At the time of the Rwandan genocide in 1994, in which some eight hundred thousand perished, the nation's TFR was 6.5, and it had one of the world's youngest population profiles. Again, this struggle was entirely ethnic and tribal in nature, without any religious connotations. In most cases, Christians were killing Christians. Sometimes, as in Mali, undoubted examples of religious extremism and guerrilla warfare combined with non-religious-based struggles—tribal and ethnic in nature—to create a cauldron of persistent violence.[26]

Of itself high fertility does not drive violence, nor does a youth bulge. But these are commonly associated with other factors that can form a toxic combination, especially when combined with extreme poverty and state weakness. We see a familiar Malthusian trap, in which population grows far beyond the means of subsistence. As in Thomas Malthus' day, the finite resources for which populations compete are land and water, as the means of producing food. Poor societies are highly vulnerable to multiple misfortunes, for which people seek scapegoats, and disasters are all the more certain as populations grow at the phenomenal rates we have observed in modern Africa. Rural regions face intensified conflicts over resources, while urban areas cannot cope with vast influxes of new residents. The weakness of government leaves citizens highly dependent on private organizations, whether that means political parties and factions or older ethnic and tribal structures. Bitter partisanship inevitably follows. In an African context, the surfeit of unemployed young adults provides fertile recruiting grounds for gangs, militias, or extremist sects.

The potential causes of conflict are many and obvious. Social conditions and economic opportunities determine the nature of that unrest and turbulence, and especially whether it will be channeled into political behavior.

How Violence Becomes Religious

But if conflict and violence are probable, why should it so commonly manifest in religious forms? Nothing in any particular religion determines that its adherents should act violently. Despite the apparently pacific and otherworldly core of its teaching, even Buddhists produce fanatics and extremists. The simple fact that Islam and Christianity coexist in Africa does not mean that wars and pogroms are inevitable. In much of sub-Saharan Africa, the two faiths exist amiably side by side, and many extended families have both Muslim and Christian members.

Yet many points of potential stress exist between the two religions, due in large part to the head-spinning pace of change in recent decades, both religious and demographic. In most of Africa, Islam is the older and better-established religion, and Muslims long regarded their social and political role as thoroughly established, and indeed incontestable. Those assumptions were upended by the mushroom growth of Christianity. I have already described the rapid transformation of the religious balance in Nigeria within just a few short decades. The relative change was even greater in Burkina Faso, where Christianity was only introduced at the end of the nineteenth century but today Christians make up almost a quarter of the population. Here and in many similar lands, the question arises of how much further those Christian numbers might grow, even to the point of outnumbering Muslims or making mass conversions from the ranks of Islam. Christians, on their side, fear Muslim violence and retaliation, and circulate florid conspiracy theories about sinister plans to create purely Islamic societies across Africa. Both sides thus fear the other, allowing each side to justify any violent actions as a form of self-defense.[27]

Profoundly aggravating tensions is the shifting role of women and thus of notions of gender roles and family obligations. Although to a smaller degree than in other parts of the world, many African women have been affected by different forms of modernization, by new social expectations, and by aspirations to pursue education and a career. Progressive and modern women pose a special threat to traditional concepts of Islam, and conservative Muslims often blame such departures from the familiar on the influence of Western media and of Christianity. Christians thus find themselves blamed for assaults on Islamic values, especially within the confines of the family. Even seemingly minor disagreements or perceived slights can provoke large-scale destruction, as each side seeks scapegoats for failures and disasters.

As often occurs globally, religion also offers tempting solutions for people unnerved or appalled by fast and overwhelming social change, by urbanization, modernization, population expansion, and Westernization. Those solutions can be strictly practical, in terms of the welfare and education services that religious institutions provide to poor people, especially in large cities. Religious responses also take ideological forms. In an Islamic context, the conspicuous failures of African states and economic systems have persuaded many to seek to return to a mythic past of religious purity. That has created a favorable environment for fundamentalist and uncompromising expressions of faith, which have made any kind of religious accommodation far more difficult. Across most of traditionally Muslim West Africa, religious behavior was expressed through membership in the various Sufi orders. If not tolerant in any Western sense, adherents were open-minded about relations with other faiths.

Recently, globalized forms of Islam emanating chiefly from the Arab Middle East have been very influential, demanding more rigid adherence to the faith as defined in Salafi tradition. This rejected most Sufi customs and institutions as almost pagan in nature. Newer kinds of Islam had the impact they did because of the changing nature of African societies, with the growth of young populations, concentrated in sprawling cities. The spread of new versions of Islam could be observed by the changing character of African mosques, which had once followed local styles and customs. Newer examples hewed closely to Middle Eastern and Arab design and precursors. Among Christians Western and particularly American styles of worship have largely supplanted older native forms.

Inevitably against such a background, social conflicts define themselves in terms of religious communities, and neither faith can claim any monopoly of victimhood. One side attacks the other, only to be met by counterattacks, as gangs and militias mobilize on each side. Respective places of worship become targets, with great loss of life. At that point religious savagery generates its own peculiar dynamic of blow and counterblow. In extreme cases religious confrontations can escalate to the level of outright warfare, as has occurred in countries like the Central African Republic. For some groups the quest for purity has involved revolutionary violence. The Islamist group Boko Haram, which has posed a deadly threat to the country's government as much as to neighboring Christians, takes its title from a slogan meaning "Western education is forbidden." That controversial "education" is a shorthand for an expansive package of ideas and beliefs, especially concerning attitudes to gender and family.[28]

In 2019 the Islamic State movement was largely uprooted from its bases in the Near East. In a well-publicized statement, the group's then-leader and "Caliph" Abu Bakr al-Baghdadi pledged to continue the fight, and he emphasized the new battlefronts emerging in Burkina Faso, Mali, and northern Nigeria. Observers felt that he was declaring these regions of West Africa as the movement's new heart—potentially, even a new Afghanistan. Consciously or otherwise, he was selecting the regions of Africa—and of the world—with the very highest fertility rates and the most marked youth bulges. Whether he understood the demographic context, he was exactly correct in identifying the most promising theaters for violence of the most extreme and fanatical kind.[29]

In passing we might note how such endemic conflicts shape and limit our knowledge of the underlying situation. Kenya is only one of many nations where exact census information is hard to come by because it might reveal the growth or reduction of particular ethnic or religious groups, and that in turn would further drive confrontation. In Nigeria any attempt at seeking accurate information about the relative strength of Christians and Muslims is a deeply dangerous and risky venture. Demographic data, in such countries, can be acutely destabilizing. At no point can demography be separated from religion.

Troubling Futures

Nor are the signs for future relations encouraging. Quite apart from religious confrontations on a global scale, Africa has specific issues that would both enhance conflict and ensure its religious nature. As much as any region on the planet, Africa stands to suffer badly from climate change. By a horrible combination of circumstances, the areas under greatest threat are precisely those that presently exhibit the most energetic demographic growth and the fastest upsurge of religious communities.[30]

This is most evident in the region of seven spectacular bodies of water known as the Great Lakes. Some of these drain into the Congo River to the west, and others into the Nile, which runs over four thousand miles to the Mediterranean. Those water systems are essential for the continued flourishing of some of the world's most populous, and most rapidly growing, nations. These countries in the Nile/Great Lakes territories have some of the world's highest fertility rates, which remain far above replacement, and commonly at or above 4.5. Between 1900 and 2050, the populations of most of these territories will have grown by a factor of twenty- or thirty-fold or more. This story has a powerful religious dimension. Taken together the Nile Valley and Great Lakes countries account for a large share of the numerical growth of both Christianity and Islam worldwide over the past century. All countries in the region have mixed populations of Christians, Muslims, and (sometimes) animists, and most have experienced tensions between majority and minority communities.

In coming decades poverty and resource conflicts will contribute mightily to religious and ethnic struggles, all of which are grounded in demography. The communities of the Nile and Great Lakes regions stand in a precarious balance with their environment, and population growth makes the situation much worse. Water resources are already profoundly stressed, even before we take account of the developing role of climate change and temperature rises in the Tropics. That same process is already taking its toll on the countries of the Western Sahel, in countries like Mali and Burkina Faso. Over decades whole new areas of the continent could become arid, uninhabitable wastelands. In multiple nations we would expect violent tugs-of-war over the remaining fertile lands and water supplies. Long historical precedent suggests that such apocalyptic transformations will spawn social conflicts, together with the scapegoating and persecutions of unpopular minorities. Religious civil wars would leave a pernicious legacy of failed states.[31]

Will Things Change?

As fertility rates have tumbled across Asia and Latin America, Africa stands out as ever more distinctive in its preservation of older patterns. The obvious question is whether, or rather when, Africa will join that larger trend. That question is critical to all future projections of global futures, not least in matters such as the use of natural resources and levels of carbon emissions. To put the matter in extreme terms, we might just imagine a Uganda with 100 million people in 2050, but must we assume that it will continue doubling every quarter century or so thereafter, to reach 400 million by 2100? Nobody seriously expects such an endless extrapolation, and the growth presumably has to stop sometime, or at least to slow. But how soon might that occur?

As we have seen in the case of Kenya, some countries have indeed experienced lower fertility, and similar changes are likely to befall those countries making economic strides—the present and potential Lion economies. Increasingly, the demand for labor should draw ever more women into full-time paid employment, particularly in emerging service sectors. These economic changes have broad social consequences, not least in terms of bolstering middle- and upper-middle-class groups, with all the aspirations we would expect. Adding to pressure for change are the African migrant communities in Europe or North America, who cannot fail to imbibe conventional Western attitudes to gender and family, which they bring home with them to their relatives. Ideally those various groups—more literate and globally minded—should increasingly press for better government and public services, to reduce levels of insecurity. Families that have some trust in the state and social order are less likely to see the need to have large numbers of children to support them and to contribute to income. We would expect to see more Western-style debates over issues of gender and sexuality—although framed strictly in terms of African traditions. Current UN projections do indeed envisage a fertility drop, to 3.0 by 2030 and 2.5 by 2050, and at that point we would see something like the benevolent effects of a demographic transition.

Religion itself should also play a key role in forcing change, with Christianity to the fore. Although African churches often adopt stances that appear reactionary by Euro-American standards, many have in practice made serious contributions to the advancement of women. Even if women cannot be ordained in particular denominations, churches have encouraged the education of girls, and African churches have a lively culture of Christian feminism. Churches have also served as effective vehicles for the distribution of medical information and facilities. Christian women are more likely than their predecessors to think seriously about family limitation—although again, the continent has a long way to go.

Much like the churches of an older Europe, very conservative ideologies have combined with practical deeds that have raised the aspirations of believers.[32]

South Africa

Despite its abundant and multifaceted problems, the nation of South Africa leads the way in such a demographic shift. Together with Nigeria the country has the largest economy in Africa, and it is sometimes included among the group of emerging economies known as the BRICS—Brazil, Russia, India, China, South Africa. Except for the last, all these countries have low or ultralow TFRs, and South Africa might plausibly be heading in that direction. Its TFR has fallen from over 6.4 in 1960 to around 2.3 in 2017, approaching replacement. This sets the country sharply apart from the rest of sub-Saharan Africa and begins to resemble the changes we have noted in Southeast Asia. Declining fertility in South Africa finds echoes in nearby nations to which it is tied culturally and economically, such as Lesotho and Swaziland. Relatively prosperous Botswana, for instance, had a 2017 TFR of 2.56, again far below the sub-Saharan norm.[33]

Predictably, those shifts in fertility also have their religious echoes. As in any African country, South Africa has thriving and very numerous Christian churches, and a Western observer is struck by the popularity of charismatic practices, especially spiritual healing. Witchcraft belief is strong and widespread, and sometimes leads to outbreaks of violent persecution. Having said that, in many ways South Africans live in a remarkably secular society—or at least, secular by African standards. The national constitution is a highly progressive document that commands strict secularism. Among other things it was the world's first country to enshrine gay equality in its constitution, while in 2006 it became the first African nation to legitimize same-sex marriage—and so far, the only one on the continent to do so. (Neighboring Botswana legalized gay sexual activity in 2019.) Since the start of the century, secular values have become steadily more popular. According to a Win-Gallup poll, between 2005 and 2012, the number of South Africans who considered themselves religious fell from 83 percent to 64 percent. Perhaps this change just represents people being freer to be candid about their lack of beliefs than in earlier years, but even so, that suggests a minor cultural revolution.

Nobody is suggesting that South Africa is on the verge of secularization. Socially and religiously South Africa is a radically polarized country. It has its flourishing urban elites, who do very well from the nation's technological orientation and its consumer boom. At the same time, the coming of democracy certainly did not solve the problem of those desperately poor people living in the slums and townships or scratching a living in the countryside, those who depend on the hopes of religion to find the courage to confront everyday life. That remains true even apart from any possible consequences of climate change. Such people are not going to abandon their faith overnight. As in the rest of Africa, megachurches, prosperity teachings, and miracle crusades still have a thriving future. Even so, even the glimmerings of a decline in religiosity are surprising enough in the African context and in one of the continent's most influential countries.

Conceivably South Africa might be blazing a trail in terms of demographic change and also in religious life. But if we are looking at continental trends, it will be a decade or two before they reach such presently very fertile (and exceedingly religious) lands as Uganda or the DRC. Even assuming that a trend of this kind can be predicted to flow in particular directions—which is debatable—then change will not come overnight. The high fertility rates in most of Africa still have a long way to fall, and those youth bulge populations are all in place, ready to start their families. Africa will long continue to occupy the role I have outlined, at once as a large and growing share of global population and moreover as the future heartland of both Christianity and Islam.

7

TWO-TIER ISLAM

I f fears of a global population explosion have dimmed, those nightmares remain very much alive in the context of the Islamic world. European observers dread the growth of high-fertility Islamic populations, which they fear would swamp old-stock residents. As to what such a society might look like, pessimists point to those chaotic lands and failed states that share the common features of a dominant Islamic faith and very high fertility rates. Outside Africa the world's highest rates—TFRs of 5.0 or 6.0—are chiefly found in Islamic nations, and specifically in such notorious centers of violence, turmoil, and fanaticism as Afghanistan, Iraq, Yemen, and the Palestinian territories (the West Bank and the Gaza Strip).[1] On the African continent, that high-fertility list would also include Egypt, Mali, the collapsed states of the Horn of Africa, and other regions of that Arc of Crisis. Although it is not a definitive criterion for extremism and mayhem, all play host to movements affiliated to al-Qaeda, or the Islamic State, or both. For many in the West, such appalling examples inevitably stir fears of what an Islamized future might look like.[2]

But such grim visions are multiply flawed. For one thing there is no necessary correlation between Islam and violence or social disorder. The cases of some mainly Christian nations in Africa show that Islamic societies as such have no monopoly on state failure or on the turbulence that results from extremely high fertility. More generally many Islamic nations deviate sharply from the pernicious stereotype derived from Yemen or Afghanistan. Radically contradicting the commonplace view, some Islamic societies are now experiencing the full effects of the demographic transition. I have already mentioned the almost shocking declines of fertility in Iran, but this is no bizarre exception. Fertility rates are moving swiftly toward European rates, most notably in Indonesia, in the Arab Maghreb of Northwest Africa, and in the Arabian Peninsula itself. Even Saudi Arabia is now below replacement. David P. Goldman's sweeping study of global demographic change is entitled *How Civilizations Die (and Why Islam Is Dying Too)*.[3] So stark are the distinctions between the two types of nation, and their social profile, that I have spoken of a two-tier Islam.

In these matters as so much else, to speak of a predominantly Muslim nation as "Islamic" actually tells us next to nothing about some significant characteristics of that society. If demographic change overthrows conventional assumptions about the concept of a Third World, it is no less destructive to any simplistic understandings of Islam. The implications for global security are far reaching.

An Islamic Difference?

The question then arises whether or when such a demographic decline might be followed by anything like secularization—however we define it—or at least a challenge to institutional religious forms. But attempts at analysis or prediction face serious difficulties. When broadly European demographic conditions spread to other societies, they are associated with many other features, such as economic conditions and attitudes to women, family, sexuality, and religiosity. While the demographic changes have indeed occurred in Islamic nations, we see only limited effects of this broader kind, and especially in matters of religiosity. By no rational standard can Saudi Arabia, say, be said to be moving in secular directions. Of course a crushing majority of Pakistanis (94 percent) say that religion is very important to them, but so do most residents of low-fertility Iran (78 percent). What does this mean for the pattern so commonly observed elsewhere, of the predictable linkage between fertility and faith?[4]

Actually, many reasons explain the different outcomes in the Islamic world, including the very recent character of the Islamic fertility decline, just over the past decade or two. Political factors also play their part, above all the distinctive role of government. In many societies people are free to express changed attitudes to religion or the secular, but in most Islamic nations that is simply not the case, because religion has traditionally been so absolutely bound up with fundamental notions of authority and government. Conversely, secular or nonreligious attitudes have often been linked with subversive views, socialist or Communist, and as such were stigmatized and heavily penalized. In highly authoritarian nations rooted in religious ideology, it is extremely difficult to change official stances or legal realities, even when popular attitudes and mores are transforming rapidly.

Adding to this resistance has been the wave of revolutionary movements and activism that has shaken so many Islamic nations since the 1990s, and that has forced governments to tread carefully in matters of social experiment. As we will see in countries like Algeria and Indonesia, even when social trends do seem to be moving away from religion and orthodoxy, threats of violence are highly effective in restoring older norms. Even if intimidation cannot compel personal belief, it can be quite effective in ensuring public conformity to expectations, for instance in enforcing the observance of fasts, suppressing alcohol, and requiring women to wear a headscarf.

No less important, the definition of faith in Islamic societies is very different from that of other religious traditions, which makes any kind of secular movement hard to imagine but also difficult to measure even when it does occur. This problem becomes apparent whenever we try to give population estimates for different faith communities. However carefully such data are gathered, Muslims and Christians differ substantially in how they define themselves and their religious identity. Very much as we saw in the case of East Asia, the notion of religion in Islamic societies is hard to separate from culture, as the two are linked in a comprehensive way that has not been true in the Christian West since Early Modern times. "Being religious" means different things in different societies—and so, of necessity, does becoming secular. If "belonging" to religion means something very different in the Christian world, then so does ceasing to belong.

That different concept of religion and faith profoundly affects how people identify themselves in surveys and how they are counted in global overviews of religious loyalties. Islamic countries rely on a default criterion, in that members of the society who do not belong to some other faith are automatically counted as Muslims, regardless of any active commitment or belief they might affirm. If not actively religious by nature, then they are at least assumed to be "cultural Muslims." In contrast, depending on the particular survey, Christians and other groups are counted by some degree of affiliation or membership, and no allowance is made for those more generic "cultural Christians." That is a particular problem in Europe, where the count of "Muslims" basically involves everyone who stems from a country with an official adherence to Islam, regardless of their individual attitudes or outlook. In turn, that question of definition affects anything we say about secularization or forsaking a particular faith. When we ask Europeans about their attitudes to religion, Christians might describe abandoning the faith, in a way that Muslims do not, because the latter still retain those cultural aspects. Although overt ex-Muslims certainly do exist, it takes real effort and courage to proclaim such a status, in evident contrast to ex-Christians.

In most of the Islamic world—not all—any kind of secularity is still a distant prospect. But the underlying demographic revolution is still very much in progress, and it is indeed having a multifaceted religious impact.

The Growth of Islam

In its modern history, the faith of Islam has benefited mightily from demographic change. In 1900 the number of Muslims was around 200 or 220 million, perhaps 12 or 13 percent of humanity, compared to a present-day figure of between 1.5 and 1.8 billion—a quarter of the whole. (As I noted, issues of definition make exact statistics difficult to assess, but the broad patterns of change are clear enough.) Roughly, the Muslim proportion of the world's people has doubled since the start of the twentieth century. Both in absolute and relative terms, that is phenomenal growth in a short historical period. Conversions have played a significant part in that story, but demography matters more. Muslims have been blessed by their location in the most fertile and fastest-growing centers of global population. While Christians have benefited from the expansion of numbers in Africa, at the same time they have been held back by the birth dearth in Europe and the traditional West. Whereas Christians in 1900 outnumbered Muslims by 2.8 to 1, the figure today is 1.5 to 1, and by 2050 it should be 1.3 to 1. Put another way there are four times as many Christians alive as there were in 1900; but over the same period, Muslims have grown seven- or eightfold.[5]

Through most of the twentieth century, most Islamic nations retained the very high fertility rates that we have already characterized as the premodern or Third World model. That image of Islamic fertility contributed to European nightmares about being swamped by immigrants from the Middle East and South Asia. As historian Niall Ferguson remarked, "The greatest of all the strengths of radical Islam . . . is that it has demography on its side. The Western culture against which it has declared holy war cannot possibly match the capacity of traditional Muslim societies when it comes to reproduction." Or as scholar Fouad Ajami wrote in 2004, in deadly contrast to Europe, "fertility rates in the Islamic world are altogether different: they are 3.2 in Algeria, 3.4 in Egypt and Morocco, 5.2 in Iraq and 6.1 in Saudi Arabia. This is Europe's neighborhood, and its contemporary fate. . . . Nemesis is near."[6]

But over the past generation, that pattern has transformed, as Islamic nations have diversified considerably. Some Islamic nations retain very high fertility rates, but cockpit nations like Yemen, Iraq, and Afghanistan are in no sense "normal," nor are they typical of the wider Islamic world. If we just take the example of Saudi Arabia, its fertility rate is no longer the 6.1 of Ajami's jeremiad, it is now below replacement, and (as we will see) other examples on his list look equally unrecognizable to modern eyes. Broadly we can speak of two categories of nation covered within the broad spectrum of Islam, with fertility as a key marker. Some are stubbornly conservative, with very high fertility rates and the associated attitudes to gender and family. In others, though, change has already come and is proceeding apace. Some nations are profoundly reactionary and even "medieval" in style, others are modernized and progressive.

The Old Order

Against the European model sketched earlier, with its low fertility, high stability, and high sense of individualism, we can set another pattern, another package of values associated with high fertility. This might be characterized by such themes and labels as more communal and communitarian, tradition oriented, less gender equal and sexually regimented, honor oriented, more aggressive and unstable, and above all, unquestioningly committed to religious values. Religion is critical as a primary expression and justification of larger values and of definitions of identity. Prominent among the more conservative Islamic nations demographically are Pakistan and Egypt, which play such a key political and cultural role in the Islamic world. Both remain societies of high (rather than extreme) fertility. In terms of their religiosity, their attitudes to gender roles, and their high fertility, they epitomize a traditional order of Islamic societies, from which others are beginning to break away.

The demographic role in Islamic growth is obvious from the Indian subcontinent, which in numerical terms has long been the powerhouse of that religion. In 1900 Muslims were a major component of the population of British India, in what would later be the nation-states of India, Pakistan, and Bangladesh. This area then contained at least 65 million Muslims, perhaps as many as 80 million. Today the same region has 530 million Muslims, almost a third of the whole global figure. After Indonesia those three countries in the subcontinent contain the world's largest Muslim populations, with Pakistan ranked in second place.[7] That growth was entirely the consequence of high fertility, rather than conversions. Through the late 1980s, Pakistan retained a TFR well above 6.0, and only in the past decade has it fallen below 4.0. Since 1960 the country's total population has soared from 46 million to 210 million, and Muslims account for 95 percent of that total.[8]

Although significantly less developed than neighboring India, Pakistan has a complex and developing economy that is projected to grow quickly in coming years. Presently, though, it remains a deeply conservative country socially, and especially in the large rural regions. Religious adherence goes far beyond mere formal practice. Islamist parties play a critical role in national affairs, and some have a controversial foothold in the military and the intelligence apparatus. The country has a notorious record of enforcing its loosely framed and draconian blasphemy law, which is commonly directed against Christians and other religious minorities. Far from being imposed from above by a political or clerical elite, such laws receive enthusiastic support from a broad mass of a zealous public. Pakistan also has large activist and militant Islamic organizations, including some violent sects and private militias, so that religious dissenters of all kinds face the threat of vigilante actions and terrorism. The victims include Muslims as well as groups that diverge from Sunni Muslim orthodoxy. It is actively dangerous to espouse any religious belief other than mainstream orthodoxy.

Against this background it is not surprising that women's social opportunities are strictly limited by both religious and communal sanctions. The enforcement of "modesty" codes and chastity can be ferocious, with family members expected to defend family honor by violence when considered necessary. Around the world honor killings abound in high-fertility family-centered societies, but historically they have tended to decline when fertility rates fall and women's role rises. The ideology of honor, in fact, remains one of the key divisions between societies worldwide and a gauge of development rarely appreciated by policy makers. Significantly from this point of view, Pakistan has the world's highest rate of honor killings per capita. The country thus fits the classic stereotype of an Islamic society, marked by high fertility and conspicuously high religiosity.[9]

Egypt

Allowing for a very different history, similar observations can be made about another key Muslim country, namely Egypt. With some 90 million Muslims, Egypt is by far the most important Arab country among the most populous Islamic nations. The country's population has grown substantially over the past century or so, from 10 million in 1900 to 30 million by 1966 and 100 million today. Although its fertility rate has fallen since the 1980s, following government programs to promote family planning, it is still well above replacement rate, with a TFR of 3.2. Even today the country has a very young population comparable to many black African nations, and 52 percent of Egyptians are aged 24 or less. (Pakistan's figure is closely comparable.) Nineteen percent of Egyptians fall into the 15 to 24 category, the classic youth bulge profile. The country's president Abdel Fattah al-Sisi has described uncontrollable population growth as the greatest peril confronting Egypt, apart from terrorism. His government has sponsored campaigns urging families to believe that "Two is Enough." If such efforts fail, the country could easily reach a midcentury population of 150 million, which is quite unsustainable in terms of food resources, and especially access to water.[10]

As in Pakistan religious loyalties remain very strong in Egypt, with the one salient difference that Egypt has a large and visible religious minority in the form of Coptic Christians, who constitute 8 or 10 percent of the population. But nationally Islam is critical at all stages of life, as mosques and religious organizations perform many of the social and educational functions that the state is unable or unwilling to fulfill. Islamic religious structures retain a high degree of public respect, especially the Al-Azhar University. Islamic beliefs and practices receive strong encouragement from popular media, from radio and television, and through the work of what in a Christian context might be called televangelists. Some of the most popular Internet sites are explicitly religious, for instance, teaching lessons from the Quran. Competitions in which children recite Quran passages have a popular following similar to that of major sporting events in other countries. Islam, in this sense, is very much alive and well in Egypt and in its most traditional guise. Over and above this, radical Islamist organizations and political parties have been highly active, although most are severely constrained by the present military-dominated government. From 2011 through 2013, the fundamentalist Muslim Brotherhood ruled the country, until being overthrown in a coup. Terrorist movements remain powerful and lethally active. Again as in Pakistan, Islamist zeal is often expressed though attacks on religious Others, which in Egypt's case means Coptic Christians.[11]

Many Egyptian women work outside the home, but as in Pakistan, their roles are highly constrained by concepts of family and honor. One gauge of this is the popularity of female circumcision ("female genital mutilation"), which is inflicted to preserve girls' chastity and to ensure their total commitment to marriage and childbearing. The practice is not demanded by Islamic scriptures or early traditions, but it is commonly cited as a religious requirement or duty. In that sense the practice is analogous to honor killings, as a social practice designed to defend family honor but which becomes inextricably bound to religious obligations. Female circumcision is widely practiced across North and Northeast Africa, most frequently in such very high fertility countries as Somalia, Sudan, and Mali, and in Egypt itself. Despite official campaigns to regulate female circumcision in Egypt, some 80 percent of women have undergone the procedure. That number has been declining for some years, especially among the educated, but the practice remains very widespread.[12]

A Surprising New World

For most Western observers, Egypt and Pakistan represent what they assume to be Islamic normality, especially in terms of pervasive piety and gender repression. But other Islamic societies are very different indeed. Some of the world's very lowest fertility rates are actually found among Muslim populations in the Balkans, in predominantly Muslim nations like Albania and Bosnia. Despite their Islamic underpinnings, such nations practice an open-minded form of faith, which is accommodating to other religions, and religious restrictions on women's roles are widely ignored. Such countries also report a high proportion of atheists or of Nones, followers of no religion.[13]

The tiny populations of such Balkan countries means that they play little role in the larger Islamic world, but very different is the case of Iran, a populous state and a strong regional power, which is at the heart of Shia Islam. As with Pakistan the country is overwhelmingly Muslim in faith. For most Western observers, Iran represents a stereotype of Islam at its most regressive and repressive. The Islamic revolution of 1979 was the first of its kind in the modern world, and it created a theocratic regime pledged to enforce a rigid concept of Islamic order throughout society. Women were required to pursue traditional roles, and to follow the strictest standards in modesty, dress, and public behavior. Any deviations were punished by the violence of local militias and popular policing units. Radical Islamist policies were supported by mass demonstrations that could draw supporters in the hundreds of thousands. Formally the regime in power today is a direct continuation of that zealot new order created forty years ago.[14]

Against that background Iran's recent demographic history must take us aback. Through the twentieth century, the country had classic Third World fertility, with fertility rates approaching 7.0 in the 1960s, falling to 6.0 in the mid-1980s. The country's population grew from 10 million in 1900 to 65 million in 2000 and 82 million today. But that last number should surprise. If Iran had maintained its earlier fertility history, then we should extrapolate a current population of over 100 million. Where did those missing 20 million young Iranians go? From the mid-1980s, fertility rates began to plunge with a suddenness scarcely paralleled even in Europe. Iran's TFR reached 2.2 in 2000, and 1.66 by 2016. To put that in perspective, Denmark's rate in that year was slightly higher, at 1.71. In a few short years—basically, in the 1990s—Iran moved from a Third World population profile into European or First World conditions. Iran's population growth rate fell from 4 percent annually in the early 1980s to just 1 percent by 2015.[15]

Iran's demographic revolution has its roots in the era of the earlier monarch, the Shah, who was overthrown in 1979. Whatever its failings his regime struggled to modernize Iran, which meant enhancing the role of women and reducing population growth. His policies promoted women's education with a view to bringing more women into the workforce, so that they would have less interest in raising large families. Initially his policies had little effect, and they were soon reversed. After the Islamic Revolution, the government restricted access to abortion and divorce and closed the day-care facilities that allowed women to work outside the home. These natalist policies had some success during the Iran-Iraq War of the 1980s, when childbearing was a patriotic duty, but Iranian women soon resumed their progress toward social participation.

Partly this liberalization resulted from reform efforts within the ruling elite, and the government resumed family planning efforts in 1993. Beyond offering contraceptive services, official agencies offered information and classes about birth control for couples planning to marry. But social change acquired its own momentum, running far beyond what the reformers had sought, as young people showed growing disenchantment with official ideology. Women flocked into higher education and into the workplace. By 2000 women made up 60 percent of university entrants, and women soon accounted for two-thirds of university graduates. Such advances have alarmed conservatives, and battles to restrict women's access to higher education have raged over the past decade. Women also sought jobs, and the rate of female participation in the labor force grew steadily into the new century. Women in Iran today are far more likely to be in gainful employment than those of most nations of the Middle East or North Africa.[16]

At many points the country's social statistics suggest attitudes to family and marriage on broadly European lines. The country's rates for marriage remain historically low and declining, and the explanations include very high urban rents and prices generally, and extravagantly expensive weddings. But the consequences sound quite familiar from other parts of the world. The country has a large number of unmarried adults. Singles often live at home with parents, or else couples live together unofficially in "white marriages," which are highly disapproved of by officialdom. These are distinct from temporary marriages permitted under Islamic law, but which younger people scorn. Although worthwhile figures are hard to come by, white marriages are reported to be common, and all those trends conspire to postpone childbearing.[17]

So marked are these various changes, and so troubling for the unreconstructed Islamist rulers, that in 2010 the country's then-president Ahmadinejad warned that "this is what is wrong with the West. Negative population growth will cause extinction of our identity and culture. The fact that we have accepted this places us on the wrong path. To want to consume more rather than having children is an act of genocide." In 2013 Supreme Leader Ayatollah Ali Khamenei called for a new wave of natalist policies, with the goal of driving the population up to 150 or 200 million by the end of the century. By common consensus such a venture had little chance of success.[18]

These changes have far-reaching implications for a country's stability and security. In the late 1970s, Iran demonstrated the kind of turbulence so characteristic of a youth bulge, when vast numbers of young people could easily be mobilized to rise against the Shah's regime. That same youth bulge allowed the regime not just to pursue its war with neighboring Iraq through the following decade but to do so with tactics that were outrageously wasteful of human lives, notably, human wave assaults on enemy lines. But those lives were there to be squandered. Ayatollah Khomeini dreamed of defending his revolution with a "twenty million man army."[19]

The situation today is utterly different, as that youth bulge has vanished. The proportion of Iranians aged 15 to 24 is just 14 percent, high by European standards (the Italian figure is below 10 percent) but among the lowest in the Islamic world. The country's median age is today over 30. If that situation does not of itself bring stability or peace, it certainly contributes. The young people are just not there to be galvanized into mobs and militias. Most positively Iran is among the Islamic nations most strongly experiencing the benefits of a demographic dividend, with significant growth in disposable income.[20]

That demographic change may contribute to explaining the remarkable longevity of the Islamic Republic, now in its fifth decade. It has persisted despite repeated economic and military disasters and widespread evidence of disaffection and popular rejection. But in order for it to evaporate like the Shah's regime before it, we would have to imagine a popular upsurge of the disaffected, who of their nature tend to be weighted to the young. But that population cohort no longer exists, so that the odds of mass popular protests are far smaller than they might have been otherwise. In Iran at least, youth bulges are not what they once were. Moreover, demographic contraction has made families more prosperous and less willing to risk all on political adventures. The regime thus benefits from a demographic paradox. Demographic changes have potentially introduced many social changes that foster disaffection. Yet those very same changes make it less likely that the regime would succumb to any popular turbulence, since the new demographic order is of its nature far more stable than that of earlier eras. This does not mean that protests are wholly absent, and a severe crisis in 2009 proved deeply dangerous for the regime, but the scale and seriousness were quite different from 1979.[21]

Toward the Secular?

The fact that fertility rates usually correlate with religiosity raises intriguing questions in the Iranian context. We are so accustomed to thinking of Iran as a byword for Islamic zeal, indeed for the application of modern revolutionary warfare tactics to the advancement of Islamic rule. While governments may adopt more or less hard-line policies, there is no question that the nation's governing elite and institutions remain committed to those goals. How can we contemplate any secular drift within that context?

Yet a decline in religiosity does indeed appear to be occurring—and gathering force. The repressive nature of the regime makes it difficult to gather reliable survey data, but the accumulated anecdotal evidence is indicative. Numerous journalistic reports have commented on the extremely low attendance at Iranian mosques, including at what should notionally be major set-piece events, like the weekly prayers at Tehran University. Repeatedly, religious authorities have been embarrassed by the very small numbers appearing at such events.[22] A consensus estimate suggests that regular Friday attendance runs around 1 or 2 percent of the population. One 2018 report noted that

> mosques all over Iran are empty at prayer times. In 2015 a Revolutionary Guard commander, Ziaeddin Hozni, revealed that only about 3,000 of the country's 57,000 Shiite mosques were fully operational. And of the 3,000, some were only functioning during the religious months of Ramadan and Muharram. The Shiites have usually been less diligent than Sunnis in mosque attendance, but lack of attendance is striking in an explicitly Shiite state run by mullahs.[23]

The article in question bore the suggestive title "The Secular Republic of Iran."

The religious establishment has suffered from its close association with the government and its attendant corruption and ineptitude. The more the government sought to use Friday prayers to spread political messages, the more resentment and resistance they encountered from ordinary believers. Within a Shia system, which relies heavily on clergy, disaffection focuses on both the clerical profession and individual mullahs. To use a familiar European term, anticlericalism is widespread. As in Europe, rejection of religious institutions does not necessarily mean hostility to religion as such, and pilgrimage remains popular. But it is unsettling to find such a secular drift in any Islamic country, leave alone one with the history of Iran. Again, although this is anecdotal, Iranian-born journalist Sohrab Ahmari remarks that "living in an Islamic theocracy—where God appears in the form of flog-gings and judicial amputations, scowling ayatollahs and secret police—has a way of souring one on things divine. Years later, I read a wise young Iranian dissident who argued that if the Islamic Republic collapsed one day it would leave behind the world's largest community of atheists." As he rightly says, "that is a perfectly plausible theory," but it remains to be tested.[24]

One curious aspect of this anticlerical phenomenon has been a pop-ular sympathy for Americans and their nation, who stand for everything the regime is against. If a country is hostile to Islamic theocracy, many Iranians feel, then clearly it must be a friend of the Iranian people. Amer-ican travelers cite the agreeably cordial reception they find in the country. During the 2016 U.S. presidential election, American visitors were startled to find Iranians so enthused about Democratic candidate Bernie Sanders. On further examination this was not based on particular awareness of Sanders' policies. Iranians just assumed that a leftist or socialist could be relied on to be opposed to religion and clericalism and would thus push a secular agenda.

Also recalling European conditions has been a sizable movement away from institutional forms of religion to more individualistic and loosely orga-nized forms of spirituality. Sufi mystical orders exercise a vast appeal for those seeking a passionate personal spirituality far removed from the repressive structures of the Islamic Republic, especially among young adults. Already a decade ago, scholars estimated that Sufi numbers in the country had grown from 100,000 before the revolution to perhaps 5 million—although any precise estimates must be treated cautiously. In turn the regime has made the Sufi orders a special target for persecution.[25]

If Iran were a European or East Asian nation, demographic trends would lead us to predict some likely developments in the near future. Those would include a substantial growth of privatized forms of faith and the emergence of publicly avowed Nones and of groups actively rejecting the need for religion. We would also expect significant shifts in public morality and the tolerance of alternate forms of sexuality, even including same-sex marriage. Obviously that latter prospect remains distant as long as the Isla-mist regime survives in anything like its current form, and it presently shows no signs whatever of crumbling. Any forms of gay or lesbian expression are severely penalized, to the point of inflicting the death penalty. (Weirdly, the country is much more generous on transgender issues.) Nor are there any signs of the regime liberalizing on these or other matters.[26]

Dictatorships can crumble rapidly, and the Shah's regime seemed impregnable only a couple of years before its collapse. Any government that could survive the near-catastrophe of the protests in 2009 is far more resilient than we might suspect. The Islamic Republic thus remains in place, and chances of a popular revolution are few.[27] What we can say with confidence is that Iran's demographic reshaping is associated with larger cultural revolutions, which cannot fail to have their impact in the long term. To push speculation to its reasonable limits, might Iran potentially become the Trojan Horse of liberal values in the larger Middle East?

The Maghrib

If they are not yet near the Iranian stage, other crucial Islamic countries are undergoing a demographic transition, with all the cultural and political consequences that implies. Particularly affected is the Maghrib region of Northwest Africa, in nations like Algeria, Morocco, and Tunisia. Changes here are all the more impressive because this region not long since had signally high TFRs, and the Algerian figure in the mid-1960s stood above 7.5—burdensome even for the African continent. The nation's population exploded, from 10 million in 1956 to 30 million at the end of the century. But the fertility rate was plummeting, falling from roughly 6.0 to 3.0 just in the years between 1985 and 1997, and it reached 2.5 in 2005. That fall coincides closely with the Iranian transition, both in degree and chronology. The Algerian figure then stabilized, and it remains above replacement, but even so, that is a staggering change in a very short period.[28]

Other countries in the region followed similar trajectories. Morocco's rate is around 2.4, Tunisia's is 2.1. It is not just in Europe that we observe the principle that a closer a woman lives to Rome, the fewer children she has: the same appears to be true on the other side of the Mediterranean. Even Libya, where the state has all but collapsed, is around 2.2, although accurate information is difficult to come by. Median ages have risen accordingly, to 28 or 29 across the region, as youth bulges have shrunk or vanished. These figures stand out all the more sharply when set against Egyptian conditions. With the glaring exception of Libya, the region has started to enjoy its demographic dividend.

As in Iran, changes in women's conditions reliably drive broader transformations. After achieving independence in 1962, Algeria espoused a radical socialist ideology and encouraged the social advancement of women.

Acknowledging the conservative religious sentiments of many Algerians, the government exercised tact in framing its social policies, so that in the 1980s it introduced widespread programs of "birth spacing" rather than the more incendiary and Western "birth control."[29] The country thus followed the pro-development policies adopted by nations worldwide in that era, while paying due attention to local concerns and potential resistance—pursuing "the art of the possible." But the schemes had their effects, and contraceptive usage almost doubled between 1987 and 2000, to reach 55 percent of married women aged 15 to 49. Women's age at first marriage also grew steeply, from 17 or 18 to the late twenties. In Morocco the proportion of never-married women in their late thirties reached European levels and was actually higher than in the United States. Against this background women were able to take advantage of the professional and economic opportunities offered to them. By 2003 Algerian women accounted for over 60 percent of graduates in tertiary education, and they now represent sizable majorities of the nation's lawyers and its judges. Women are well represented in the workforce generally, if nowhere near European levels.[30]

Other factors peculiar to this region encourage new attitudes to gender and family. For one thing, Maghrib nations have long been deeply involved in sending migrants to Western Europe, and many of those retain ties with their families in the home nations. Inevitably then visiting relatives import new European attitudes and aspirations, especially from highly liberal societies like France or the Netherlands. Moreover, many residents of the Maghrib nations enthusiastically follow Western media, commonly by satellite dish. They usually do this in pursuit of sport and light entertainment, but it is hard to watch Western productions without imbibing some of the associated values, attitudes, and social interactions. Religious conservatives in the region regularly preach against these imported evils, which in their view pollute traditional values and mores.

Such profound social changes should logically have had a significant impact on religious beliefs and practices, but the outcome was complicated by the rise of revolutionary politics and Islamic militancy across much of the Islamic world. Although its origins were complex, that upsurge was in part driven by resentment of Westernization and of the overturning of familiar gender assumptions. In the 1990s Algeria suffered a bloody Islamist insurgency that detonated a civil war, which killed at least a hundred thousand. That movement in turn spilled over into neighboring regions, sparking terrorist attacks in Europe and boosting new insurgencies in West Africa. Within Algeria itself the continuing power of Islamist militancy encouraged public conformity to religious values, as many women adopted Islamic dress to avert violence. The movement also had its impact on recent reforms, as contraceptive use even declined slightly and the previously plunging fertility rate stabilized. That reaction did not end progress in gender matters, but it did proclaim limits to future change.[31]

In other nations, though, liberalization was more advanced. In politically conservative Morocco, the state deliberately promotes more open and tolerant forms of Islam, to the point of encouraging women's participation as leaders of religious communities. Official institutions train women as scholars, and women become spiritual guides, *morchidat,* who are clergy in all but name. That well-publicized program has the specific goal of defusing potential Islamic extremism, but it also acknowledges the expanded role for women thought suitable in a developing society. It brings into the religious realm the kind of visible activism that women have acquired in secular society. If it is not a secular development, it does represent an accommodation to new social and demographic conditions.[32]

The country in this region with the sharpest fall in fertility rates is Tunisia, which among the Arab nations has moved closest to European conditions. Among other gauges of change, its proportion of people aged 15 to 24 is below 14 percent, that is, even lower than the Iranian figure, and the country's median age is 32. Based on these criteria, in 2008 U.S. demographer Richard Cincotta predicted that the country would democratize within a decade or so. At the time this projection was greeted with extreme skepticism, because Tunisia seemed so firmly in the grip of a classic authoritarian regime under a dictatorial president. But Cincotta's view was grounded on the belief that an aging and demographically stable society is far better educated and better informed, with higher aspirations, and less willing to tolerate unreasonable political constraints.[33] His opinions were decisively vindicated in 2011 when Tunisia became the epicenter of the Arab Spring movement, with its calls for progressivism and democratic rights. That movement subsequently spread across much of the Middle East, overthrowing seemingly invulnerable dictatorships. In most cases countries failed to replace those old orders with sustainable new democratic regimes, and the consequences for Syria and Libya were catastrophic.[34]

But Tunisia's social and demographic foundations ensured far greater success there. The country elected to government the moderate Islamist party en-Nahda, which remains strictly democratic, and the country enjoys broad civil and political rights. The government has even proposed moves toward gender equality in inheritance and other matters, which are strikingly unusual for Islamic North Africa. Journalist Ursula Lindsey remarks that the country is "renowned for being at the vanguard of women's rights in the Arab world." Oddly, it even enjoys a bellwether role in LGBT rights. Although homosexual acts are illegal, gay populations are sufficiently visible to support pressure groups and public events, including a thoroughly aboveground Queer Film Festival.[35] If demographic change does not herald outright secularization, it marks a shift away from tight religious restrictions that contradict shifting public opinion.

However significant these transformations are for the Maghrib region itself, they are doubly significant for Europe, as the Maghrib has long been the source of most Muslim immigration in Western Europe. If the present fertility decline continues, Europe will have to look much farther afield to find the migrants it needs in order to survive—perhaps into black Christian Africa. Visions of "swamping" by Islam depend on assumed birth rates that are now a distant memory.

Indonesia

The experience of the Maghrib parallels that of Indonesia, which remains by some margin the most populous Islamic nation. In the past half century, the nation's overall population has risen from 120 million to 270 million today. If we assume that the Muslim share of the population is around 80 to 85 percent, then that would mean that Indonesia today has some 220 Muslims, up from 60 million in the mid-twentieth century. One out of every eight Muslims worldwide is Indonesian. Put another way, the number of Muslims just in Indonesia today is not far short of what the *global* total was back in 1900. Yet Indonesia's fertility rate has declined substantially from its high late twentieth-century rates of between 5.0 and 6.0, to reach replacement by 2018. This places the country clearly in the low-tier group of Islamic fertility rates. The country's median age approaches 31, above that of Iran.

The fertility decline in Indonesia echoes conditions in neighboring countries of Southeast Asia, the Tigers and Dragons, and it has become significantly more prosperous. Its nominal GDP per capita is around $4,000, which places it in the middle rank of nations, not far removed from the Maghrib nations. Typically for Pacific Rim nations, that recent development has especially drawn women into the workforce, and that has had the predictable effect on family size. Contraceptive use runs at over 60 percent. By the standards of the Islamic world, women are visible in public life and the professions, and the country has had a woman president.[36]

For many reasons these changes should be reflected in attitudes to morality and sexuality, and to the religious institutions that seek to regulate them, and we might imagine some drift to the secular. In fact the country grants limited rights to LGBT citizens, so that private consensual acts are not formally illegal in most of the country, with the exception of a couple of hard-line Islamist-dominated provinces. Again by the standards of the larger

Islamic world, this represents a relatively liberal stance, but it is striking that it has not gone further. Again in the specific case of LGBT rights, formal tolerance can easily break down in face of sudden outbreaks of persecution from reactionary Islamists.[37]

Islam in Indonesia is a complicated phenomenon that is difficult to pigeonhole into categories of moderation or extremism. In most ways the country's religious affairs are easygoing and tolerant, and a strictly main-stream and moderate tradition is institutionalized through some very large popular organizations that mobilize tens of millions of members. It is also open to debate how many of the country's Muslims share any great passion for the faith. The number of notional Muslims skyrocketed in the 1960s for a particular and practical reason. For years the country had a great many secularists who espoused no religion—what we might today call Nones. This situation changed following a wave of anti-Communist massacres that claimed half a million lives, and it became perilous to own an identity card that did not show an explicit religious label. The number of self-described Muslims grew sharply within a couple of years, regardless of any change in actual levels of belief.[38]

Yet at the same time, the intensity of Islamic enthusiasm has undoubt-edly grown in recent years, as part of the general global upsurge. Indonesia in particular also has a serious and troubling current of militant and vio-lent organizations, which serve as a persistent threat. Moderates have to be constantly aware of that potential danger, and even mainstream institutions will with little warning lurch from their customary tolerance to quite repres-sive and fundamentalist positions. An example occurred in 2014, when a prominent Christian gained the powerful position of mayor of Jakarta with the support of Islamic organizations. Shortly afterward, he was tried and imprisoned for alleged blasphemy against the faith of Islam, following pressure from hard-line militants. That potential for repression makes any attempt at religious liberalization perilous and establishes a strict bound-ary to potential change. Indonesia is very different from Pakistan, but any potential dissident has to be constantly aware of sudden shifts in political mood and the threat of actual violence.

The Arabian Peninsula

If the most significant Shia Muslim nation—Iran—is entering a very dif-ferent demographic age, so is its principal Sunni rival, Saudi Arabia. That country is of course the legendary bastion of uncompromising Islamic faith and piety and of traditional attitudes to family and motherhood.

Yet things are changing. Twenty years ago I was working on my book *The Next Christendom*, in which I tried to project the populations of various nations in order to sketch the likely religious maps of the mid-twenty-first century. At that point Saudi Arabia had a famously rapid rate of population growth, rising from 3 million in 1945 to 6 million in 1969 and 20 million in 1997, and that spectacular growth seemed likely to continue indefinitely. I followed the best estimates of the time in projecting that the country was destined to reach 40 million people by 2020 and 60 or 70 million by 2050. But matters have changed quite dramatically since then. Saudi Arabia presently has 33 million people, and by 2050 that number may rise just to 46 million. The disparity in estimates results from a fundamental shift in fertility. Until the early 1980s, the country's fertility rate was above 7.0, but that fell to 3.0 by 2010, and by 2018, it was just over 2.0. If we grade the Islamic nations by fertility trends, then Saudi Arabia is clearly part of the low-fertility regions, alongside such peninsular neighbors as the United Arab Emirates (UAE), Kuwait, and Qatar—all now well below replacement. The median ages of all these countries are already in the upper twenties and should rise to 30 within a very few years.[39]

That fertility decline has caused real concern in the peninsular nations. The UAE has made a major commitment to natalist policies, using government grants and subsidies to encourage additional children and offering assistance to help new couples establish homes. The government also promotes nurseries in places of employment, to ease the lives of working mothers. However useful in many ways, abundant past precedent suggests that such policies are unlikely to reverse the demographic slide. Once begun, the pressures toward fertility decline are hard to resist.[40]

More than in most cases, that Saudi change demands explanation, implying as it does such a radical alteration in women's attitudes and behavior. Like Iran, Saudi Arabia is celebrated (or notorious) for its rigid interpretation of Islam and its associated moral codes. Other religions are not officially permitted in the country, and gender restrictions are ferociously enforced. Until recently Islamic values were asserted in a heavy-handed way by an officially sanctioned vigilante force, the religious police or Committee for the Promotion of Virtue and the Prevention of Vice. These are the Mutaween—"those who make others obey." Although recent reformist authorities have curbed the group's powers, very strong social mores prevent any deviation from orthodoxy in dress or behavior. Until 2018, the country did not even allow women to drive, and women are always under the legal authority of a spouse or male relative. School and college classrooms practice strict gender segregation. Gays and other sexual nonconformists face brutal legal penalties. If we imagine the world's nations graphed according to their degree of social and moral repression, Saudi Arabia would stand at an extreme end of the bell curve.[41]

Yet against that background, the demographic evidence suggests a near revolution within families and households, and a really fundamental rethinking of concepts of family and the place of children. How can we resolve this paradox? As in Iran we must draw a clear line between the workings of the state and the regime—whether in its secular or spiritual aspects—and the attitudes of ordinary people. We can speculate as to the exact reasons why families are behaving differently, but access to reliable contraception plays a critical role, as does education. Whatever the discrimination faced by Saudi women, many have taken wholeheartedly to education and to higher education. For the past several years, women have constituted a solid majority of university students and of new graduates. Beyond those reasons we also note exposure to Western media as well as direct contact with the Western world through travel. As in many other societies, fertility rates have fallen because of a sharply rising age of marriage among Saudi women, as they have found other avenues in life that they wish to explore.

As elsewhere, political pressures and outright repression prevent any overt challenges to existing Saudi standards and mores. In recent years this has been painfully apparent in the stern official sanctions visited upon women whose only offense is to seek to drive. Such a response obviously grows out of entrenched conservatism, but that has to be understood against the broader political context of the kingdom and state, where authority is grounded in religious authorities and ideologies. Any relaxation in those foundations would endanger the existence of the state.

To present a wildly improbable hypothetical, let us assume that countries like Iran, Algeria, or Saudi Arabia were as open to free expression and political debate as Germany or the United States. Based on the tendencies we have observed in other countries, we would expect a quite swift transition in views toward sexual morality and a growing hostility to religious institutions that are seen as repressive. At some point we would expect the first same-sex weddings to be scheduled in Tehran, and even in Riyadh. Obviously, such a scenario is not going to happen any time in the near future. But the implacable conservatism of public policy in those nations should not lead us to assume that those laws will always reflect a solid moral consensus. The main trend in the coming decade is likely to be an ever-larger chasm between private sentiment and public moral codes, and a progressive discrediting of religious establishments, as is beginning in Iran.

Migration

However else changing fertility rates might affect society, we can already
see one marked trend in the Arabian peninsula, and that is the emergence
of real and unprecedented religious diversity. The general pattern is familiar enough from Europe, where a shortage of labor demanded immigration, which had the unintended additional consequence of importing the
religious beliefs of the newcomers. Quite unintentionally Europe acquired
a sizable and growing Islamic minority. Changing only a few details, that is
exactly what happened to the Arab nations of the Gulf. Oil wealth brought
immense prosperity across the region, which rapidly evolved from quite
backward tribal societies to extremely rich urban communities. Much like
contemporary Europe, nations here urgently needed immigrants to do the
jobs that locals would not or could not do, and falling fertility rates made
that demand even more acute. Lacking any plausible alternatives, governments freely accepted and encouraged mass immigration, although without
thinking through the long-term consequences. Foreign workers make up at
least 30 percent of the population of Saudi Arabia and a far higher proportion in the states of the Arab Gulf.[42]

In just a few decades, the peninsular states have become strikingly
diverse in terms of ethnicity but also of religion. Just as Europeans were sur-
prised to find so many Muslims among them, so the peninsular states now
became home to many Christians. Christians are well represented among
newcomers from India, Sri Lanka, and the Philippines, while many Arab
migrants are also Christian. So are many European and U.S. expatriates.
Any remarks about the religious situation in Saudi Arabia are complicated
by the country's official refusal to allow any non-Muslim worship, so by
definition there can be no active Christian presence to study. In practice,
estimates of the country's Christian population range from 5 to 10 percent,
a significant number in the traditional heart of the Islamic world. Christians make up 17 percent of the total population of Kuwait, 14 percent of
Bahrain, 9 percent of both the UAE and Qatar. Taking the whole Arab Gulf
region, the Christian population is between 5 and 10 percent, a number that
is actually higher than the Muslim proportion of the European Union.

Although Christians are strictly prohibited from evangelizing among
Muslims, Gulf states have treated their religious minorities quite generously,
allowing the erection of many impressive churches and even cathedrals.
Some flourishing megachurches serve thousands of worshipers. Local Muslims find these conspicuous expressions of a once unfamiliar faith quite as
startling as do Europeans witnessing sizable new mosques being erected in
their once homogeneous neighborhoods.

Ever-contracting populations of native residents make it all but impossible that the peninsular countries will become any less dependent on foreign labor, so that Christian numbers are likely to increase in coming decades. Demographic change contributes to making these Islamic nations look ever more European in their diversity, as well as social patterns. The question then arises of how long the monarchical regimes can maintain political structures designed for far simpler conditions.

Acknowledging Revolution

Western observers commonly draw a sharp distinction between a fertile, tradition-bound, and pious Islamic world and a decadent West in the process of losing its Judeo-Christian heritage. Such an image is outdated, and far too broad in its generalizations. Much more likely, Islamic nations themselves will in coming years face systematic crises and controversies over issues of morality, gender, sexuality, and ultimately the definition of religious authority. Commentators have long debated future relations between Islam and the West, however controversial and loaded each of those labels might be. In coming decades some of the most important conflicts and cultural clashes might be those within the larger world of Islam, with fertility as a critical marker—divisions between nations and within particular societies themselves.

If indeed multiple Islamic nations do in fact stand on the verge of a rapid decline in religious practice and religious structures, that is potentially one of the most significant unheralded stories in contemporary global politics. It cries out to be acknowledged and internalized by policy makers.

8

GO FORTH AND DIVIDE

Fertile societies tend to be more religious; religious societies are more fertile. I have been addressing these contrasts at a global level, comparing (for instance) Western Europe with West Africa. But very diverse communities can coexist within the frontiers of a single nation-state. The resulting demographic and religious polarization underlies political situations and conflicts in some critically significant countries. In some instances the fact that a society seems to be drifting away from older forms of religiosity can mean that a state pays more attention to the politics of God, not less.

Many countries are divided between prosperous and progressive communities and poorer, less educated societies, and commonly that divide follows urban/rural lines. Both demography and religion mark critical dividers, which both symbolize and accentuate larger conflicts of class, race, wealth, and ethnicity. Such a situation offers rich rewards for a movement or party to exploit these intermingled causes of faith and fertility, but the actual outcomes vary according to the political situation. In parts of Europe, political movements summon old-stock white populations to unite against the intrusion of immigrant Muslims and to reassert the presumed values of an older and more homogeneous society. This is the model followed by rightist regimes in a country like Hungary.[1]

But another response is also possible, namely for a party or regime to ally with the numerous and growing high-fertility population against the declining elites—to espouse values of the rising faithful against the shrinking secularists. If a country practices electoral democracy, that means that a party or movement appealing to those traditional religious values will find a rock-solid political base, a secure bastion against secular liberalism, feminism, and cosmopolitanism. The more the educated and progressive population complains about such policies, the easier it is to stigmatize them as enemies of faith, or of the nation, and that in turn reinforces the loyalty of the poor and excluded, the fertile and faithful. Governments can also pledge to work for higher fertility and more babies, in an attempt to restore national strength and integrity, but such policies also proclaim the superiority of the values of the poor and faithful.

Such demographic differences, in fact, provide an excellent foundation for populist or authoritarian politics. The word "populist" refers, obviously, to "the people," but the question then arises of which people are being favored and lauded. Imagine a society with two very different communities: one will double its numbers in a generation or so, the other might shrink at a comparable rate. When a government has to choose between two such distinct "peoples"—two demographic regions—it is highly tempting to turn to the one with all the voters and potentially all the young party militants. Politicians, like businesspeople, understand the principle of investing in growth.[2]

I will discuss this political/demographic phenomenon with reference to four very different countries that in their various ways are extraordinarily important for Western policy makers, namely Turkey, India, Israel, and Russia. In each case radical and uneven demographic change has over the past decade produced conditions favorable to populist politics. To varying degrees these politics are grounded in an overwhelming religious justification and summon the nation to return to a supposed original purity and authenticity. During the 2010s four visible and controversial "strongman" leaders symbolized these political trends. In their diverse ways, Turkey's Recep Tayyip Erdoğan, India's Narendra Modi, and Israel's Benjamin Netanyahu all pursued a rational response to demographic realities—and so, in his way, did Vladimir Putin. They follow what Lyndon Johnson famously proclaimed as the first law of politics: they know how to count. That law will continue to apply long after the specific individuals have passed from the political scene. (Throughout this chapter I will be drawing on the important work of international relations scholar Monica Duffy Toft.)[3]

Differential fertility rates within particular nations help explain some of the thorniest and most troubling situations in the modern world. Through bitter experience Western governments have now learned to take religion seriously as a factor in political decision-making. Increasingly they have to come to terms with the demographic laws that underlie and shape those religious currents.[4]

The Lebanese Warning

To illustrate the processes that are at work in many nations today, we can turn to an example from recent history. In twentieth-century Lebanon, a sizable demographic differential between faiths, and between economic groups, all but destroyed the nation. While this is an extreme example of "demographic disintegration," it does highlight some significant and enduring themes.[5]

In the 1940s Lebanon was divided among several diverse religious groups. In order to create a working political model, the country divided power and political offices according to the numerical strength of particular communities, according to a census conducted in 1932. With 53 percent of the population, Christians dominated the emerging country, with Maronites the largest denomination, and Sunni Muslims also received a sizable share of the spoils. Largely ignored in this calculus were the Shi'ite Muslims, who were poor and largely rural. That confessional model worked for some decades, but it became increasingly divorced from demographic reality, as the census was never updated. Maronites especially were very European in orientation, more likely to be urban, prosperous, and educated, and their fertility rate fell sharply. Sunni Muslims, who were relatively prosperous, shared that trend to a somewhat lesser degree. But the largest change occurred among the country's Shia Muslims, who bred prolifically. They grew from perhaps 20 percent of the population in the 1940s to at least 30 percent by the start of the twenty-first century—some estimates suggest 40 percent. As I have noted in other settings, the deep sensitivity of such census figures makes it all but impossible to find more realistic statistics.

The resulting imbalances and distortions of power contributed to the country's lengthy civil war (1975–1990), in which the Shi'ites played an increasingly prominent and dynamic role. Groups like Hezbollah made the Shi'ites a formidable military force, regionally and globally. The resulting civil war destabilized the region. It even came close to bringing down a U.S. president, as the Reagan administration struggled to rescue Western hostages in that land, provoking the Iran–Contra debacle. Following the years of agonizing strife, Christian numbers suffered further from migration, and today the Christian share of the country is at most 40 percent.

Lebanese conditions were (and are) highly distinctive, but that grim story does offer lessons that can be widely applied today. Instead of such a patchwork of faiths and denominations, imagine a country where the vast majority of people follow one particular faith tradition. But despite that notional homogeneity, variations in prosperity and location (city versus countryside) will affect how that religion is practiced. Wealthier and educated city dwellers commonly differ from rural populations in their degree of religious fervor, their respect for clerical authority, their openness to religious diversity, their tolerance for other faiths or traditions, and their willingness to espouse fundamentalist approaches to faith or scripture. We would also expect divergent attitudes to key issues of gender, sexuality, and family. That elite or more liberal community will have far lower birth rates than its poorer compatriots, so that inevitably the poorer and pious constituencies will grow both in absolute and relative terms. In a sense the religious do inherit the earth—but the struggles in which they have to engage mean that it can be a damaged and impoverished earth.

The Lebanese model illustrates how differential patterns of fertility divide nations, reflecting and exaggerating issues of class, race, wealth, ethnicity—and above all, of religion. When those differences are sufficiently acute, they can lead to outright disintegration or state failure. That Lebanese example has in recent years been much on the minds of European policy makers, who have imagined worst-case scenarios for the demographic futures of their own countries, with rising levels of Muslim immigration. However poorly grounded such apocalyptic imaginings might be, religious and ethnic disparities can have grave social effects.

Turkey's Two Faces

If other countries have channeled their demographic divisions into relatively peaceful politics, they have nevertheless proved deeply divisive. Turkey offers an egregious example. Over the past decade, the country's affairs have been critical to the larger Middle East and have attracted keen interest from the United States, Russia, and Israel, among others. In the 2010s Turkish attitudes and decisions shaped the struggle against the Islamic State and the response to the Syrian civil wars. Any worthwhile attempt to understand those issues must of necessity draw heavily on demographic concerns and the differential demographics of a divided nation. Matters of fertility—and the hopes and fears they arouse—are essential to understanding the rise and fall of political parties and causes, the creation of national ideologies, and the relations between a central government and its dissident minorities.[6]

Since 2002 Turkey has been dominated politically by the Justice and Development Party (AKP). That party is led by Erdoğan, who since 2014 has served as the country's president. Originally presented as a standard-bearer for a moderate and pragmatic form of Islamism, the party has become steadily more authoritarian. Erdoğan himself has emerged as a charismatic strongman practicing an authoritarian populism. His government appeals to its poorer and more religious citizens by preaching much more conservative versions of the country's dominant faith, a startling departure from the country's recent history.[7]

That Islamist drift is difficult to comprehend without some knowledge of modern Turkish history. In its modern form, the country emerged in the 1920s from the wreckage of the historic Ottoman Empire. Under the leadership of Mustafa Kemal Atatürk ("Father of the Turks"), the country made a radical leap to modernization, enforced by stern government intervention. Turks were required to forsake traditional clothes for Western dress, and the language was to be written in a Western-style alphabet. The country became aggressively secular in its public life, prohibiting conspicuous signs of religious faith and suppressing the once powerful Sufi orders. While Islamic life was accepted and tolerated, the country's religious institutions were under the firm hand of a central Presidency of Religious Affairs, the Diyanet. Secularist and Kemalist views were deeply entrenched in the political and military establishment, which struggled to resist the new wave of Islamic politics sweeping much of the region in the late twentieth century. One major flashpoint was women's use of headscarves, the hijab, which were strictly forbidden in institutions of public education.[8]

Matters have changed thoroughly under the AKP, as Islamic institutions, newspapers, and media outlets have all flourished. The government has approved the wearing of hijabs in universities and even by women police officers. Erdoğan has openly advocated far-reaching policies of Islamization, including restrictions on alcohol and the prohibition of public displays of suggestive activity, including kissing. His government has actively favored the building or restoration of mosques and of historic Ottoman sites. From a Western perspective, this all falls far short of the atrocities of the Islamic State, but in Turkish terms it is startling enough, even revolutionary. Recalling the country's former regime, when the Sultan also claimed to be the Caliph of Islam, critics describe Erdoğan's rule as "neo-Ottoman."

Turkey's Demographic Divide

Erdoğan's promotion of faith can be understood only against the country's unusual demographic patterns. Overall Turkey's fertility rate is a little below replacement at 2.0, but that simple fact obscures enormous regional variations. The country can roughly be divided into four zones, stretching from west to east. The western quarter is thoroughly European in demographic terms, with sub-Danish fertility rates of around 1.5. That is not surprising in light of the close ties uniting those regions to Europe, the impact of European media, and the extensive Turkish migration to lands like Germany and the Netherlands. Naturally, many of those migrants brought European ways and attitudes home with them. But the nation's other regions exhibit quite different patterns. Fertility rates rise steadily as we travel farther east into Anatolia, until the upland east has very high rates resembling those of neighboring Iraq or Syria. The far-western province of Edirne has a TFR of 1.5, while in the southeast Şanlıurfa is over 4.34. That disparity is far greater than we find between liberal and conservative regions of the United States. Turkey's median age is 31.5—high by Middle Eastern standards, but again, the rate varies a great deal from west to east, as older westerners confront younger easterners. "Europe" and the Third World—Sterilia and Fertilia—jostle each other within one nation.[9]

As we would expect, that demographic gradation closely tracks expressions of religious zeal. The high-fertility regions of eastern and central Turkey are much more religious than the secular west, and this is where we find the Quran Belt that so regularly supports Islamic and fundamentalist causes. It simply makes electoral sense for the government to respond to the interests of that populous and growing area, and to drift ever more steadily in Islamist directions. In the 2015 elections, the AKP did badly in western and coastal regions with fertility rates well below replacement. Conversely, it won its greatest successes in the high-fertility regions of south-central Turkey, between Konya and Malatya, and in many eastern sections. The very high-fertility region of Şanlıurfa is an AKP fortress. As so often around the world, religious parties find their electoral strongholds in high-fertility areas.

But there is a complicating fact here, which further contributes to the demographic underpinnings of the country's politics. It may seem odd at first that those triumphs in south-central regions were not wholly replicated farther east in the very high-fertility areas of the far southeast, around cities like Diyarbakir. In fact the AKP met its sturdiest opposition there. But besides the fast-breeding Turks in those eastern regions, we also find members of a significant non-Turkish minority who likewise display extremely high fertility. These are what the Turkish government euphemistically calls the "Mountain Turks" but which are properly known as Kurds. Turkey's Kurdish minority, usually estimated at around 15 to 20 percent of the population, is expanding rapidly, posing a demographic threat that dominates the thinking and the rhetoric of President Erdoğan. Throughout his time in office, the president has consistently and repeatedly stressed these demographic themes, to the bafflement or contempt of Western observers, for whom such causes do not resonate in the slightest.[10] Erdoğan has issued apocalyptic warnings that Turkey will possess a national Kurdish majority within just a couple of decades, far earlier than most demographers would predict. Fears of Kurdish growth or domination go far toward explaining why, over the past decade, the Turkish government so often preferred to act militarily against that Kurdish community, rather than against the Islamic State that most Western observers viewed as a critical danger to regional stability and peace. From a Turkish point of view, though, the Islamic State was an irritant, while the Kurds posed an existential demographic threat.

In the face of seemingly imminent demographic catastrophe, Turkey faces limited options. Like many other countries in a similar position, the government can deploy the usual array of incentives to encourage non-Kurdish citizens to start breeding again—even those Western-oriented secularists—and to get the national fertility rate closer to 3.0 than 2.0. As the president has said, "If you have a young population, the future is yours. . . . But when we look at the increase, if we continue like this, alarm bells are ringing for 2037–40." He has urged Turkish people that "at least three children you must have, before it's too late," and further describes abortion as a "plan to wipe the country off the world stage."[11] He tries to persuade Turkish families living in Europe to have five children, as part of an explicit scheme to promote Turkish and Islamic values. Beyond the usual natalist incentives, the government extols religious, Islamic identities as a means of reviving fertility. Ideally, a return to conservative versions of Islam might inspire Turkish (and specifically non-Kurdish) families to reassert traditional values and to have more children.[12]

For several reasons, then, in the current demographic environment, it makes excellent sense for a Turkish government to favor its poorer and more faithful population, to extol Islamic values, and to berate the "West" for its malign influences. Numbers alone mean that a leader has little to lose by espousing ever more vociferous Islamic policies and rhetoric, all of which are going to be well received in the Quran Belt. Whatever happens to Erdoğan personally, or to his party, those underlying demographic facts are not going to vanish overnight. Nor are the lessons for future political parties and movements. For that reason, over the next decade or two, Islamism will play a major and continuing role in this country on Europe's doorstep.

Saffron India

In India as in Turkey, demographic divisions have provoked a drift away from secularism, and a national leader has mobilized the politics of faith in what constitutes a major deviation from the country's recent history. Turkey itself is overwhelmingly Muslim, and resulting controversies thus occur between Muslims or else they set conservative Muslims against secularists. In India, by contrast, the political appeal to conservative religion has involved ugly confrontations with the country's other religions, with their very sizable populations.[13]

As in Turkey, official secularism was deeply rooted in the Indian political tradition. Numerically the population is overwhelmingly Hindu (reportedly around 80 percent today) but with a substantial Muslim minority (14 percent), as well as Sikhs, Jains, Christians, and others. The Muslim minority, which constitutes almost 200 million people, represents the world's third-largest Islamic community, exceeded only by the nations of Indonesia and Pakistan. Globally one Muslim out of every eight or nine is an Indian citizen. All these estimates of religious strength should be taken with some skepticism, as census figures have also been criticized for their alleged exaggeration of Hindu strength and the systematic undercounting of minorities. But even if they are close to correct, the estimates demonstrate a large Hindu predominance in the population. When the country gained its independence from Britain in 1947, the new government was conscious of the need to avoid giving preference to any one faith, and that rhetoric was fundamental to the long-dominant Congress Party. Majoritarianism, from this perspective, invited religious discord and oppression. Official secularism was, and is, essential to preventing an overt Hindu hegemony.[14]

The Congress Party suffered a historic electoral defeat in 1977, and in recent years the country has often been ruled by a coalition dominated by the hard-line Hindu Bharatiya Janata Party (the Indian People's Party, or BJP). In 2014 the party won a historic triumph in the national elections, taking almost a third of the popular vote, making Narendra Modi prime minister. The party secured a convincing parliamentary majority, which it substantially increased in new elections in 2019.[15]

Although following constitutional and democratic forms, the BJP traces its origins to an extreme Hindu sect called the RSS, the Rashtriya Swayamsevak Sangh, which began in the 1920s as a paramilitary movement with close parallels to European fascism. Modi himself began his political career in the RSS. The fact that so many Indians have voted for the BJP does not of itself signify a rising tide of religious commitment, still less of bigotry, and the party owed its upsurge to hopes that it would implement much-needed economic reforms. In some areas even Muslims cast their votes for Modi's party. Yet that 2014 political victory sparked an alarming escalation of extremist Hindu rhetoric and activism. As in Turkey, the country's recent governments have openly asserted the country's dominant religion, and in conservative and fundamentalist forms, with the political/religious Indian nationalism known as Hindutva. In Indian terms this Hindu surge constitutes a "saffron wave," like the red wave that we associated with Communism in other contexts.[16]

The effects of this saffron wave have been extensive and wide ranging. Governments at the national and state level have operated on the assumption that India needs to return to its supposedly authentic native roots, which are Hindu, with the downplaying or even removal of other faiths that are viewed as recent importations. That especially means Islam and Christianity, both of which have in truth been on Indian soil for many centuries. Among other issues this official stance places severe burdens on anyone seeking to convert to such a "non-Indian" faith. Extremists have projected their opposition to conversion into the remote past, suggesting that any Indians belonging to "foreign" religions—including Christianity—were descended from people deceptively or forcibly lured away from the true (Hindu) faith. From that point of view, their modern-day descendants must be strongly encouraged to return to their spiritual home. In effect such policies deny the legitimacy of any and all non-Hindu religions on Indian soil. One notorious example of this approach came in 1992 when the RSS led attacks that demolished a venerated mosque in Ayodhya, in Uttar Pradesh, on the grounds that it stood on the site of an older Hindu temple. Other old established Islamic centers have been threatened.[17]

The ultimate goal of the hard-liners, voiced with varying degrees of frankness, is a fully Hindu India. That has been symbolized by the growing replacement of familiar names for cities with new official designations supposedly more in tune with historic national authenticity. Bombay has become Mumbai, Madras is now Chennai, Calcutta is Kolkata, and so on—often to the discomfort or anger of local residents.

Particularly over the last decade, religious minorities have suffered from vigilantism and mob violence. One common flashpoint is the protection of cows, which are sacred in the Hindu tradition. Although Muslims are licensed to trade in cattle, Hindu extremists—like the violent Bajrang Dal group—ignore those permissions and engage in mob attacks, which have claimed dozens of lives. Although moderate parties reject vigilantism, the attacks have made cow protection central to the political agenda and have forced even Congress politicians at the state level to advocate the establishment of "cow sanctuaries." In a very few years, extremist religious agendas have reshaped the substance of Indian politics. Again as in Turkey, religious extremists actively benefit from external criticism of acts of intolerance or violence, as these are presented as part of foreign conspiracies, orchestrated through a hostile global media. Those external currents are contrasted with the pure goals of domestic national and religious movements, whether that means Islamism in Turkey or Hindutva in India.[18]

The Politics of Indian Demography

As in Turkey, such a reactionary tilt is surprising in light of long secularist traditions, not to mention the obvious practical advantages of avoiding interfaith conflict. Apart from the vast size of India's Muslim population, the country's Islamic neighbor of Pakistan is a potent military rival, and both countries possess large stockpiles of nuclear weapons. But again demography largely explains the change. Until quite recently most of India was a very high-fertility society, but over the past twenty years, the chasm between different regions has become obvious. Militant Hindu policies are designed to appeal to the high-fertility regions where fundamentalist religion remains popular.

Enormous disparities exist within the vast territories of what is better thought of as a subcontinent rather than merely a nation. Some states still have high fertility: over 3.0 in the populous areas of Uttar Pradesh and Bihar. Together with Madhya Pradesh, those states already claim some 375 million people, considerably more than the contemporary United States. These are also key centers of Hindu numerical and cultural strength of the "cow belt." When Indian political observers describe the country's Hindu heartlands, they also describe high-fertility provinces like Rajasthan, Madhya Pradesh, and Chhattisgarh—all presently with TFRs over 2.5. (It is powerful testimony to the global change that such rates are now considered "high.") But other states and territories are below replacement, often significantly so. Half of all Indians now live in states with sub-replacement fertility rates. Maharashtra, with over 100 million inhabitants, has a TFR of 1.8. West Bengal and Punjab stand at 1.6, while most of southern India looks strongly "European": Karnataka, Tamil Nadu, Kerala, and Andhra Pradesh all have TFRs around 1.7 or 1.8. The capital of West Bengal, by the way, is Kolkata/Calcutta, which not long ago so often starred in apocalyptic images of the global Population Bomb.[19]

The reasons for fertility decline echo what we have already seen in so many other nations. These include economic growth, a shift to service industries, the growth of higher education, a boom in high tech, and throughout, a fundamental shift in the social and economic position of women. Those trends are most marked in states with the sharpest falls in fertility rates, especially in southern India, while the poorer and more backward areas in the north remain highly fertile. Just using the crude measure of gross domestic product, not adjusted for population, then India's wealthiest states are Maharashtra and Tamil Nadu, both marked by sub-replacement rates.[20] That fertility division also has a much wider cultural and social impact, which aligns closely with such other features as prosperity, education, and above all, religiosity. Discussing southern exceptionalism, *Economist* journalist "Banyan" comments that

> the south has long been readier than the north to agitate against the strictures of caste. Southerners are more relaxed about religion: Banyan's driver

in Chennai patronized various Hindu temples but went to church too. The most religiously strident are as likely to be atheists. Nearly every town in Tamil Nadu boasts a statue of the great social reformer E. V. Ramasamy, or *Periyar*. He used to burn images of the Hindu god Rama, at whose supposed birthplace the BJP wants to build a temple.[21]

The BJP and allied hard-line parties inevitably find their strongest and most enduring support in the high-fertility regions, especially the lands of deep and conservative Hindu faith. In 2018 the party suffered electoral setbacks, including in the contests for several legislative assemblies, and even such heartland territories as Madhya Pradesh were lost. The areas that retained their saffron loyalties at such a moment correspond well to the country's centers of high fertility. That included critical states in the northeast, including Uttar Pradesh and Bihar, as well as Jharkand, Assam, and Haryana. The party did badly in low-fertility states like the Punjab and West Bengal and in most of what we might call the solid south. Once again fertility is not the exclusive explanation here, and the strength of Sikh numbers in Punjab makes that state a tough proposition for them. Southern India, moreover, is the historic heartland of Christian numbers and loyalties. Generally the strength or weakness of fertility offers a solid guide to likely BJP prospects and of saffron causes generally.

Besides religion, language also plays a role, as the BJP appeals both to religious Hindus and to speakers of the Hindi language. Modi's party uses the nationalist slogan "Hindi—Hindu—Hindustan," which seamlessly integrates religious and linguistic causes. Although many languages are spoken, by far the most common is Hindi, which is the first language of over 40 percent of the country. As in religious matters, Indian politicians long strove to avoid giving excessive preference to the dominant language, so that minority tongues would be suitably respected and accommodated, along with their cultures. But that attempt at balance has weakened greatly in recent years, as demographic change destabilizes older structures and safeguards. The high-fertility states that are growing most rapidly in population—such as Bihar, Uttar Pradesh, and Madhya Pradesh—also stand out because they are also the largest Hindi-speaking states. Conversely six of the states marked by historically low fertility are dominated by speakers of non-Hindi languages (Bengali, Marathi, Telugu, Tamil, Malayalam, and others). These include the two northern states of West Bengal and Maharashtra and the four large southern states. Inevitably in coming decades the numbers of Hindi speakers will grow substantially, and so will their political clout.[22]

Matters may of course change in the near future, and Indian parties and coalitions have been subject to quite sudden schisms and transformations. But whatever the exact party label, the saffron cause will not go away, and it will continue to be mapped together with high fertility. So, on their side, will be liberal and progressive movements, with issues of gender and religious pluralism at the forefront of debate.

Israel and the Difference Engine

Israel, like India, is a robust democracy, but in both countries, demographic divisions have powered forms of explicitly religious politics that would have shocked the countries' respective founders. In Israel religion has come to the fore politically in ways that could scarcely have been contemplated in the 1940s, and this process must be understood through demographics. Specifically we turn to the differential demographics that result from varying degrees of wealth and education and competing views of women's proper role. That "difference engine" powerfully shapes political alignments.[23]

The state of Israel was proclaimed in 1948, just nine months after Indian independence, and as with India, its founders were largely secular, anticlerical, and (often) socialist. Although the new Israel was a home for the Jewish people, there was no expectation that strictly religious concerns would be of great significance. Two factors overturned this expectation, and demography played a significant role in both. One driver of change was the heavy immigration of Sephardic Jews from North Africa and the Middle East, who resented what they saw as the pride and condescension of the dominant European Zionist elites. Poorer Jewish communities were much more open to calls to religious faith and practice and to explicit Jewish politics. By the 1970s the poorer Mizrahi (Sephardic) population became ever more important, chiefly because of sharply higher fertility rates and larger family sizes, and they defined their grievances in religious terms.[24]

Increasingly, ethnic and religious politics merged with nationalist causes. The two Arab-Israeli wars of 1967 and 1973 revolutionized the country's politics. The 1967 war extended Israeli control over the West Bank and other territories, as well as Jerusalem, stirring religious and even messianic excitement. International efforts to end or limit that expansion galvanized conservative resentment, and in 1973 rightist and conservative parties allied to form the new Likud Party, which appealed strongly to blue-collar voters of Mizrahi background. There was also intense activity on the Far Right, and the potent movement Gush Emunim was committed to widespread settlement over the whole land claimed for Israel.

By 1977 Likud was offering an intoxicating blend of anti-elite messages, condemning traditional elites as corrupt puppets of foreign governments, who wished to dismember and betray the land. At once, they argued, the old elites betrayed both God's law and public security. The election of May 1977 marked a "revolution" (HaMahapakh), as Menachem Begin became prime minister as head of a coalition dominated by rightist and religious elements. A later Likud incumbent in that office is the long-serving Benjamin Netanyahu (1996–1999, 2009–present).[25]

Again the demographic component of this story must be stressed. Into the 1970s even fervent Western supporters of Israel had worried about the low fertility of the country's Jews when compared with Palestinian Arabs. In a private conversation, President Richard Nixon responded to a question about the country's long-term future by grimly turning his thumb downward. Ultimately, he believed, differential demography would doom the new state, which would fall to the weight of Arab numbers. Secular Jews continued their downward trajectory in fertility, but any threat of population decline was compensated by the high fertility of the Mizrahi. The Jewish population further benefited from mass immigration from the former Soviet Union.

The Orthodox and Israel's Future

But the decisive demographic change came from growth among Israel's Orthodox and ultra-Orthodox populations, which represents the second key factor in reversing the country's secular orientation. In the early years, these groups had been a minor component of the population, but their numbers boomed spectacularly. Partly this was a result of recruiting new followers, as many previously secular Israelis found a new religious commitment. Mainly, though, this was a story of much higher fertility among the Orthodox and especially the ultra-Orthodox, in particular the Haredim, whose fertility rates were and are extraordinary. Not only did their rates resist the general decline common to Western societies, but they remained at levels that we more commonly associate with Africa—often of 6.0 or higher. Israel's position as a sophisticated and wealthy nation also meant that infant mortality rates remained very low, so the overall numbers of the ultra-Orthodox have soared, both in absolute and relative terms. In 2010 Haredim constituted 10 percent of the Israeli population, around 750,000 individuals, up from 300,000 in the 1980s. That total exceeded a million (12 percent) by 2017. By 2050 Haredim will make up at least a quarter of Israel's population and perhaps a third by the 2060s. That number does not take account of other Orthodox who do not form part of the "ultra" camp. Beyond being fervently religious, the ultra-Orthodox have a high veneration for rabbinic authority, and religious leaders are key figures in political debate.[26]

Since the 1980s, specifically religious issues have played an ever more crucial part of Israel's politics. That is especially evident in issues of domestic policy, such as the enforcement of Sabbath laws. Particularly contentious is the definition of Jewish status in a country where that decides a person's right to residence and citizenship. It has become much harder to secure that recognition for individuals who do not meet the sternest Orthodox criteria for Jewish status, and especially for those who converted according to the standards of Reform or Conservative Judaism. Such conflicts provoke bitter controversies with American Jews, who are customarily much more liberal on such issues. As issues of marriage are subject to the authority of the Chief Rabbinate, the country does not recognize same-sex marriage, and any attempt to expand gay rights meets ferocious opposition from religious conservatives, from the Orthodox and ultra-Orthodox. In contrast to the familiar language of secularization, one recent book analyzes "the religionization of Israeli society." Different religious attitudes have also driven harder-line policies in external matters, in issues such as the settlement of the occupied territories, and in relations with neighboring Arab states.[27]

Scarcely less sensitive is the relationship between race, religion, and citizenship. Around a fifth of Israeli citizens are of Arab origin, a population quite distinct from Arabs living in the occupied territories. The great majority are Muslim by faith, with some Christians. Since the foundation of the state, that citizenship has been taken to imply equal rights to Jewish Israelis, although that position was anathema to extremists, who envisioned the nation in purely Jewish terms. One notorious advocate of that view was American Orthodox rabbi Meir Kahane, whose followers have been denounced by Israeli authorities as racist or fascist. Yet in 2019 Prime Minister Netanyahu espoused that explosive position, declaring that "Israel is not a state of all its citizens. . . . Israel is the nation-state of the Jewish people—and it alone." Only a generation ago, such a stance would have appeared too extreme for mainstream politics, and it was promptly denounced by the country's president. But Netanyahu's views appealed to the conservative and religious Right, and he even formed an alliance with the Kahane-linked sect, Jewish Power. Such connections infuriated liberals and centrists, who were no less concerned with multiple corruption charges facing the prime minister. Nevertheless, Netanyahu stunned critics by retaining power following elections in 2019. Netanyahu's policy stances, and his amazing powers of political endurance, must be understood in the context of the rapidly shifting demographic foundations of Israeli politics—of "religionization."[28]

In most senses Israel closely resembles a Western or European society, with its democratic system and very advanced technology. Large sections of the population remain secular and indifferent to Jewish religious causes, although faithful to Jewish identity and culture. Israel has a powerful liberal and progressive strand, committed to feminist and gay rights causes. Within Israel such attitudes are most obvious in a center like Tel Aviv, which is proverbially feminist, secular, and gay friendly. A 2006 film about this world was titled *The Bubble* (*Ha-Buah*), suggesting its distance from the growing power of religious forces, and religious politics, within the larger society. But in recent years, the country's sophisticated mass media have had to address the very different communities emerging among the Orthodox or ultra-Orthodox. Against *The Bubble* we can set so many Israeli films of recent years that portray the dilemmas of that pervasively religious world—*Eyes Wide Open* (2009), *Fill the Void* (2012), and *The Women's Balcony* (2016), or the television series *Shtisel* (2013–present). Together these constitute a whole new genre, reflecting the critical significance of those communities. Each in its way addresses the situation of women within those communities. It is almost as if the two sets of films are describing two countries, two worlds, and in a sense they are.

As in India or Turkey, a world of high fertility and devout religiosity confronts a secular rival with extremely low fertility rates. The prospects for the long term clearly favor the religious side, and canny politicians fully recognize that fact. Meanwhile, liberal secularists increasingly find themselves consigned to a bubble.

Putin's Christian Russia

In the cases described so far, differential demographic patterns persuaded political leaders to ally with surging religious populations, at the expense of secular progressives. In Russia acute demographic pressures have likewise promoted religious politics, but of a very different character. In this instance the fast-rising religious population is not the country's previously dominant Christians but rather the Muslims. Instead of allying with that rising tide, the country's rulers have presented it as a systematic challenge, demanding a sweeping political response. The divergent demography of Russia's Muslim minorities provides an essential context for that country's recent history and the religious policies of Vladimir Putin.

At first sight the Russia experience fits poorly with the other countries I have discussed. By most standard measures, Russia is not at the vanguard of Christian zeal, and in terms of religious enthusiasm, it is not too far removed from Scandinavian or Baltic patterns. Its levels of church attendance are low even by the standards of Western Europe: over 60 percent of Russians report their attendance as seldom or never, and the proportion who report praying daily is among the lowest in Europe. Only some 16 percent of Russians say that religion is very important to them. Yet that is not the impression we might form from the ostentatious support shown by Putin for Orthodoxy and the country's historic Christian heritage, and his government's intimate alliance with the church. At least in public life, Christianity plays a prominent role, which increasingly marks a division from the fading story of Christian politics in Europe proper.[29]

The fall of the Soviet Union in 1991 created a sense of optimism among Western observers who hoped that the successor states—which chiefly meant Russia—would share Western values of economic liberalization and political cooperation. Yet since 1999 the country has been led by Vladimir Putin, who has sought to restore former Soviet strength and has acted aggressively toward neighbors, especially Ukraine. Putin centralized power and patronage in his own hands, while promoting the rhetoric and propaganda of a great Russian state. As with other strong charismatic leaders like Modi and Erdoğan, he has presented his activities as aimed at restoring bygone national splendors, which have often been framed in religious and specifically Orthodox Christian terms. Putin has vigorously sought support for his vision from nationalist thinkers and groups and from the Orthodox church. His behavior can easily be understood in terms of the disappointments and fears of the country's former military and intelligence establishments, who were appalled by the loss of old Soviet certainties and the sense of inferiority to a triumphant West. But demographic factors are also at play, and these are intimately bound up with religion.[30]

Fertility and the Fate of Russia

The Russia that emerged in the 1990s inherited the grim demographic circumstances of the former Soviet Union, in which fertility rates were alarmingly low and high death rates reduced life spans to levels that we more commonly associate with Africa. Matters grew much worse during the extreme social and economic crisis of the 1990s. In 1999 the country's TFR reached a historic low of 1.17, although it has subsequently rebounded to 1.7. The country's birth rate places it around the 180th rank among all the world's nations. Russia's population today stands at 145 million, which will likely fall to around 130 million by 2050. In 2017 Russia's economy minister aptly described its demographic situation as "one of the most difficult in the world." Or, as Putin himself has reputedly declared, "Demography is a vital issue. . . . Either we'll continue to exist, or we won't."[31]

Russian observers fear that the vast expanse of Russian land space and the country's wealth of resources might attract the aggressive attention of more populous neighboring nations—most conspicuously China. But the link between demography and religion poses a special threat. Since Soviet times the country's Muslim minorities have proved much more fertile than Slavic and other European populations, and the Russian successor state inherited that reality. Presently the country's Muslims have a TFR of over 2.3, significantly higher than that of Slavic peoples. Besides Muslims with historic Russian roots, the country has also attracted many migrants from Central Asia, where high fertility rates remain common. Muslims are numerous in regions like the Caucasus, but they also have a strong and visible urban presence in the great cities, especially Moscow itself. In 2018 a record 320,000 Muslims attended mosques in Moscow during the Eid al-Adha religious festival.[32]

As so often, precise figures are hard to come by, but Muslims make up at least 15 percent of the Russian population. The country's Grand Mufti places the number at 25 million, or 18 percent of the whole, and further projects that the proportion could exceed 30 percent by the mid-2030s. That represents a far higher Muslim share of the population than in European nations that agonize over the threat of "Islamization." Of itself such a growth of Muslim populations need have no major effects on Russian society, particularly since many of those people tend to be secular in orientation. But the vision of a near-future Russia that is one-third Muslim demands a profound rethinking of traditional narratives about that country's history and its long-standing claim to represent one of the critical centers of Christianity. Such a vision is of course profoundly disturbing to the country's Orthodox Church.[33]

In other situations, as we have seen, governments have allied with the rising and more fertile population, but Russia offers a different response to its own demographic crisis. Putin himself has repeatedly expressed alarm about the situation and has sought to raise birth rates by means of financial incentives. The religious element is more complex. Putin has made favorable remarks about Islam and supported the opening of impressive new mosques. But the prospect of a growing Islamic presence has shaped his presidency in multiple ways and guided Russian policy. Above all, Russia has to be constantly aware of the Muslim nations that constitute its Near Abroad—nations like Turkey and Iran—and to intervene forcefully to prevent the creation of radical or extremist regimes that could provide a disturbing example for the country's own Muslims. This awareness underlies Russian intervention in the Caucasus and the Near East, and above all its incendiary military presence in Syria. Demographic trends within the

Russian homeland mean that the country cannot fail to have an activist policy in the Near East.

The main impact has been in guiding Putin's domestic religious policy and the potent assistance and encouragement his regime has given to the Orthodox Church. In his rhetoric Putin comes close to presenting himself as a successor of the faithful tsars of old, the bastions of faith and orthodoxy. Supporting this image has been the array of senior Orthodox clerics who regularly appear with him on public occasions. Putin has often spoken in fulsome terms about Russia's Christian heritage, describing the country's conversion as "the starting point for the formation and development of Russian statehood, the true spiritual birth of our ancestors, the determination of their identity. Identity, the flowering of national culture and education." Based on such words, some far-right theorists have even granted Putin a messianic or apocalyptic role in history.[34]

Obviously we have no way of assessing the sincerity of such declarations from Putin, any more than we can judge the religious credentials of leaders like Erdoğan, Modi, or Netanyahu. But in the Russian context, such views have had their practical impact on state-church relations, which have been very amicable. We see this in the state support for the restoration of historic cathedrals and churches, or for supporting and favoring the country's impressive monastic revival. Meanwhile, the government has cooperated with Orthodox leaders in making life difficult for rival Christian denominations and for smaller Christian sects. Legal reforms have expanded the church's role in public education and made it easier for church authorities to regain properties seized in the times of Soviet persecution.[35]

Most visible among such policies has been granting the church a potent role in determining issues of public morality. Russia diverges sharply from European nations in its restrictive attitudes to LGBT rights, and official policies are closely aligned to those of the Orthodox Church. In 2013, the church's Patriarch Kirill warned that same-sex marriages were "a very dangerous sign of the Apocalypse," and that any attempt to separate law from morality risked following the same path as Nazi Germany (or alternatively, Soviet totalitarianism).[36] That apocalyptic framing is by no means exceptional of recent church statements, which have posited an ever-growing gulf between the Christian nature of the Russian state and the dangerous amoral secularism of the West. Whatever the roots of the sentiment, overwhelming public opposition means that there is no likelihood of any legalization of same-sex marriage in the near future.

Pro-church policies have even shaped Russian foreign policy. In what at first sight looks like a remarkable throwback to the ecclesiastical politics of several centuries ago, the Russian regime has even become deeply involved in the struggle between the rival patriarchates claiming authority over Russia (Moscow) and Ukraine (Kiev). As hostility between the two countries grew, in 2018–2019 the Ukrainian patriarchate sought its independence and autonomy, sparking furious Russian diplomatic and intelligence efforts to prevent the secession.[37] It is difficult in such circumstances to know whether to characterize the church as an arm of the Russian state or vice versa.

The church-state alliance is founded on shared demographic concerns. Orthodox leaders too express alarm about population decline and hope to reverse it by a reaffirmation of traditional family structures and gender roles. Such a reorientation would include a rejection of the strong cultural tolerance for abortion, which dates back to early Soviet times. From this perspective a faithful Orthodox Russia would again be a fertile Russia, which would assume its proper role as a core center of the Christian world. A revival of conservative religious values and mores would thus be an immense boon to the Putin government and to any likely successor.

Even without the demographic crisis, it is very likely that Putin would have sought the authoritarian position he has obtained and probably that he would have gained the allegiance of the Orthodox Church. But that crisis, and its prominence in public discourse, have contributed powerfully to the strong religious coloring that the regime has affected.

The Revenge of God

In the late twentieth century, observers were often taken aback to witness the resurgence of religion and faith as elements in world politics, of what Gilles Kepel termed in 1991 *The Revenge of God*.[38] The most egregious example of that process was of course the rise of political Islam, which was first manifested in struggles in Iran, Lebanon, and Afghanistan, and then in terrorism worldwide. But all the major religions experienced some reassertion of faith in public life, sometimes with violent overtones. To that extent the manifestation of religious politics is nothing new.

What is new is the strong demographic foundation of so many of these situations as they affect various nations. When we encounter a situation in which governments espouse conservative or fundamentalist religious views, it is often helpful to determine the particular constituencies to whom they are seeking to appeal and moreover, whether the conflicts in that particular society are rooted in demographic change. As I have suggested here, such a context can certainly be traced in several high-profile contemporary nations, and other examples would not be hard to find. In politics as much as any area of life, faith is so often bound up with fertility.

CONCLUSION

9

LIVING IN A LOW-FERTILITY WORLD

An Empty Planet?

In their 2019 book *Empty Planet*, John Ibbitson and Darrell Bricker imaginatively surveyed the long-term effects of demographic decline and population contraction.[1] Like those prolific texts on the population explosion from the late 1960s, the book forced readers to contemplate global trends by extrapolating present realities. But the momentous title does need to be examined. Although the "empty" concept grabs attention, nobody believes that the human race will breed itself out of existence, that the planet literally will be empty. If we extrapolate present trends, then by some predictions, Japan will have bred itself entirely out of existence within a couple of centuries.

The response to any such claims about "If this goes on . . ." is that generally, it doesn't. Trend lines usually do not carry on indefinitely or eternally. As we have seen, demographic trends can reverse, often quite suddenly, and societies can to some extent pull out of what appear to be catastrophic dives in the fertility rate: just think of Russia since the late 1990s. But that Russian case also reinforces the basic point that much or most of the planet does seem destined for fertility rates far lower than in previous eras, and the implications demand careful consideration. For the foreseeable future—for several decades at least—most of the non-African world does face the prospect of a contracting and steeply aging population. If not an empty planet, then we might well be contemplating a more sparsely populated world. The implications are sobering. When in 1937 economist John Maynard Keynes attacked Malthusian ideas of overpopulation, he offered the prophetic comment that "I only wish to warn you that the chaining up of the one devil may, if we are careless, only serve to loose another still fiercer and more intractable"—that is, steep and sudden population decline.[2]

What might that "devil" mean for religion? If in fact faith and fertility are bound together so tightly, does that mean that a world of very low fertility will also be one of low or sharply diminished religiosity—even of the end of religion as we have known it? In religious terms at least, would we indeed be contemplating an empty planet?[3]

If that were indeed the outcome, many of the changes would be welcomed by many religious believers themselves. The core idea, after all, is that at a certain stage of social development, families view themselves with greater security so that they need no longer fear heavy rates of child mortality, while they can rely on a degree of social provision from the state. In consequence it becomes possible for women to devote themselves to goals other than maternity, while children are viewed as more than simple sources of labor. In every way these developments are entirely to be welcomed, and the decline of institutional religion is a small price to pay for these gains.

But such an apocalyptic vision can be countered in several ways, and we need to be careful about what we mean when we speak of religion. Undoubtedly the fertility shift will transform religions and religious practice, in ways that we are just beginning to appreciate, and congregations of all kinds, and all faiths, need to adapt to those new realities, just as they must absorb the implications of new kinds of technology. Crucially, the changes that we have seen in Europe portend grim times for organized institutional faith, but not necessarily for faith itself. Religious and spiritual attitudes remain alive and even vigorous, even if they seek nontraditional channels for expression. And although it is just not possible to extrapolate those European developments around the world, it seems probable that parallel distinctions must be made elsewhere. Churches and other religious bodies are not passive victims of change but have the capacity to take decisions that could profoundly affect their response to social currents. Any such planning must begin with a full consciousness of the demographic dimension, in all its complexity.[4]

We need not speak in terms of a collapse of religion as such, still less of extinction. But this does imply a real transformation of many older assumptions about ways of "being religious." All the world's religions will be fundamentally changed by these factors, and some are better prepared to cope than others. Whether secular or religious, "progress" is complex and multifaceted.

Mapping Religious Futures

Some trends in global faith can be mapped with great confidence because they do not assume any knowledge of future demographic shifts. Over the past half century, the enormous demographic differential between Europe and Africa or Asia has meant an ever-growing disparity in overall numbers, and specifically in the adherents of different faiths. This has revolutionized the global map of Christianity and moved the faith's center of gravity ever farther to the south. Whatever church or denomination we look at, we see an epochal move away from North American or European nations. That change has happened, is happening, and will continue to happen, at least for some decades to come.

It might well be that in coming decades, the remaining regions presently marked by very high fertility—especially in Africa—will come to share "European" demographic conditions. But even if that did occur, that would only gradually interrupt the long-term trends described here. Assume for the sake of argument that much of Africa will experience such a steep fertility decline around 2030, as seems probable. Even if that did happen, a time lag would delay the appearance of any obvious results in the practical realm. That generation born in the 2020s would grow to adulthood in the 2040s, when they would likely be pouring into the churches and mosques in their millions. Such a fertility decline would not thus prevent Nigeria, Ethiopia, and the Democratic Republic of the Congo ranking among the leading Christian nations by 2050. It would not prevent African nations overwhelmingly dominating the Anglican Communion by that date, or the mainline Protestant denominations, nor would it halt the growing African hold on the Roman Catholic Church. Such a hypothetical shift might slow the long-term growth of booming African-derived denominations like Nigeria's Redeemed Christian Church of God, but it would not prevent them ranking among the world's more numerous denominations by midcentury. Nor would it interfere with the burgeoning African presence in Islam. In religious terms as well as secular, the midcentury world will look much more African.

I admit to a personal investment in such projections. In 2002 my book *The Next Christendom* explored the shift of Christianity to the Global South, suggesting that this move would become ever more marked as the century progressed.[5] The book actually spread awareness of the concept of the Global South in American Christian circles. Since the book was written, the main change that has occurred has been the plunge in fertility rates in many nations across Latin America and East Asia, which certainly affects any detailed estimates of Christian numbers. As I have suggested, the whole concept of the Global South demands fundamental reexamination, as does any assumption that the three continents of Africa, Asia, and Latin America automatically share any particular characteristics. However common that idea was for twentieth-century policy makers, it is looking distinctly shopworn. It becomes ever less accurate as immigration continues to transform the ethnic and religious constitution of the old Global North, or the West, or whatever we term it. If in the 1960s a "white West" confronted a rest of the world made up of people of color, that contrast has faded fast.

What has not been affected is my conclusion that by 2050, Christian numbers will be ever more concentrated in nations like the Philippines, Brazil, and India, even if the actual numbers are somewhat smaller than I suggested. What has become still more glaringly obvious over time is that, as predicted, Africa will indeed contain the world's largest Christian population, and that around one-third of Christians will live on the African continent. That is quite apart from African migrants in the global diaspora, chiefly in Europe and North America. Christianity, by that stage, would indeed be at its core a religion of Africa and the African Diaspora. Today, if anything, my projections seem conservative. African numerical dominance within that faith will arrive sooner than I argued and will be still more sizable.

For other faiths too, the near future can be projected with some confidence. Within Judaism, it might be that in a decade or two, Orthodox and ultra-Orthodox families will move toward the fertility patterns more standard across Euro-American societies, although there are presently few signs of any such development. But even if that change did occur, it would not interfere with the transformation of Judaism in more religious and Orthodox directions—certainly in Israel but also in other major centers, above all the United States. In the context of Israel, the country in twenty or thirty years will almost certainly have a far more religious cast than the Zionist pioneers might ever have envisaged and might even have the kind of clerical and millenarian tone that we today associate with Iran. Conversely, the prospects for progressive strands, such as the Reform tradition, are not promising.

At least as we look to the midcentury, such projections remain solid across faith boundaries. Matters might of course change toward the end of the century, but any such long-term prophecies—beyond twenty or thirty years—are necessarily speculative anyway. They depend on unforeseeable developments in technology, politics, and the economy, so they are more in the realm of prophecy rather than extrapolation. They also offer the wonderful advantage that nobody who makes such predictions will live long enough to see them disproved.

The End of Faith?

Some very credible social scientists believe that the fertility revolution heralds the destruction of religion in any form we have known, if not the actual abolition of religious faith as such. In the short term, such analyses are chiefly based on European experience, but the long-term implications have global relevance. One of the leading scholars on the religious implications of demographic change is David Voas, who declares unequivocally that

> religion is in decline across the Western world. Whether measured by belonging, believing, participation in services, or how important it is felt to be, religion is losing ground. Older generations die out and are replaced by less religious younger generations. Modernization has predictable and permanent effects, one of which I call the secular transition. . . . Certain major transformations—such as the industrial revolution or the demographic transition (the decline first in mortality and then in fertility)—occur exactly once in each society. These transitions are very difficult to undo. Backtracking is exceptional and temporary: slavery isn't restored after it's been abolished, nor do women lose the vote once granted. A transition is permanent, not cyclical or recurring; once out, the toothpaste won't go back into the tube. Secularization is such a transition.[6]

Whatever caveats we offer about the term *secularization*, Voas is speaking broadly of a decline in actual belief, rather than just institutional structures. Callum Brown is still more explicit. As he writes, "The Western World is becoming atheist. In the space of three generations churchgoing and religious belief have become alien to millions. We are in the midst of one of humankind's great cultural changes."[7] Although these scholars are discussing the West, there is no intrinsic reason why the changes that have overtaken Western religion should not have their impact on a global scale and, ultimately, even in Africa. If such views are correct, then Christianity has a specific expiration date, to be followed after some delay by the other great faiths. At some not-too-distant point, perhaps in the mid-twenty-second century, God would become an extinct species.

Several objections present themselves. One is superficial, namely that earlier prophecies about the end of religion have proved wildly wrong, so why should these be different? Educated people in the 1790s were certain that Christianity had reached its final days, yet a century of faith followed. In the 1960s even the best-informed global observer would not have predicted the highly religious coloring of politics in the coming century. God took his revenge. Repeatedly through history, religion and religions have declined to the point of apparent extinction, only to be restored (or replaced) by fervent new groupings that tried to respond to popular needs and hungers. That precedent might yet recur. Having said that, scholars like Voas and Brown are basing themselves not on impressions but on very large quantitative bodies of evidence covering many countries and spanning long periods. Their analyses demand respect.

More serious is the response that "never" is a very long time, and that matters can change in ways that seem inconceivable to us today. In appropriate circumstances toothpaste might indeed return to the tube. In its brief period in power, the Islamic State actually did succeed in restoring a medieval set of social and gender arrangements, complete with slavery, in real-life manifestation of something like the world of *The Handmaid's Tale*. However briefly, the group's horrific power extended over eight million people, in an area the size of Hungary. If indeed that example proved "exceptional and temporary," who can say whether future efforts might be vastly more successful? For a benevolent example of social reaction, we look again at Orthodox and ultra-Orthodox Jews. In those communities we find families who exemplified both the demographic and the secular transitions but whose daughters accepted new lives of religious commitment and who are happily deciding to bear six or seven children.

In both those instances, we are looking at tiny populations. But some highly credentialed and authoritative scholars suggest that groups like the ultra-Orthodox are one manifestation of a much larger phenomenon, in which the conservative preference for large families will over time ensure the preservation and extension of religious views. I have already noted Eric Kaufmann's argument in *Shall the Religious Inherit the Earth?*, and he is by no means the only thinker to advance such views. From that point of view, it is the religiously unaffiliated who will decline over time, rather than the faithful or fundamentalist. We need not agree with those views, either in whole or in part, to recognize that a legitimate debate does exist.[8]

Other global factors might well forestall or even prevent any so-called secular transition. Vast areas and populations very probably will be affected by sweeping changes in conditions that could subvert possible notions of secular security. Climate change is the obvious example and one that in the long term could indeed sustain or revive ideas of religious belonging, as well as believing. If Europe (say), or even the United States, has passed through the twin transitions, then those areas will still be importing migrants from other parts of the world that have not. Far from placing confidence in the destruction of any particular world faith, we should remain open to the possibility of other new faiths yet to come. To say that is not to make a prediction; still less is it to hope for cataclysms sufficiently terrifying to maintain religious faith. Rather, it is to remain open to the spectrum of future possibilities.

New Worlds of Faith

Quite apart from such macro-level speculations, we can scarcely contest the statement that "religion is in decline across the Western world" or that this decline is deeply rooted in social conditions. The question then arises of how religious institutions of any kind will continue to operate in a low-fertility environment, where fertility rates are consistently around 1.6 or so. Based on recent experience, we can make some assessments of the problems that need to be met and the capacity of institutions to respond to them. As previously, I will here draw mainly on Christian churches for examples, although most of the points apply equally across religious frontiers.

The changes we witness affect attitudes to the spiritual realm to a far smaller degree than they transform the assumptions by which institutions work. Spirituality, broadly defined, continues to fascinate, as do notions of holiness and of holy places. The current vogue for pilgrimage shows no sign of waning, fully justifying the language of resacralization or reenchantment.

But in terms of the structures on which institutions so long depended, so many of those circumstances probably have changed irrevocably, at least in the West. In so many instances, the toothpaste really cannot be returned to the tube. We see this for instance in the decline of children's role as a primary raison d'être of churches. On a related theme, religious institutions must respond to the utterly changed situation of women, which in all societies has been the most significant force driving demographic change. Debates about women's role in religious institutions generally focus on questions of clerical roles or ordination, but the changes run far deeper than that. At all levels women have long been vital to congregational activities, not least in matters of food, entertainment, and provision of social and community services. As in the case of childcare and education, such contributions can no longer be counted on when women are fully engaged in the workplace. Any attempts to draw women into religious organizations have to use an egalitarian approach, assuming that the subjects are employed workers as well as mothers or family members. Alongside such key building blocks as voluntarism, egalitarianism, and decentralization, a movement must offer full participation to the laity.

Beyond such an idealized account of those future models, we can see some real-world attempts to respond to the new environment.

New Movements

The demographic shift had its origins in Europe, and it is here especially that we see the pioneering efforts to adjust to the new situation. One of the most telling realizations is that churches can no longer rely on mass public devotion or even sympathy and must rather focus on the role of creative minorities. Churches have to relearn operating as minority communities within a predominantly nonreligious environment. The best-known advocate of this position was the former pope Benedict XVI, who remarked that "the mass Church may be something lovely, but it is not necessarily the Church's only way of being."[9]

Europe's churches have enjoyed some successes in moving beyond the "mass church" concept, emphasizing instead communities and networks that operate freely and flexibly in highly mobile environments. The church can no longer count on the participation of 60 or 70 percent of the community coming to church every week but having little involvement beyond that, but they can rely on the devotion and commitment of a much more committed and informed core, say of 5 percent. There now exist a range of so-called new ecclesial movements, which demand intense commitment and participation from believers. These often draw on intense forms of personal spirituality or from charismatic traditions. Ideally those devout activist groups and new religious orders should serve as leaven or yeast within the larger community and as the foundation for a new and wider evangelization. Such movements are often heavily invested in the idea of pilgrimage. Although created in response to European conditions, such groupings might be particularly appropriate for the low-fertility worlds of East Asia and Latin America.[10]

What these new forms have in common is that they are fitted for a world that is individualistic rather than communal, in which assumptions about mass participation in religious institutions no longer apply, any more than in mass economic production. Nor do they assume such once fundamental institutions as the family with children or communities sending children to common schools or churches. Participation is based on personal choice and a decision to opt in, and they are open to older people and singles. These grassroots groups are decentralized and highly media savvy, offering major spiritual rewards in exchange for massive investment in time and commitment.

The Anglican church has responded similarly to the steep decline of mass church attendance, by a new focus on neo-Pentecostal movements and charismatic networks, some of which have evolved into flourishing megachurches far removed from older visions of the parish. The Church of

England is also the source of another scheme that moves beyond traditional concepts of the parish, and of older assumptions about social organization. The charismatic Anglican parish of Holy Trinity, Brompton—a de facto megachurch—created the Alpha Course, an innovative form of evangelization and Christian education that does not assume a society revolving around families and children. Individuals contact and recruit each other through nonhierarchical networking and commit to attending a series of ten dinners, with wide-ranging conversation and a video presentation. The whole series is intended to lead to a "decision for Christ." The Alpha model has been widely adopted worldwide, and over twenty million people have participated.[11]

Such new movements and strategies have to be placed in context. They certainly have not averted a dramatic decline in church numbers and influence in Europe, nor have comparable measures in Latin America. Successive crises involving sexual abuse by clergy continue to cast a long shadow. But in the longer term, these innovations suggest possible means by which congregations can respond to the very different social environment created by the demographic revolution. In particular they show an admirable willingness to recognize the inadequacies of models and assumptions derived from high-fertility environments.

None of the features outlined here is in any sense distinctive to Christianity. In fact the list of criteria I have outlined applies very well to the Sufi orders that for centuries have been such a prominent feature of Islam, although they have so often faced violent attacks and persecution in the modern day. Yet in their voluntary structure and mystical emphasis, they might yet be an ideal institution for future Islamic societies. Significantly, the best-publicized Sufi revival in the modern Islamic world has occurred in Iran, where the demographic transition has had the greatest impact.

An Aging World

Nowhere is that need to rethink assumptions more obvious than in issues of aging. A low-fertility society is marked by decreasing numbers of children and an increasing share of elderly people, and especially the very old, people in their eighties or older. That number will only grow as medical technologies advance. By all logic these vast new populations of the elderly should provide the basis for a fundamental rethinking of institutional religion and of congregational life. Generally, all religious institutions need to consider adapting to congregations with a much older demographic profile and away from the old emphasis on younger families. It is presently an open question what such a shift might mean in terms of theology, liturgy, or pastoral practice.

The scale of this aging trend is dramatic. In 1970, around 10 percent of Americans were aged over 65, as against 15 percent in 2017, and that proportion will rise steeply. A 2016 report by the Population Reference Bureau remarked, "The number of Americans ages 65 and older is projected to nearly double from 52 million in 2018 to 95 million by 2060, and the 65-and-older age group's share of the total population will rise from 16 percent to 23 percent." Related to this trend, the U.S. Census Bureau notes another forthcoming landmark, namely that around the year 2030, older people—those over 65—will outnumber the nation's children. That will be the first time in U.S. history that such a situation has occurred, but that is likely to become the new normal.[12]

Such a change would indeed be far-reaching in its effects, but the United States is actually behind other advanced countries in the process of national graying. Already over a quarter of Japanese are over 65: indeed, 20 percent are now more than 70.[13] Much of Europe is moving in that direction. Gradually, similar conditions will affect all nations that have gone through the demographic shift, across Asia and Latin America. Present-day Japan might be the bellwether for much of the globe—with the caveat that very few countries have anything like the economic muscle needed to offer an appropriate response. Adding to the impact of this change is the decline of traditional family structures in which older people might once have found support and companionship. Quite apart from immediate physical and medical needs, the plight of the lonely elderly will in coming decades be one of the most pressing social situations.

Governments at all levels have discussed plans to respond to the impending situation. Japan has given much thought to redesigning cities and transportation systems in ways that will make life easier for older people with reduced capacities in vision or mobility. But what about the churches and other religious institutions that potentially could provide older people with their most promising opportunities for social interaction, not to mention practical support networks? Congregations obviously serve an enormous range of clienteles, but most or all will have to confront these issues in coming years. Few, though, have responded with anything like the systematic care or thought that is usually reflected in the activities offered to children, with schools and programs, and commonly with pastors specifically allotted to that age range.

Nor, more generally, do Christian thinkers and writers devote nearly as much time to developing theologies of aging, to discussing the implications for spirituality. There are some important exceptions to this rule, but presently they are far outnumbered by works directed to young and teenaged audiences. The main exception to that rule would be in books about preparation for death, which are commonplace and which vastly outnumber works intended to advise people how to live for several decades after their retirement from an active career. How can or should religious institutions target their distinctive messages to the elderly?[14]

Many religious congregations already find themselves dominated by the elderly, with few or no children or young families. Such communities face little chance of growing, although the structures of denominations commonly mean that they will survive in some form. In the case of mainline Christian churches, such elderly congregations continue indefinitely because of the investment of earlier generations, which have left substantial endowments and imposing facilities. Increasingly, such age structures will of necessity become more commonplace and among communities without those long-term resources. Congregations will be forced to ask just how long they can realistically survive as institutional entities before being terminated or at least consolidated into larger bodies. The experience of the Roman Catholic Church in closing or consolidating older urban parishes will serve as a precedent for many other denominations that are presently thriving and expanding. The traumatic nature of such changes in the Catholic context—and the fierce opposition that often arises—will also be reproduced across the denominational spectrum. By midcentury, the heartrending politics of church closures due to congregations "aging out" will be a critical and deeply divisive theme in denominational affairs.

Immigrant Communities

If we imagine communities that are homogeneous or isolated, then a move to low fertility will indeed imply aging and gradual decline. But as we know well, that demographic shift implies a substantial immigrant presence, with the consequent expansion of diversity in the community in question, and that in turn transforms religious life in multiple ways. A society with so many people who are either aged, retired, or not in regular paid work can only be sustained by the steady importation of new groups to perform the work and pay taxes, and that must mean immigrants from high-fertility societies. Whatever other tensions or conflicts might arise from such a trend, those migrants are likely to be much more committed to their distinctive religious forms, which in a European context generally means either Islam or Christianity. After those communities have been in the new country for a few decades, their religious forms increasingly become a part of the native religious landscape. How well or badly those religious forms adapt to host societies varies enormously in particular instances, but immigration can play a dynamic role in supporting and enhancing religious life. That principle should be thoroughly familiar to students of American history, where religion has so often been reshaped by repeated waves of immigration.

That model is familiar enough, but deciding on an appropriate response poses dilemmas for older religious institutions. As we have seen, some host countries have adopted a nativist response, seeing the newcomers as threats, and perhaps trying to build up the numbers of the older communities. This is the solution attempted in Eastern European nations like Hungary. More commonly churches themselves have sought to be hospitable and welcoming but with no well-thought-out agenda about future relationships with those new communities.

Imagine a Catholic church in a European nation, its congregation almost entirely composed of old-stock white believers, finding itself in the company of multiple new and thriving institutions. In the case of mosques, the older church might seek to promote friendly relations and even interfaith endeavors, but they would at best be good neighbors. Much more challenging are immigrant Christian churches, of various denominations, which would likely have a very young age profile, contributing to the vigor and enthusiasm of their services. Some of those communities might themselves be Catholic, albeit of a very different character. The older church might treat these emerging congregations merely in a neighborly way, much like the mosques, but other opportunities for much deeper involvement and cooperation present themselves. If in fact the immigrant churches did conspicuously represent the future of faith in a particular community, then it would make excellent sense for the different congregations to work together as far as possible. Above all, each church would need to perform an honest and searching inventory of its own strengths and weaknesses, to determine what it can offer its neighbors and what are its most pressing needs.

Ideally, the fact of such diversity should provide older congregations with tremendous opportunities to revive and reinvigorate themselves, to overcome the burdens posed by demographic challenges and by aging. In that sense the immigrant congregations would themselves serve as leaven, just like the emerging movements and networks. But this can happen only if both sides can confront the many cultural challenges that await any such meeting of old and new forms of faith. No less than confronting the dilemmas of aging, this situation demands a real rethinking of basic assumptions about faith and practice.

Again, the examples chosen here are mainly Christian, with direct relevance to Europe or North America, but as I have suggested, similar patterns and debates occur elsewhere. If Christians confront a new Islamic presence, then Muslims in regions like the Arab Gulf similarly find themselves in the vicinity of new Christian neighbors and congregations, and again, that is a direct response to shifts in fertility. Even if faiths do not communicate directly, beyond formal politeness, they will often adopt styles or tactics from those new neighbors. In recent years some Muslim preachers have enjoyed transcontinental success as (in effect) televangelists, deploying contemporary communications technologies but also borrowing freely from Christian approaches and rhetoric. The more faiths come into contact, the more we can expect of such cross-pollination.

Moral Messages

However it may change, institutional religion will survive for the foreseeable future. Just how far the messages that those bodies preach will change over time is a much more open question. In some cases churches might find success in shifting their doctrinal emphasis away from themes that have become so controversial, especially in matters of sexuality and sexual identity. Reducing the emphasis on sexual themes in moral teaching is a predictable and perhaps inevitable way in which religious institutions can respond to a new demographic environment.

Initially in Europe, and then farther afield, the demographic transition led to growing gulfs between religious teaching and a general moral consensus over many issues of sexuality and gender roles. In a growing number of countries, the gulf between official religious teachings and secular attitudes has done much to undermine religious affiliations and encourage hostility toward the churches. This divergence has been most evident in matters of homosexuality but also of sexual behavior more generally defined. That gap becomes a chasm where younger people and young adults are concerned. Abortion is one of the few areas in which a sizable share of the population still opposes progressive or liberal views, or at least seeks to draw limits.

Religions of all kinds face a grave dilemma. How far should they continue in public opposition to behaviors or ideas that have become thoroughly acceptable to most of their actual and potential membership? To take an example, the Roman Catholic Church has always taught the sinfulness of artificial means of contraception, a policy reasserted in 1968 by Pope Paul VI. But if the policy has not changed—and indeed is usually declared to be unchangeable—lay Catholics widely ignore it. Catholic clergy are well aware of that unofficial dissidence, and few would make contraception the subject of a sermon, still less a morality campaign. When churches organize politically on issues such as divorce or same-sex marriage, they know that they do so contrary to the opinions of large sections of the faithful.

Substantial areas of sexual morality play a far smaller part in church teachings and activism than would have been imaginable a few decades ago, and we must ask how far such a trend will move in future. In coming decades, and by no means only in the West, a growing number of major Christian denominations will have clergy who are openly gay or transgender, and will be performing same-sex marriages. In such institutions it would be very surprising indeed to hear sermons about sins such as fornication or adultery, still less homosexuality. Even more conservative churches have become much more open to more accepting attitudes on homosexuality.

This does not of course mean that religious institutions worldwide are in any sense abandoning their traditional focus on sexual behavior as a centerpiece of moral enforcement and exhortation. The Islamic world proves slow to change on such matters, even in those societies marked by rapid changes in gender roles and imploding fertility rates. Consistently, communities with traditional fertility patterns tend to be much more conservative on these fundamental issues, all the more so when reasserting their values against liberal rivals. That contrast is especially evident within Judaism, where the Orthodox and ultra-Orthodox remain strongly committed to traditional sexual norms. Even within Christianity very conservative attitudes persist in the high-fertility societies of Africa, which has led to bitter confrontations within some global denominations. Debates over homosexuality have caused an open schism within the Anglican Communion, and such divisions have echoed through other Protestant churches. Such attitudes have a special impact on Western societies because of the presence of those immigrant churches, which retain the attitudes of their home societies.

Church Going

Religious institutions will be transformed by demographic changes, and their success and continued existence will depend on how far they can adapt to a radically changed world. Some traditions, some denominations, will decline in the process, and some might fail altogether. But that is quite different from forecasting the end of religion as such. Even when formal institutions are in crisis or decline, ample signs of religious sentiment or enthusiasm remain undimmed.

In understanding this paradox, we might usefully turn to a literary work that actually tells us as much about religious developments as a great many longer works of sophisticated sociological inquiry. In 1955 English poet Philip Larkin published "Church Going," a title that refers both to the act of visiting churches and to the possibility that such churches might vanish or go away.[15] In the poem a passing cyclist, presumably an agnostic like Larkin himself, steps into a deserted church. Finding nothing of special aesthetic interest, he leaves fairly rapidly but is still puzzled at why he even bothered to stop. What exactly is the remaining pull of a place that is notionally holy? And if, as seems obvious, religion is in such sharp decline, what will be the ultimate fate of such places when they fall into disuse and ruin? Larkin speculates that they might become objects of superstitious terror, unlucky places. Or perhaps they will be special and magical, thin spaces, where people might believe that they witness the dead walking. Superstition might endure a while, but ultimately, even that will fade. So what happens when disbelief has gone, along with faith itself?

However grim the speculations, Larkin returns to his basic dilemma of why he so enjoys and appreciates these places, which are the venues for rituals and prayers in which he does not believe. Yes, churches and creeds may fade, but holy places remain, and they powerfully focus our desires and hopes, our need for rootedness and continuity:

> A serious house on serious earth it is
> In whose blent air all our compulsions meet
> Are recognized and robed as destinies.

People will always need to seek the "serious," most obviously in places linked to the dead, and to bygone traditions:

> And that much never can be obsolete
> Since someone will forever be surprising
> A hunger in himself to be more serious
> And gravitating with it to this ground
> Which he once heard was proper to grow wise in
> If only that so many dead lie round.

In any era religion responds to a deep-seated need for connection to the "serious" past. That connection might be a sacred place, but it might be to something more generic—to bodies of practice and ritual, to culture and especially music. Here too we can find the serious, the significant, the rooted, which together form the irreducible core of religion.

The demographic revolution subverts or renders irrelevant so many of the features and activities that religions have long been accustomed to viewing as essential to their existence and their work. As those features fade, so religions of all kinds are forced to reconsider what their core purpose actually is, what is for them the heart of the matter. That exercise in rethinking could be prolonged and even painful, but the potential opportunities are rich indeed, and at a time of special human need. An empty planet needs far more than empty faith.

NOTES

1 Fertility and Faith

1   Jay Winter and Michael Teitelbaum, *The Global Spread of Fertility Decline: Population, Fear, and Uncertainty* (New Haven, Conn.: Yale University Press, 2013); Steven Philip Kramer, *The Other Population Crisis: What Governments Can Do about Falling Birth Rates* (Washington, D.C.: Woodrow Wilson Center Press with Johns Hopkins University Press, 2014); Paul Morland, *The Human Tide: How Population Shaped the Modern World* (New York: Public Affairs, 2019). Throughout, I have drawn on Massimo Livi-Bacci, *A Concise History of World Population*, 6th ed. (Hoboken, N.J.: John Wiley & Sons, 2017); and Detlef Pollack and Gergely Rosta, *Religion and Modernity: An International Comparison*, trans. David West (Oxford: Oxford University Press, 2017).

2   One early recognition of the religious change came in Joseph Claude Harris, "The Future Church," *America*, March 18, 2002.

3   The linkage with religion is noted in Lyman Stone, *Declining Fertility in America* (Washington, D.C.: American Enterprise Institute, 2018), 15–16, https://www.aei.org/research-products/report/declining-fertility-in-america/.

4   Morland, *The Human Tide*.

5   For various means of measuring fertility, see the convenient discussion by Gretchen Livingston, "Is U.S. Fertility at an All-Time Low? Two of Three Measures Point to Yes," *Fact Tank* (blog), Pew Research Cen-

ter, May 22, 2019, https://www.pewresearch.org/fact-tank/2019/05/22/
u-s-fertility-rate-explained/. See also Max Roser, "Fertility Rate," Our
World in Data, last modified December 2, 2017, https://ourworldindata
.org/fertility-rate.

6   "What Explains America's Mysterious Baby Bust?" *Economist*, November 24, 2018, https://www.economist.com/united-states/2018/11/24/what
-explains-americas-mysterious-baby-bust.

7   The best source for demographic data of all kinds is the United Nations Population Division, which offers a massive range of data and reports: see, for
instance, "Fertility," United Nations Department of Economic and Social
Affairs: Population, https://www.un.org/en/development/desa/population/
theme/fertility/index.asp. Fertility rates and other demographic data are
widely available online. One readily convenient source is the country-by-
country figures in The World Factbook, Central Intelligence Agency, https://
www.cia.gov/library/publications/the-world-factbook/. Valuable data is
available through the Population Reference Bureau, https://www.prb.org/;
World Population Review, http://worldpopulationreview.com/; and Roser,
"Fertility Rate." See also the World Data Atlas, Knoema, https://knoema
.com/atlas. Throughout this book I draw on studies by the Pew Research
Center: see, for instance, *The Global Religious Landscape* (Washington,
D.C.: Pew Research Center, 2012), https://www.pewforum.org/2012/12/
18/global-religious-landscape-exec/; "Sub-Saharan Africa," in *The Future
of World Religions: Population Growth Projections, 2010–2050* (Washington, D.C.: Pew Research Center, 2015), 163–65, https://www.pewforum
.org/2015/04/02/sub-saharan-africa/; or *The Changing Global Religious
Landscape* (Washington, D.C.: Pew Research Center, 2017), https://www
.pewforum.org/2017/04/05/the-changing-global-religious-landscape/. For
a heroic effort to reconstruct historical populations, see Jan Lahmeyer, Po-
pulstat (website), http://www.populstat.info/.

8   John R. Weeks and Debbie L. Fugate, eds., *The Youth Bulge: Challenge
or Opportunity?* (New York: International Debate Education Association,
2012). For Fertilia and Sterilia, see Livi-Bacci, *A Concise History of World
Population*.

9   "Fertility Rates," OECD Data, https://data.oecd.org/pop/fertility-rates
.htm. For the rates of the most advanced nations, see Christine Tamir,
"G7 Nations Stand Out for Their Low Birth Rates, Aging Populations,"
Fact Tank (blog), Pew Research Center, August 23, 2019, https://www
.pewresearch.org/fact-tank/2019/08/23/g7-nations-stand-out-for-their-low
-birth-rates-aging-populations/.

10 "Country Comparison: Median Age," The World Factbook, Central Intelligence Agency, https://www.cia.gov/library/publications/the-world-factbook/fields/343rank.html. For Japan, see Toshihiko Hara, *A Shrinking Society: Post-demographic Transition in Japan* (Tokyo: Springer Japan, 2015).

11 Dirk J. van de Kaa, "Europe's Second Demographic Transition," *Population Bulletin* 42, no. 1 (1987): 1–57; Ron Lesthaeghe, "The Unfolding Story of the Second Demographic Transition," *Population and Development Review* 36, no. 2 (2010): 211–51; Ron Lesthaeghe, "The Second Demographic Transition: A Concise Overview of Its Development," *Proceedings of the National Academy of Sciences of the United States of America* 111, no. 51 (2014): 18112–15; Batool Zaidi and S. Philip Morgan, "The Second Demographic Transition Theory: A Review and Appraisal," *Annual Review of Sociology* 43, no. 1 (2017): 473–92.

12 Jean Raspail, *The Camp of the Saints*, trans. Norman Shapiro (New York: Scribner, 1975). For population fears and the related policies, see Matthew Connelly, *Fatal Misconception: The Struggle to Control World Population* (Cambridge, Mass.: Belknap Press of Harvard University Press, 2008); John F. May, *World Population Policies: Their Origin, Evolution, and Impact* (Dordrecht: Springer Netherlands, 2012); Richard Togman, *Nationalizing Sex: Fertility, Fear, and Power* (New York: Oxford University Press, 2019).

13 John C. Caldwell, "The Globalization of Fertility Behavior," in *Global Fertility Transition*, ed. Rodolfo A. Bulatao and John B. Casterline (New York: Population Council, 2001), 93–115.

14 Ellen Chesler and Terry McGovern, eds., *Women and Girls Rising: Progress and Resistance around the World* (New York: Routledge, 2016).

15 For the relationship between gender and demographic change, see the essays collected in Nancy E. Riley and Jan Brunson, eds., *International Handbook on Gender and Demographic Processes* (Dordrecht: Springer Netherlands, 2018).

16 For the impact of aging, see Susan A. McDaniel and Zachary Zimmer, eds., *Global Ageing in the Twenty-First Century: Challenges, Opportunities and Implications* (Farnham: Ashgate, 2013); Donald T. Rowland, *Population Aging: The Transformation of Societies* (Dordrecht: Springer Netherlands, 2012).

17 One excellent survey of religious demography is Todd M. Johnson and Brian J. Grim, *The World's Religions in Figures: An Introduction to International Religious Demography* (Malden, Mass.: Wiley-Blackwell, 2013).

18 Rachel M. McCleary, ed., *The Oxford Handbook of the Economics of Religion* (New York: Oxford University Press, 2011).

19 *The Gender Gap in Religion around the World* (Washington, D.C.: Pew Research Center, 2016), https://www.pewforum.org/2016/03/22/the-gender -gap-in-religion-around-the-world/; Marta Trzebiatowska and Steve Bruce, *Why Are Women More Religious Than Men?* (Oxford: Oxford University Press, 2012); Kristin Aune, Sonya Sharma, and Giselle Vincett, eds., *Women and Religion in the West: Challenging Secularization* (Aldershot: Ashgate, 2008).

20 Philip Jenkins, *God's Continent: Christianity, Islam, and Europe's Religious Crisis* (New York: Oxford University Press, 2007).

21 Alicia H. Munnell, Anqi Chen, and Geoffrey T. Sanzenbacher, *Is the Drop in Fertility Temporary or Permanent?* (Chestnut Hill, Mass.: Center for Retirement Research at Boston College, 2018), 6, https://crr.bc.edu/briefs/ is-the-drop-in-fertility-temporary-or-permanent/; Michael Hout, Andrew Greeley, and Melissa J. Wilde, "The Demographic Imperative in Religious Change in the United States," *American Journal of Sociology* 107, no. 2 (2001): 468–500; Kevin McQuillan, "When Does Religion Influence Fertility?" *Population and Development Review* 30, no. 1 (2004): 25–56; Renzo Derosas and Frans van Poppel, eds., *Religion and the Decline of Fertility in the Western World* (Dordrecht: Springer Netherlands, 2006); Eric P. Kaufmann and Vegard Skirbekk, "'Go Forth and Multiply': The Politics of Religious Demography," in *Political Demography: How Population Changes Are Reshaping International Security and National Politics*, ed. Jack A. Goldstone, Eric P. Kaufmann, and Monica Duffy Toft (Boulder: Paradigm, 2011), 194–211; Sandra Hubert, *The Impact of Religiosity on Fertility: A Comparative Analysis of France, Hungary, Norway, and Germany* (Wiesbaden: Springer VS, 2015); Nitzan Peri-Rotem, "Religion and Fertility in Western Europe: Trends across Cohorts in Britain, France and the Netherlands," *European Journal of Population* 32, no. 2 (2016): 231–65.

    Some important recent studies point to a steep fertility decline now occurring among conservative Protestants: see especially Samuel L. Perry and Cyrus Schleifer, "Are the Faithful Becoming Less Fruitful? The Decline of Conservative Protestant Fertility and the Growing Importance of Religious Practice and Belief in Childbearing in the US," *Social Science Research* 78 (2019): 137–55. Even so, monthly church attendance emerged as a factor combatting fertility decline.

22 Pippa Norris and Ronald Inglehart, *Sacred and Secular: Religion and Politics Worldwide*, 2nd ed. (New York: Cambridge University Press, 2011); Pippa Norris and Ronald Inglehart, "Are High Levels of Existential Security Conducive to Secularization? A Response to Our Critics," in *The*

Changing World Religion Map: Sacred Places, Identities, Practices and Politics, ed. Stanley D. Brunn (Dordrecht: Springer Netherlands, 2015), 5:3389–408.

23 Mark L. Haas, "A Geriatric Peace? The Future of U.S. Power in a World of Aging Populations," *International Security* 32, no. 1 (2007): 112–47; Jonathan V. Last, "Demography Is Destiny," *Weekly Standard*, April 23, 2012, https://www.washingtonexaminer.com/weekly-standard/demography-is -destiny.

24 For the origins of the Gibson quote, see Garson O'Toole, "The Future Has Arrived—It's Just Not Evenly Distributed Yet," Quote Investigator, January 24, 2012, https://quoteinvestigator.com/2012/01/24/future-has -arrived/.

25 Philip Jenkins, *The Next Christendom: The Coming of Global Christianity*, 3rd ed. (New York: Oxford University Press, 2011).

26 The fragment of Polybius is quoted from Bill Thayer, "Fragments of Book XXXVI," Polybius: The Histories (website), http://penelope.uchicago.edu/ Thayer/E/Roman/Texts/Polybius/36*.html.

27 Paul R. Ehrlich, *The Population Bomb* (New York: Ballantine, 1968); Harry Harrison, *Make Room! Make Room!* (New York: Doubleday, 1966). Compare John Brunner, *Stand on Zanzibar* (New York: Doubleday, 1968); Togman, *Nationalizing Sex*.

28 Ben J. Wattenberg, *The Birth Dearth: What Happens When People in Free Countries Don't Have Enough Babies?* (New York: Pharos, 1987); Doug Saunders, *The Myth of the Muslim Tide: Do Immigrants Threaten the West?* (New York: Vintage, 2012); Winter and Teitelbaum, *The Global Spread of Fertility Decline*; Andrew Brown, "The Myth of Eurabia: How a Far-Right Conspiracy Theory Went Mainstream," *Guardian*, August 16, 2019, https:// www.theguardian.com/world/2019/aug/16/the-myth-of-eurabia-how-a-far -right-conspiracy-theory-went-mainstream.

29 Margaret Atwood, *The Handmaid's Tale* (Toronto: McClelland & Stewart, 1985); P. D. James, *The Children of Men* (London: Faber & Faber, 1992). Compare Brian W. Aldiss' 1964 novel *Greybeard* (London: Faber & Faber) for a similar scenario.

30 Phillip Longman, *The Empty Cradle: How Falling Birthrates Threaten World Prosperity and What to Do about It* (New York: Basic Books, 2004); Fred R. Harris, ed., *The Baby Bust: Who Will Do the Work? Who Will Pay the Taxes?* (Lanham, Md.: Rowman & Littlefield, 2006); Richard Jackson, Neil Howe, Rebecca Strauss, and Keisuke Nakashima, *The Graying of the Great Powers: Demography and Geopolitics in the 21st Century* (Washington, D.C.: Center for Strategic & International Studies, 2008);

Fred Pearce, *The Coming Population Crash and Our Planet's Surprising Future* (Boston: Beacon Press, 2010); Ted C. Fishman, *Shock of Gray: The Aging of the World's Population and How It Pits Young against Old, Child against Parent, Worker against Boss, Company against Rival, and Nation against Nation* (New York: Scribner, 2010); Susan Yoshihara and Douglas A. Sylva, eds., *Population Decline and the Remaking of Great Power Politics* (Washington, D.C.: Potomac Books, 2011); Martin C. Libicki, Howard J. Shatz, and Julie E. Taylor, *Global Demographic Change and Its Implications for Military Power* (Santa Monica: RAND, 2011); Jorgen Randers, *2052: A Global Forecast for the Next Forty Years* (White River Junction, Vt.: Chelsea Green, 2012); Jonathan V. Last, *What to Expect When No One's Expecting: America's Coming Demographic Disaster* (New York: Encounter Books, 2013); *2050: Implications of Demographic Trends in the OSCE Region, Hearing before the Commission on Security and Cooperation in Europe*, 112th Cong., 1st sess. (2011). Darrell Bricker and John Ibbitson, *Empty Planet: The Shock of Global Population Decline* (New York: Random House, 2019). For aging, see Peter G. Peterson, *Gray Dawn: How the Coming Age Wave Will Transform America—and the World* (New York: Times Books, 1999); George Magnus, *The Age of Aging: How Demographics Are Changing the Global Economy and Our World* (Chichester: Wiley, 2012).

31 For more technical analyses of the relationship between religion and demography, see Derosas and van Poppel, *Religion and the Decline of Fertility*.

32 Callum G. Brown, *Religion and the Demographic Revolution: Women and Secularisation in Canada, Ireland, UK and USA since the 1960s* (Woodbridge: Boydell Press, 2012).

33 Mary Eberstadt, *How the West Really Lost God: A New Theory of Secularization* (West Conshohocken, Pa.: Templeton Press, 2013).

34 David P. Goldman, *How Civilizations Die (and Why Islam Is Dying Too)* (Washington, D.C.: Regnery, 2011).

35 Eric Kaufmann, *Shall the Religious Inherit the Earth? Demography and Politics in the Twenty-First Century* (London: Profile Books, 2011); Eric Kaufmann and W. Bradford Wilcox, eds., *Whither the Child? Causes and Consequences of Low Fertility* (Boulder: Paradigm, 2013). Compare Joshua Ramos, "Demographics as Destiny: Globalization and the Resurgence of Religion through Fertility," *Journal for Cultural and Religious Theory* 12, no. 3 (2013): 125–39; Marcin Stonawski, Vegard Skirbekk, Eric Kaufmann, and Anne Goujon, "The End of Secularisation through Demography? Projections of Spanish Religiosity," *Journal of Contempo-*

rary Religion 30, no. 1 (2015): 1–21; Eric Kaufmann, "Why Is Secularization Likely to Stall in America by 2050? A Response to Laurie DeRose," *Institute for Family Studies* (blog), July 24, 2019, https://ifstudies.org/blog/why-is-secularization-likely-to-stall-in-america-by-2050-a-response-to-laurie-derose.

2 Europe's Revolution

1   Russell Shorto, "No Babies?" *New York Times Magazine*, June 29, 2008; Massimo Livi-Bacci, *A Concise History of World Population*, 6th ed. (Hoboken, N.J.: John Wiley & Sons, 2017).

2   Emil Reich, *Germany's Swelled Head*, 2nd ed. (London: Melrose, 1914). For Germany, see Michael J. Kendzia and Klaus F. Zimmermann, "Celebrating 150 Years of Analyzing Fertility Trends in Germany" (Discussion Paper No. 6355, Forschungsinstitut zur Zukunft der Arbeit, Bonn, 2012).

3   Netherlands statistics are summarized at *Wikipedia*, s.v. "Demography of the Netherlands," last modified October 20, 2019, 21:54, https://en.wikipedia.org/wiki/Demography_of_the_Netherlands.

4   Guido Alfani and Cormac Ó Gráda, eds., *Famine in European History* (New York: Cambridge University Press, 2017). For death rates, see Richard G. Rogers and Eileen M. Crimmins, eds., *International Handbook of Adult Mortality* (Dordrecht: Springer Netherlands, 2011).

5   Carlo A. Corsini and Pier Paolo Viazzo, eds., *The Decline of Infant and Child Mortality: The European Experience, 1750–1990* (The Hague: Martinus Nijhoff, 1997). For infant mortality rates, see, for instance, "Netherlands—Infant Mortality Rate," World Data Atlas, Knoema, https://knoema.com/atlas/Netherlands/topics/Demographics/Mortality/Infant-mortality-rate; Peter Yin and Marsha Shine, "Misinterpretations of Increases in Life Expectancy in Gerontology Textbooks," *Gerontologist* 25, no. 1 (1985): 78–82.

6   Livi-Bacci, *A Concise History of World Population*; John Caldwell, "Social Upheaval and Fertility Decline," *Journal of Family History* 29, no. 4 (2004): 382–406; Renzo Derosas and Frans van Poppel, eds., *Religion and the Decline of Fertility in the Western World* (Dordrecht: Springer Netherlands, 2006); Jay Winter, "Demography," in *A Companion to World War I*, ed. John Horne (Chichester: Wiley-Blackwell, 2010), 248–62; Ian Kershaw, *To Hell and Back: Europe, 1914–1949* (New York: Viking, 2015).

7   Richard Togman, *Nationalizing Sex: Fertility, Fear, and Power* (New York: Oxford University Press, 2019).

8   For the 1930 encyclical *Casti Connubii*, see Pius XI, *Casti Connubii*, The Holy See, https://w2.vatican.va/content/pius-xi/en/encyclicals/documents/hf_p-xi_enc_19301231_casti-connubii.html. See also Trent MacNamara, *Birth Control and American Modernity: A History of Popular Ideas* (Cambridge: Cambridge University Press, 2018).

9   Steven Mihm, "How a Homemade Baby Boom May Be the Only Way to Save Us from Decline under Trump," *Dallas Morning News*, January 5, 2017, https://www.dallasnews.com/opinion/commentary/2017/01/05/baby-boom-just-grow-population-economy.

10 Clarence L. Barber, "On the Origins of the Great Depression," *Southern Economic Journal* 44, no. 3 (1978): 432–56; Claude Diebolt and Faustine Perrin, *Understanding Demographic Transitions: An Overview of French Historical Statistics* (Cham: Springer International, 2017); Herbert S. Klein, "The U.S. Baby Bust in Historical Perspective," in *The Baby Bust: Who Will Do the Work? Who Will Pay the Taxes?* ed. Fred R. Harris (Lanham, Md.: Rowman & Littlefield, 2006), 113–47.

11 C. M. Kornbluth, "The Marching Morons," *Galaxy Science Fiction*, April 1951, 128–58, https://archive.org/stream/Galaxy_v02n01_1951-04#page/n129/mode/2up; Allan C. Carlson, *The Swedish Experiment in Family Politics: The Myrdals and the Interwar Population Crisis* (New Brunswick, N.J.: Transaction, 1990); Lauren E. Forcucci, "Battle for Births: The Fascist Pronatalist Campaign in Italy 1925 to 1938," *Journal of the Society for the Anthropology of Europe* 10, no. 1 (2010): 4–13; Paul Morland, *The Human Tide: How Population Shaped the Modern World* (New York: Public Affairs, 2019).

12 Halvor Gille, "An International Survey of Recent Fertility Trends," in *Demographic and Economic Change in Developed Countries*, ed. George B. Roberts (New York: Columbia University Press, 1960), 17–35; Tomas Frejka and Jean-Paul Sardon, *Childbearing Trends and Prospects in Low-Fertility Countries: A Cohort Analysis* (Dordrecht: Kluwer Academic, 2004); Jeremy Greenwood, Ananth Seshadri, and Guillaume Vandenbroucke, "The Baby Boom and Baby Bust," *American Economic Review* 95, no. 1 (2005): 183–207.

13 David S. Reher, "Baby Booms, Busts, and Population Ageing in the Developed World," *Population Studies* 69, no. S1 (2015): S57–68.

14 Nicholas Crafts and Gianni Toniolo, eds., *Economic Growth in Europe since 1945* (New York: Cambridge University Press, 1996).

15 Herrick Chapman, *France's Long Reconstruction: In Search of the Modern Republic* (Cambridge, Mass.: Harvard University Press, 2018); Sarah

Fishman, *From Vichy to the Sexual Revolution: Gender and Family Life in Postwar France* (New York: Oxford University Press, 2017).

16 Corrado de Francesco, "The Growth and Crisis of Italian Higher Education during the 1960s and 1970s," *Higher Education* 7, no. 2 (1978): 193–212.

17 Ian Kershaw, *The Global Age: Europe, 1950–2017* (New York: Viking, 2018).

18 Gert Hekma and Alain Giami, eds., *Sexual Revolutions* (New York: Palgrave Macmillan, 2014).

19 Frejka and Sardon, *Childbearing Trends and Prospects.*

20 A rich source for European population data is Eurostat (website), https://ec.europa.eu/eurostat/web/population/overview.

21 For migrations, see Paul Ginsborg, *A History of Contemporary Italy: Society and Politics, 1943–1988* (New York: Palgrave Macmillan, 2003); Sergio del Molino, *La España vacía: Viaje por un país que nunca fue* (Madrid: Turner, 2016); Lorenzo Tondo, "Battle with Time: Italian Towns Face Demise by Depopulation," *Guardian*, July 12, 2019, https://www.theguardian.com/world/2019/jul/12/battle-with-time-italian-towns-face-demise-by-depopulation.

22 Eugenio F. Biagini and Mary E. Daly, eds., *The Cambridge Social History of Modern Ireland* (Cambridge: Cambridge University Press, 2017).

23 See Kershaw, *The Global Age*, for the political background.

24 "Country Comparison: Total Fertility Rate," The World Factbook, Central Intelligence Agency, https://www.cia.gov/library/publications/the-world-factbook/rankorder/2127rank.html. The tiny Faroe Islands, with a population of barely fifty thousand, actually ranked higher than France, but it scarcely counts as a nation.

25 Hardy Graupner, "German Population Plunge Expected," *Deutsche Welle*, November 7, 2006, https://www.dw.com/en/german-population-plunge-expected/a-2229744; "This Is What Italy's Population Will Look Like in 50 Years," *Local*, April 26, 2017, https://www.thelocal.it/20170426/this-is-how-italys-population-will-look-in-50-years-time; Amy Walker, "Birthrate in England and Wales at All-Time Low," *Guardian*, August 1, 2019, https://www.theguardian.com/lifeandstyle/2019/aug/01/birth-rate-in-england-and-wales-at-all-time-low; Peter Kotecki, "10 Countries at Risk of Becoming Demographic Time Bombs," *Business Insider*, August 8, 2018, https://www.businessinsider.com/10-countries-at-risk-of-becoming-demographic-time-bombs-2018-8.

26 Richard Vinen, *1968: Radical Protest and Its Enemies* (New York: Harper, 2018), 32; Callum G. Brown, *Religion and the Demographic Revolution:*

Women and Secularisation in Canada, Ireland, UK and USA since the 1960s (Woodbridge: Boydell Press, 2012).

27 Stanley Kurtz, "The End of Marriage in Scandinavia," *Weekly Standard*, February 2, 2004, https://www.washingtonexaminer.com/weekly -standard/the-end-of-marriage-in-scandinavia.

28 The quotation is from Joseph Chamie, "Out-of-Wedlock Births Rise Worldwide," *YaleGlobal Online* (blog), March 16, 2017, https://yaleglobal.yale .edu/content/out-wedlock-births-rise-worldwide; "43% of Births in the EU Are Now outside Marriage," Eurostat, August 9, 2018, https://ec.europa .eu/eurostat/web/products-eurostat-news/-/DDN-20180809-1.

29 "Country Comparison: Infant Mortality Rate," The World Factbook, Central Intelligence Agency, https://www.cia.gov/library/publications/the -world-factbook/rankorder/2091rank.html; Mark R. Montgomery and Barney Cohen, eds., *From Death to Birth: Mortality Decline and Reproductive Change* (Washington, D.C.: National Academies Press, 1998).

30 Nancy E. Riley and Jan Brunson, eds., *International Handbook on Gender and Demographic Processes* (Dordrecht: Springer Netherlands, 2018).

31 Andrew Brown and Linda Woodhead, *That Was the Church That Was: How the Church of England Lost the English People* (London: Bloomsbury, 2016), 16.

32 David E. Bloom, David Canning, and Jaypee Sevilla, *The Demographic Dividend: A New Perspective on the Economic Consequences of Population Change* (Santa Monica: RAND, 2003).

33 Eric Kaufmann and W. Bradford Wilcox, eds., *Whither the Child? Causes and Consequences of Low Fertility* (Boulder: Paradigm, 2013); Linda Hantrais, Dimiter Philipov, and Francesco C. Billari, *Policy Implications of Changing Family Formation: Study Prepared for the European Population Conference 2005* (Strasbourg: Council of Europe, 2006).

34 Livia Sz. Oláh, "Changing Families in the European Union: Trends and Policy Implications" (FamiliesAndSocieties Working Paper Series No. 44, 2015). For the "sex recession," see Greg Wilford, "Young Japanese People Are Not Having Sex," *Independent*, July 8, 2017, https://www.independent .co.uk/news/world/asia/japan-sex-problem-demographic-time-bomb-birth -rates-sex-robots-fertility-crisis-virgins-romance-porn-a7831041.html; Kate Julian, "Why Are Young People Having So Little Sex?" *Atlantic*, December 2018, https://www.theatlantic.com/magazine/archive/2018/12/the -sex-recession/573949/.

35 John Misachi, "Countries with the Highest Median Age," World Atlas, last modified October 13, 2017, https://www.worldatlas.com/articles/countries -with-the-highest-median-age.html; "Country Comparison: Median Age,"

The World Factbook, Central Intelligence Agency, https://www.cia.gov/library/publications/the-world-factbook/fields/343rank.html.

36 Jeff Desjardins, "Over the Next Year, Germany Will Hit a Scary Demographic Milestone," *Visual Capitalist* (blog), January 16, 2018, https://www.visualcapitalist.com/germany-scary-demographic-milestone/.

37 William Voegeli, "The Graying of the Welfare State," *National Review*, March 1, 2018, https://www.nationalreview.com/magazine/2018/03/19/welfare-state-cost-going-broke-population-ages/; Daron Acemoglu and Pascual Restrepo, "Secular Stagnation? The Effect of Aging on Economic Growth in the Age of Automation" (National Bureau of Economic Research Working Paper No. 23077, 2017).

38 Michaela Kreyenfeld and Dirk Konietzka, eds., *Childlessness in Europe: Contexts, Causes, and Consequences* (Cham: Springer International, 2017).

39 Pamela Beth Radcliff, *Modern Spain: 1808 to the Present* (Hoboken, N.J.: Wiley-Blackwell, 2017).

40 Biagini and Daly, *The Cambridge Social History of Modern Ireland.*

41 Howard Chiang, Anjali Arondekar, Marc Epprecht, Jennifer Evans, Ross G. Forman, Hanadi Al-Samman, Emily Skidmore, and Zeb Tortorici, eds, *Global Encyclopedia of Lesbian, Gay, Bisexual, Transgender, and Queer (LGBTQ) History* (Farmington Hills, Mich.: Charles Scribner's Sons, 2019).

42 Chiang et al., *Global Encyclopedia.*

43 Peter Gatrell, *The Unsettling of Europe: How Migration Reshaped a Continent* (New York: Basic Books, 2019). For Islam, see *Europe's Growing Muslim Population* (Washington, D.C.: Pew Research Center, 2017), https://www.pewforum.org/2017/11/29/europes-growing-muslim-population/. Several relevant essays can be found in Rogelio Sáenz, David G. Embrick, and Néstor P. Rodríguez, eds., *The International Handbook of the Demography of Race and Ethnicity* (Dordrecht: Springer Netherlands, 2015), including the studies by Elena Ambrosetti and Eralba Cela on Italy, Marie des Neiges Léonard on France, and Melissa F. Weiner on the Netherlands. For African migrants, see Stephen Smith, *The Scramble for Europe: Young Africa on Its Way to the Old Continent* (Cambridge: Polity, 2019).

44 Eric Kaufmann, *Whiteshift: Populism, Immigration and the Future of White Majorities* (London: Allen Lane, 2018). Compare Roger Eatwell and Matthew Goodwin, *National Populism: The Revolt against Liberal Democracy* (London: Pelican, 2018); Francis Fukuyama, *Identity: The De-*

mand for Dignity and the Politics of Resentment (New York: Farrar, Straus and Giroux, 2018); Morland, *The Human Tide.*

45 Derek Thompson, "The Doom Loop of Modern Liberalism," *Atlantic,* October 24, 2017, https://www.theatlantic.com/business/archive/2017/10/ immigration-modern-liberalism/543744/.

46 Günter Grass, *Headbirths: Or, the Germans Are Dying Out,* trans. Ralph Manheim (Boston, Mass.: Houghton Mifflin, 1990); Alejandro Macarrón Larumbe, *Demographic Suicide in the West and Half the World: Either More Births or Catastrophe?* (Scotts Valley, Calif.: CreateSpace, 2017). "Europe 2050: Demographic Suicide," Robert Schuman Foundation, February 12, 2018, https://www.robert-schuman.eu/en/european-issues/0462 -europe-2050-demographic-suicide.

47 Renaud Camus, *Le Grand Remplacement* (Paris: David Reinharc, 2011); "The Christchurch Manifesto: A Weapon for the Murderous Troll Culture of the Internet," *newsbeezer,* March 16, 2019, https://newsbeezer .com/canada/the-christchurch-manifesto-a-weapon-for-the-murderous -troll-culture-of-the-internet/; Angelique Chrisafis, "Right-Wing 'New Reactionaries' Stir Up Trouble among French Intellectuals," *Guardian,* October 9, 2015, https://www.theguardian.com/world/2015/oct/09/right -wing-new-reactionaries-stir-up-trouble-among-french-intellectuals; Kelly Weill, "From El Paso to Christchurch, a Racist Lie Is Fueling Terrorist Attacks," *Daily Beast,* August 5, 2019, https://www.thedailybeast.com/el -paso-shooting-racist-lie-great-replacement-fuels-terrorist-attacks.

48 Charles F. Westoff and Tomas Frejka, "Religiousness and Fertility among European Muslims," *Population and Development Review* 33, no. 4 (2007): 785–809; Jay Winter and Michael Teitelbaum, "Islam in Europe," chap. 3 in *The Global Spread of Fertility Decline: Population, Fear, and Uncertainty* (New Haven, Conn.: Yale University Press, 2013).

49 Paul Lendvai, *Orbán: Hungary's Strongman* (New York: Oxford University Press, 2017).

3 Spiritual and Secular

1 Throughout this chapter I will concentrate on Christian developments. Other religions of course had ancient roots in Europe, but Jews had suffered catastrophe in the 1940s, and Muslim populations were until recent times quite a marginal presence outside the Balkans and Southeastern Europe.

Philip Jenkins, "Is the EU's Flag Really a Marian Emblem with the Central Figure Removed?" *Aleteia* (blog), August 27, 2014, https://aleteia .org/2014/08/27/is-the-eus-flag-really-a-marian-emblem-with-the-central -figure-removed/; Grace Davie, *Religion in Modern Europe: A Memory*

Mutates (Oxford: Oxford University Press, 2000); Grace Davie, *Europe: The Exceptional Case; Parameters of Faith in the Modern World* (London: Darton, Longman & Todd, 2002); Peter Berger, Grace Davie, and Effie Fokas, *Religious America, Secular Europe? A Theme and Variations* (Burlington, Vt.: Ashgate, 2008); Detlef Pollack and Gergely Rosta, *Religion and Modernity: An International Comparison*, trans. David West (Oxford: Oxford University Press, 2017); Olivier Roy, *Is Europe Christian?* (London: Hurst, 2019). See also the essays in Abby Day and Mia Lövheim, eds., *Modernities, Memory and Mutations: Grace Davie and the Study of Religion* (Farnham: Ashgate, 2015).

2   Although see Eric Kaufmann, "Sacralization by Stealth? The Religious Consequences of Low Fertility in Europe," in *Whither the Child? Causes and Consequences of Low Fertility*, ed. Eric Kaufmann and W. Bradford Wilcox (Boulder: Paradigm, 2013), 135–56.

3   Philip Jenkins, *The Great and Holy War: How World War I Became a Religious Crusade* (San Francisco: HarperOne, 2014).

4   Philip Jenkins, *God's Continent* (New York: Oxford University Press, 2007).

5   Harry Post, *Pillarization: An Analysis of Dutch and Belgian Society* (London: Avebury, 1989).

6   Norman Barrymaine, *The Peter Townsend Story* (New York: Dutton, 1958).

7   Hugh McLeod and Werner Ustorf, eds., *The Decline of Christendom in Western Europe, 1750–2000* (Cambridge: Cambridge University Press, 2003); Nancy Christie and Michael Gauvreau, eds., *The Sixties and Beyond: Dechristianization in North America and Western Europe, 1945–2000* (Toronto: University of Toronto Press, 2013).

8   Quoted from Callum G. Brown, *The Death of Christian Britain: Understanding Secularisation, 1800–2000* (London: Routledge, 2009), 1. See also Steve Bruce, *God Is Dead: Secularization in the West* (Oxford: Blackwell, 2002); Robin Gill, *The "Empty" Church Revisited* (Aldershot: Ashgate, 2003); Callum G. Brown, *Religion and Society in Twentieth-Century Britain* (London: Pearson Longman, 2006); Jane Garnett, Matthew Grimley, Alana Harris, William Whyte, and Sarah Williams, eds., *Redefining Christian Britain: Post 1945 Perspectives* (London: SCM, 2007); Callum G. Brown, *Religion and the Demographic Revolution: Women and Secularisation in Canada, Ireland, UK and USA since the 1960s* (Woodbridge: Boydell Press, 2012); Clive D. Field, *Secularization in the Long 1960s: Numerating Religion in Britain* (Oxford: Oxford University Press, 2017). Grace Davie, *Religion in Britain since 1945: Believing without Belonging*

(Cambridge, Mass.: Blackwell, 1994); and Grace Davie, *Religion in Britain: A Persistent Paradox*, 2nd ed. (Oxford: Wiley-Blackwell, 2015). For longer-term trends, see S. J. D. Green, *The Passing of Protestant England: Secularisation and Social Change, c. 1920–1960* (Cambridge: Cambridge University Press, 2010).

9 Harriet Sherwood, "Attendance at Church of England's Sunday Services Falls Again," *Guardian*, November 14, 2018, https://www.theguardian.com/world/2018/nov/14/attendance-church-of-england-sunday-services-falls-again.

10 Kate Connolly, "Atheist Berlin to Decide on Religion's Place in Its Schools," *Guardian*, April 26, 2009, https://www.theguardian.com/world/2009/apr/26/berlin-germany-religious-education-ethics; Damian Thompson, "2067: The End of British Christianity," *Spectator*, June 13, 2015, https://www.spectator.co.uk/2015/06/2067-the-end-of-british-christianity/; Adam Becket, "Number of Self-Identifying Anglicans Falls," *Church Times*, July 11, 2019, https://www.churchtimes.co.uk/articles/2019/12-july/news/uk/number-of-self-identifying-anglicans-falls.

11 Alexandra Gowling, "Christian Practice in the Netherlands Drops to Its Lowest Point," *I Am Expat* (blog), April 29, 2014, https://www.iamexpat.nl/expat-info/dutch-expat-news/christian-practice-netherlands-drops-its-lowest-point; Naftali Bendavid, "Europe's Empty Churches Go on Sale," *Wall Street Journal*, January 2, 2015, https://www.wsj.com/articles/europes-empty-churches-go-on-sale-1420245359; Jonathan Evans, "Once a Majority, Protestants Now Account for Fewer Than a Third of Germans," *Fact Tank* (blog), Pew Research Center, February 12, 2019, https://www.pewresearch.org/fact-tank/2019/02/12/once-a-majority-protestants-now-account-for-fewer-than-a-third-of-germans/; "German Churches to See Sharp Drop in Membership by 2060," *Fox News*, May 2, 2019, https://www.foxnews.com/world/german-churches-to-see-sharp-drop-in-membership-by-2060; Tom Heneghan, "One Fifth of All Dutch Churches Now Converted to Secular Use," *Tablet*, July 1, 2019, https://www.thetablet.co.uk/news/11831/one-fifth-of-all-dutch-churches-now-converted-to-secular-use; Christa Pongratz-Lippitt, "Latest Statistics Show German Church Faces Massive Exodus," *Tablet*, July 25, 2019, https://www.thetablet.co.uk/news/11900/latest-statistics-show-german-church-faces-massive-exodus; Christof Wolf, "How Secularized Is Germany? Cohort and Comparative Perspectives," *Social Compass* 55, no. 2 (2008): 111–26; Phil Zuckerman, "Why Are Danes and Swedes So Irreligious?" *Nordic Journal of Religion and Society* 22, no. 1 (2009): 55–69.

Several relevant essays may be found in Callum G. Brown and Michael Snape, eds., *Secularisation in the Christian World* (Farnham: Ashgate, 2010). See especially Peter van Rooden, "The Strange Death of Dutch Christendom"; Erik Sidenvall, "A Classic Case of De-Christianisation?"; and Lucian Holscher, "Europe in the Age of Secularisation." See also Detlef Pollack, Olaf Müller, and Gert Pickel, eds., *The Social Significance of Religion in the Enlarged Europe: Secularization, Individualization and Pluralization* (Farnham: Ashgate, 2012); Joep de Hart, Paul Dekker, and Loek Halman, eds., *Religion and Civil Society in Europe* (Dordrecht: Springer Netherlands, 2013).

12 Gabriella Swerling, "Record Low as 25pc of Marriages Are Religious Ceremonies, as Weddings Become 'More Social, Less Sacred,'" *Telegraph*, March 28, 2019, https://www.telegraph.co.uk/news/2019/03/28/record-low-25-marriages-religious-ceremonies-weddings-become/; Tom Heyden, "10 Ways Christening Has Changed," *BBC News Magazine*, October 23, 2013, https://www.bbc.com/news/magazine-24565994.

13 Christa Pongratz-Lippitt, "Archdiocese of Vienna to Undergo Radical Parish Reform," *National Catholic Reporter*, October 8, 2012, https://www.ncronline.org/news/world/archdiocese-vienna-undergo-radical-parish-reform; Marco Tosatti, "Return of the Vocations Crisis," *First Things*, August 10, 2017, https://www.firstthings.com/web-exclusives/2017/08/return-of-the-vocations-crisis; Jonathan Luxmoore, "Europe's Church Creatively Rethinks as Numbers Plummet," *National Catholic Reporter*, November 15, 2017, https://www.ncronline.org/news/world/europes-church-creatively-rethinks-numbers-plummet.

14 For the Augustinians, see Bendavid, "Europe's Empty Churches Go on Sale"; Jonathan Luxmoore, "Last Orders? Spain's Vanishing Monasteries," *Catholic Herald*, December 6, 2018, https://catholicherald.co.uk/magazine/spains-religious-communities-are-disappearing-at-a-rate-of-more-than-100-a-year/; "Pope Laments 'Hemorrhaging' of Priests and Nuns in Europe," *Religion News Service*, May 21, 2018, https://religionnews.com/2018/05/21/bc-eu-rel-vatican-priest-shortage1st-ld-writethru/.

15 Emily Liner, "Emily Liner on the Dwindling Numbers of Practicing Catholics in France," *Berkley Center for Religion, Peace & World Affairs* (blog), Georgetown University, March 1, 2007, https://berkleycenter.georgetown.edu/posts/emily-liner-on-the-dwindling-numbers-of-practicing-catholics-in-france; Palash Ghosh, "The Church in Decline: France's Vanishing Catholics," *International Business Times*, March 14, 2013, https://www.ibtimes.com/church-decline-frances-vanishing-catholics-1125241; Luxmoore, "Europe's Church Creatively Rethinks as Numbers Plummet."

16 "Religious Identity," in *Being Christian in Western Europe* (Washington, D.C.: Pew Research Center, 2018), 81–94, https://www.pewforum.org/2018/05/29/religious-identity/; Franco Garelli, "Religion and Civil Society in Italy and Other Latin Countries," in *Religion and Civil Society in Europe*, ed. Joep de Hart, Paul Dekker, and Loek Halman (Dordrecht: Springer Netherlands, 2013), 125–45.

17 Pollack and Rosta, *Religion and Modernity*; "Religious Commitment and Practices," in *Religious Belief and National Belonging in Central and Eastern Europe* (Washington, D.C.: Pew Research Center, 2017), 69–81, https://www.pewforum.org/2017/05/10/religious-commitment-and-practices/.

18 "How Religious Commitment Varies by Country among People of All Ages," in *The Age Gap in Religion around the World* (Washington, D.C.: Pew Research Center, 2018), 50–58, https://www.pewforum.org/2018/06/13/how-religious-commitment-varies-by-country-among-people-of-all-ages/. For "feeling religious," see Oliver Smith, "Mapped: The World's Most (and Least) Religious Countries," *Telegraph*, January 14, 2018, https://www.telegraph.co.uk/travel/maps-and-graphics/most-religious-countries-in-the-world/.

19 *Being Christian in Western Europe*, 38, https://www.pewforum.org/2018/05/29/being-christian-in-western-europe/pf_05-29-18_religion-western-europe-00-15/; "Two-Thirds of People in Netherlands Have No Religious Faith," *Dutch News*, March 14, 2016, https://www.dutchnews.nl/news/2016/03/two-thirds-of-people-in-netherlands-have-no-religious-faith/; Harriet Sherwood, "Church in Crisis as Only 2% of Young Adults Identify as C of E," *Guardian*, September 7, 2018, https://www.theguardian.com/world/2018/sep/07/church-in-crisis-as-only-2-of-young-adults-identify-as-c-of-e; Gabriella Swerling, "Atheism and Islam on the Rise in the UK as Christianity Suffers 'Dramatic Decline,'" *Telegraph*, July 11, 2019, https://www.telegraph.co.uk/news/2019/07/11/atheism-islam-rise-uk-christianity-suffers-dramatic-decline/.

20 *Eastern and Western Europeans Differ on Importance of Religion, Views of Minorities, and Key Social Issues* (Washington, D.C.: Pew Research Center, 2018), https://www.pewforum.org/2018/10/29/eastern-and-western-europeans-differ-on-importance-of-religion-views-of-minorities-and-key-social-issues/; Connolly, "Atheist Berlin to Decide on Religion's Place in Its Schools"; Lois Lee, *Recognizing the Non-religious: Reimagining the Secular* (Oxford: Oxford University Press, 2015).

21 Richard Allen Greene, "Organized Religion 'Will Be Driven Toward Extinction' in 9 Countries, Experts Predict," *Belief* (blog), CNN, March 23,

2011, http://religion.blogs.cnn.com/2011/03/23/religion-to-go-extinct-in -9-countries-experts-predict/.

22 Sandra Hubert, *The Impact of Religiosity on Fertility: A Comparative Analysis of France, Hungary, Norway, and Germany* (Wiesbaden: Springer VS, 2015).

23 For the role of children in shaping religion, see the essays in Kaufmann and Wilcox, *Whither the Child?*

24 Robert Wuthnow, *After the Baby Boomers: How Twenty- and Thirty-Somethings Are Shaping the Future of American Religion* (Princeton, N.J.: Princeton University Press, 2007), 51–70.

25 For the political context, see John Pollard, *Catholicism in Modern Italy: Religion, Society and Politics since 1861* (New York: Routledge, 2008).

26 Josephine McKenna, "Number of Priests and Nuns in Marked Decline," *Telegraph*, June 6, 2013, https://www.telegraph.co.uk/news/worldnews/ europe/vaticancityandholysee/10103961/Number-of-priests-and-nuns-in -marked-decline.html.

27 The literature on death, dying, and preparation for death is vast for the medieval and early modern periods.

28 Philip Larkin, "Aubade," All Poetry, https://allpoetry.com/poem/8495769 -Aubade-by-Philip-Larkin.

29 Jenkins, *The Great and Holy War*; Owen Davies, *A Supernatural War: Magic, Divination, and Faith during the First World War* (New York: Oxford University Press, 2018).

30 Mark Donnelly, *Sixties Britain: Culture, Society and Politics* (New York: Routledge, 2013); David Kynaston, *Modernity Britain, 1957–1962* (London: Bloomsbury, 2013); Dominic Sandbrook, *White Heat: A History of Britain in the Swinging Sixties* (London: Little, Brown, 2006).

31 For disaffiliation from the church, see Stephen Bullivant, *Mass Exodus: Catholic Disaffiliation in Britain and America since Vatican II* (Oxford: Oxford University Press, 2019); and Stephen Bullivant, "When 'No Change' Changed Everything," *Catholic Herald*, July 19, 2018, https://catholicherald .co.uk/magazine/when-no-change-changed-everything/. For confession, see John Cornwell, *The Dark Box: A Secret History of Confession* (New York: Basic Books, 2014).

32 Stephen Bullivant, "The Scary Truth about Young Europeans and the Church," *Catholic Herald*, March 22, 2018, https://catholicherald.co.uk/ issues/march-23rd-2018/the-scary-truth-about-young-europeans-and-the -church/; Philip Jenkins, "Europe, Secular by Default," *Christian Century*, June 6, 2018, 44–45.

33 *Eastern and Western Europeans Differ on Importance of Religion, Views of Minorities, and Key Social Issues.*

34 In what follows I draw heavily on Charlotte Allen, "Belgium after Danneels," *First Things*, April 4, 2019, https://www.firstthings.com/web-exclusives/2019/04/belgium-after-danneels.

35 The quote is from Jon Anderson, "Belgium's Crisis of Faith," *Catholic Herald*, October 15, 2015, https://catholicherald.co.uk/issues/october-16th-2015-2/belgiums-crisis-of-faith/. See also "Belgian Catholic Baptisms in Major Decline amid Rise of Evangelicals and Muslims," *Christian Daily Journal*, March 13, 2018, https://christiandailyjournal.com/2018/03/13/belgian-catholic-baptisms-major-decline-amid-rise-evangelicals-muslims/; Florence Taylor, "Belgium: More than 100 Churches at Risk of Closure under Archbishop's Plan," *Christian Today*, June 14, 2016, https://www.christiantoday.com/article/belgium-more-than-100-churches-at-risk-of-closure-under-archbishops-plan/88310.htm.

36 *Eastern and Western Europeans Differ on Importance of Religion, Views of Minorities, and Key Social Issues.*

37 *Religious Belief and National Belonging in Central and Eastern Europe.*

38 Philip Jenkins, "Far-Right Piety in Poland," *Christian Century*, August 1, 2018, 44–45.

39 Brian Stanley, *Christianity in the Twentieth Century: A World History* (Princeton, N.J.: Princeton University Press, 2018); Bullivant, *Mass Exodus.*

40 Philip Jenkins, "Decline and Scandal," *Christian Century*, June 15, 2010, 45.

41 Matthew Day, "Polish Catholic Church Expects 'Wave' of Child Sex Abuse Reports after Release of Film on Paedophilia," *Telegraph*, May 15, 2019, https://www.telegraph.co.uk/news/2019/05/15/polish-catholic-church-expects-wave-child-sex-abuse-reports/.

42 David Martin, *A General Theory of Secularization* (New York: Harper and Row, 1978); Rob Warner, *Secularization and Its Discontents* (New York: Continuum, 2010); Brown and Snape, *Secularisation in the Christian World*; Craig Calhoun, Mark Juergensmeyer, and Jonathan VanAntwerpen, eds., *Rethinking Secularism* (New York: Oxford University Press, 2011); Steve Bruce, *Secularization: In Defence of an Unfashionable Theory* (Oxford: Oxford University Press, 2011); Detlef Pollack, *Säkularisierung–ein moderner Mythos? Studien zum religiösen Wandel in Deutschland*, 2nd ed. (Tübingen: Mohr Siebeck, 2012); Phil Zuckerman and John R. Shook, eds., *The Oxford Handbook of Secularism* (New York: Oxford University Press, 2017).

For attacks on the theory, see Rodney Stark and Laurence R. Iannaccone, "A Supply-Side Reinterpretation of the 'Secularization' of Europe," *Journal for the Scientific Study of Religion* 33, no. 3 (1994): 230–52; Rodney Stark, "Secularization, R.I.P.," *Sociology of Religion* 60, no. 3 (1999): 249–73; Monica Duffy Toft, Daniel Philpott, and Timothy Samuel Shah, *God's Century: Resurgent Religion and Global Politics* (New York: W. W. Norton, 2011).

43 De Hart, Dekker, and Halman, *Religion and Civil Society in Europe*, 1.

44 Richard John Neuhaus, "Secularization Doesn't Just Happen," *First Things*, March 2005, https://www.firstthings.com/article/2005/03/secularization -doesnt-just-happen; Phil Zuckerman, Luke W. Galen, and Frank L. Pasquale, *The Nonreligious: Understanding Secular People and Societies* (New York: Oxford University Press, 2016).

45 Davie, *Religion in Britain since 1945*; Abby Day, *Believing in Belonging: Belief and Social Identity in the Modern World* (Oxford: Oxford University Press, 2011). But see also David Voas and Alasdair Crockett, "Religion in Britain: Neither Believing nor Belonging," *Sociology* 39, no. 1 (2005): 11–28.

46 Zuckerman, Galen, and Pasquale, *The Nonreligious*.

47 Tom Stoppard, *Jumpers* (London: Faber, 1972), act 1; Stephen Bullivant and Michael Ruse, eds., *The Oxford Handbook of Atheism* (Oxford: Oxford University Press, 2013); Callum G. Brown, *Becoming Atheist: Humanism and the Secular West* (London: Bloomsbury Academic, 2017).

48 *Eastern and Western Europeans Differ on Importance of Religion, Views of Minorities, and Key Social Issues*; Neha Sahgal, "10 Key Findings about Religion in Western Europe," *Fact Tank* (blog), Pew Research Center, May 29, 2018, https://www.pewresearch.org/fact-tank/2018/05/29/10-key -findings-about-religion-in-western-europe/.

49 *Being Christian in Western Europe*.

50 For new and diverse forms of spirituality, see Christopher Partridge, *The Re-enchantment of the West*, 2 vols. (London: T&T Clark International, 2004–2006); Paul Heelas and Linda Woodhead, with Benjamin Seel, Bronislaw Szerszynski, and Karin Tusting, *The Spiritual Revolution: Why Religion Is Giving Way to Spirituality* (Oxford: Blackwell, 2005); Kristin Aune, Sonya Sharma, and Giselle Vincett, eds., *Women and Religion in the West: Challenging Secularization* (Aldershot: Ashgate, 2008); Harvey G. Cox and Daisaku Ikeda, *The Persistence of Religion: Comparative Perspectives on Modern Spirituality* (London: I.B. Tauris, 2009); Grace Davie, "Resacralization," in *The New Blackwell Companion to the Sociology of Religion*, ed. Bryan S. Turner (Oxford: Wiley-Blackwell, 2010), 160–77;

Linda A. Mercadante, *Belief without Borders: Inside the Minds of the Spiritual But not Religious* (New York: Oxford University Press, 2014).

51 Philip Jenkins, *God's Continent: Christianity, Islam, and Europe's Religious Crisis* (New York: Oxford University Press, 2007).

52 Helena Vilaça, Enzo Pace, Inger Furseth, and Per Pettersson, eds., *The Changing Soul of Europe: Religions and Migrations in Northern and Southern Europe* (Farnham: Ashgate, 2014); *Europe's Growing Muslim Population* (Washington, D.C.: Pew Research Center, 2017), https://www.pewforum.org/2017/11/29/europes-growing-muslim-population/; David Goodhew and Antony-Paul Cooper, eds., *The Desecularisation of the City: London's Churches, 1980 to the Present* (London: Routledge, 2019).

53 David Garbin and Anna Strhan, eds., *Religion and the Global City* (London: Bloomsbury Academic, 2017).

54 See also Andrew M. Greeley, *Religion in Europe at the End of the Second Millennium* (London: Transaction, 2003).

4 The Revolution Goes Global

1 Jill Lepore, "What 2018 Looked Like Fifty Years Ago," *New Yorker*, January 7, 2019, https://www.newyorker.com/magazine/2019/01/07/what-2018-looked-like-fifty-years-ago.

2 Richard Togman, *Nationalizing Sex: Fertility, Fear, and Power* (New York: Oxford University Press, 2019).

3 Antoine van Agtmael, *The Emerging Markets Century: How a New Breed of World-Class Companies Is Overtaking the World* (New York: Free Press, 2007); Rajiv Biswas, *Emerging Markets Megatrends* (Cham: Palgrave Macmillan, 2018).

4 "Completing the Fertility Transition," United Nations Department of Economic and Social Affairs: Population Division, https://www.un.org/en/development/desa/population/publications/fertility/fertility-transition.asp; Tomas Frejka, "Half the World's Population Is Reaching below Replacement Fertility," *Institute for Family Studies* (blog), December 11, 2017, https://ifstudies.org/blog/half-the-worlds-population-is-reaching-below-replacement-fertility; James Gallagher, "'Remarkable' Decline in Fertility Rates," *BBC News*, November 9, 2018, https://www.bbc.com/news/health-46118103; Colin Lloyd, "Demographic Decline: Opportunity or Threat?" American Institute of Economic Research, September 2019, https://www.aier.org/article/demographic-decline-opportunity-or-threat/; Andre Tartar, Hannah Recht, and Yue Qiu, "The Global Fertility Crash," *Bloomberg Business Week*, October 30, 2019, https://www.bloomberg.com/graphics/2019-global-fertility-crash/.

5   Ben J. Wattenberg, "It Will Be a Smaller World After All," *New York Times*, March 8, 2003, https://www.nytimes.com/2003/03/08/opinion/it -will-be-a-smaller-world-after-all.html.

6   Hannah Ritchie and Max Roser, "Urbanization," Our World in Data, September 2018, https://ourworldindata.org/urbanization.

7   Nancy Birdsall, Allen C. Kelley, and Steven W. Sinding, eds., *Population Matters: Demographic Change, Economic Growth, and Poverty in the Developing World* (New York: Oxford University Press, 2003).

8   Ha-Joon Chang, *The East Asian Development Experience: The Miracle, the Crisis and the Future* (London: Zed Books, 2006); Michael R. Auslin, *The End of the Asian Century: War, Stagnation, and the Risks to the World's Most Dynamic Region* (New Haven, Conn.: Yale University Press, 2017).

9   Yu-Hua Chen, "Trends in Low Fertility and Policy Responses in Taiwan," *Japanese Journal of Population* 10, no. 1 (2012): 78–88; James C. T. Hsueh, "Five Stages of Demographic Transition in Taiwan," *Institute for Family Studies* (blog), February 4, 2019, https://ifstudies.org/blog/ five-stages-of-demographic-transition-in-taiwan; Benjamin Haas, "South Korea's Fertility Rate Set to Hit Record Low of 0.96," *Guardian*, September 3, 2018, https://www.theguardian.com/world/2018/sep/03/south -koreas-fertility-rate-set-to-hit-record-low; Elizabeth Llorente, "Women in South Korea Increasingly Rejecting Marriage, Motherhood, Sparking Declining Birth Rates and Workforce," *Fox News*, July 25, 2019, https:// www.foxnews.com/world/women-in-south-korea-increasingly-rejecting -marriage-motherhood-sparking-declining-birth-rates-and-workforce; Jiyeun Lee, "Korea Baby Bust Pushes World's Lowest Birth Rate Even Lower," *Bloomberg*, August 28, 2019, https://www.bloomberg.com/news/ articles/2019-08-28/korea-baby-bust-pushes-world-s-lowest-birth-rate -even-lower.

10 Joshua R. Goldstein, Tomáš Sobotka, and Aiva Jasilioniene, "The End of 'Lowest-Low' Fertility?" *Population and Development Review* 35, no. 4 (2009): 663–99. For the rank order of TFRs, see "Country Comparison: Total Fertility Rate," The World Factbook, Central Intelligence Agency, https://www.cia.gov/library/publications/the-world-factbook/rankorder/ 2127rank.html. For responses to aging, see Cristina Martinez, Tamara Weyman, and Jouke van Dijk, eds., *Demographic Transition, Labour Markets and Regional Resilience* (Cham: Springer International, 2017).

11 "Country Comparison: Median Age," The World Factbook, Central Intelligence Agency, https://www.cia.gov/library/publications/the-world-factbook/ fields/343rank.html; Tim Harper and Sunil S. Amrith, eds., *Histories of*

Health in Southeast Asia: Perspectives on the Long Twentieth Century (Bloomington: Indiana University Press, 2014).

12 Fertility rate figures from "Fertility Rate, Total (Births per Woman)," The World Bank: Data, https://data.worldbank.org/indicator/SP.DYN.TFRT .IN.

13 "East Asia/Southeast Asia: Philippines," The World Factbook, Central Intelligence Agency, https://www.cia.gov/library/publications/the-world -factbook/geos/rp.html.

14 Gyan Prakash, *Emergency Chronicles: Indira Gandhi and Democracy's Turning Point* (Princeton, N.J.: Princeton University Press, 2019).

15 Richard Madsen, "Secularism, Religious Change, and Social Conflict in Asia," in *Rethinking Secularism*, ed. Craig Calhoun, Mark Juergensmeyer, and Jonathan VanAntwerpen (New York: Oxford University Press, 2011), 248–69.

16 Toshihiko Hara, *A Shrinking Society: Post-demographic Transition in Japan* (Tokyo: Springer Japan, 2015); Jay Winter and Michael Teitelbaum, "Japan: Family Structure, Abortion, and Fertility since 1945," chap. 6 in *The Global Spread of Fertility Decline: Population, Fear, and Uncertainty* (New Haven, Conn.: Yale University Press, 2013).

17 Jason Ānanda Josephson, "The Paradoxes of Secularism in Contemporary Japan," *Nonreligion & Secularity* (blog), October 13, 2014, https:// blog.nsrn.net/2014/10/13/the-paradoxes-of-secularism-in-contemporary -japan/.

18 Kyoko Kimpara, "Religion and the Secular State in Japan," in *Religion and the Secular State: National Reports*, ed. Javier Martínez-Torrón and W. Cole Durham Jr. (Madrid: Servicio de Publicaciones de la Facultad de Derecho de la Universidad Complutense, 2014), 471–78.

19 Ronald Inglehart and Wayne E. Baker, "Modernization, Cultural Change, and the Persistence of Traditional Values," *American Sociological Review* 65, no. 1 (2000): 19–51.

20 Ian Reader, "Buddhism in Crisis? Institutional Decline in Modern Japan," *Buddhist Studies Review* 28, no. 2 (2011): 233–63; "Kyoto-Based Buddhist Group Struggles with Decline in Temples and Priests," *Japan Times*, April 24, 2017, https://www.japantimes.co.jp/news/2017/04/24/ national/kyoto-based-buddhist-group-struggles-decline-temples-priests/# .XOb0i6YpB-g. For the impact of contemporary trends in globalization, and especially gender, across the Buddhist world, see Hanna Havnevik, Ute Hüsken, Mark Teeuwen, Vladimir Tikhonov, and Koen Wellens, eds., *Buddhist Modernities: Re-inventing Tradition in the Globalizing Modern World* (New York: Routledge, 2017); Michael Jerryson, ed., *The Oxford*

Handbook of Contemporary Buddhism (New York: Oxford University Press, 2017).

21   Eric Talmadge, "In Japan, Shinto Struggles for Relevance," *Chron*, November 13, 2004, https://www.chron.com/life/houston-belief/article/In-Japan-Shinto-struggles-for-relevance-1516693.php; Justin McCurry, "Zen No More: Japan Shuns Its Buddhist Traditions as Temples Close," *Guardian*, November 6, 2015, https://www.theguardian.com/world/2015/nov/06/zen-no-more-japan-shuns-its-buddhist-traditions-as-temples-close; Isabel Reynolds, "Japan's Shinto Shrines in Crisis despite Abe Pushing Religion," *Bloomberg*, May 23, 2016, https://www.bloomberg.com/news/articles/2016-05-23/abe-shines-spotlight-on-japan-s-shinto-shrines-in-grip-of-crisis; Alana Semuels, "Can Anything Stop Rural Decline?" *Atlantic*, August 23, 2017, https://www.theatlantic.com/business/archive/2017/08/japan-rural-decline/537375/.

22   Steven Borowiec, "Why Young South Koreans Are Turning Away from Religion," *Al Jazeera*, May 28, 2017, https://www.aljazeera.com/indepth/features/2017/05/young-south-koreans-turning-religion-170524144746222.html.

23   Lucy Williamson, "South Korea's Buddhists [*sic*] Monks Tackle Modern Challenges," *BBC News*, June 27, 2012, https://www.bbc.com/news/world-asia-18482726; Ben Jackson, "Karma Back! Buddhist Ad Campaign Tries to Reverse Falling Numbers," *Korea Exposé*, January 30, 2018, http://www.koreaexpose.com/buddhist-south-korea-declining-jogye/.

24   "Young Adults around the World Are Less Religious by Several Measures," in *The Age Gap in Religion around the World* (Washington, D.C.: Pew Research Center, 2018), 30–49, https://www.pewforum.org/2018/06/13/young-adults-around-the-world-are-less-religious-by-several-measures/.

25   Nick Street, "How Korea's 'Nones' Differ from Religiously Unaffiliated Americans," Center for Religion and Civic Culture, USC Dornsife, February 24, 2016, https://crcc.usc.edu/how-korean-religious-nones-differ-from-unaffiliated-americans/.

26   Thomas Fuller, "Monks Lose Relevance as Thailand Grows Richer," *New York Times*, December 19, 2012, https://www.nytimes.com/2012/12/19/world/asia/thai-buddhist-monks-struggle-to-stay-relevant.html; "Decline of Buddhism in Thailand," *Religion & Ethics Newsweekly*, May 24, 2013, https://www.pbs.org/wnet/religionandethics/2013/05/24/may-24-2013-decline-of-buddhism-in-thailand/18432/.

27   "Scandal-Hit Thai Temple Helps to Stage Mass Buddhist Event in Myanmar," *Reuters*, January 21, 2018, https://www.reuters.com/article/us-myanmar-buddhism/scandal-hit-thai-temple-helps-to-stage-mass-buddhist-event-in-myanmar-idUSKBN1FA0LS; George Styllis, "Thai

Crackdown Targets Buddhist Monks amid Accusations of Embezzlement and Fraud," *Washington Post*, June 24, 2018, https://www.washingtonpost .com/world/asia_pacific/thai-crackdown-targets-buddhist-monks-amid -accusations-of-embezzlement-and-fraud/2018/06/24/67847242-7000 -11e8-bd50-b80389a4e569_story.html.

28 Howard Chiang, Anjali Arondekar, Marc Epprecht, Jennifer Evans, Ross G. Forman, Hanadi Al-Samman, Emily Skidmore, and Zeb Tortorici, eds., *Global Encyclopedia of Lesbian, Gay, Bisexual, Transgender, and Queer (LGBTQ) History* (Farmington Hills, Mich.: Charles Scribner's Sons, 2019).

29 Shannon van Sant, "Taiwan Celebrates Same-Sex Marriage with a Mass Wedding Banquet," *NPR*, May 26, 2019, https://www.npr.org/2019/05/26/ 727139304/taiwan-celebrates-same-sex-marriage-with-a-mass-wedding -banquet.

30 Thomas Scharping, *Birth Control in China, 1949–2000: Population Policy and Demographic Development* (London: Routledge, 2002); Isabelle At-tané and Baochang Gu, eds., *Analysing China's Population: Social Change in a New Demographic Era* (Dordrecht: Springer Netherlands, 2014).

31 Scott Neuman and Rob Schmitz, "Despite the End of China's One-Child Policy, Births Are Still Lagging," *NPR*, July 16, 2018, https://www.npr .org/2018/07/16/629361870/despite-the-end-of-chinas-one-child-policy -births-are-still-lagging; Mei Fong, "China's Lost Little Emperors . . . How the 'One-Child Policy' Will Haunt the Country for Decades," *Guardian*, September 2, 2018, https://www.theguardian.com/commentisfree/2018/ sep/02/chinas-lost-little-emperors-how-the-one-child-policy-will-haunt-the -nation-for-decades.

32 "How Religious Commitment Varies by Country among People of All Ages," in *The Age Gap in Religion around the World* (Washington, D.C.: Pew Research Center, 2018), 50–58, https://www.pewforum.org/2018/06/ 13/how-religious-commitment-varies-by-country-among-people-of-all-ages/; Ian Johnson, *The Souls of China: The Return to Religion after Mao* (New York: Vintage, 2017).

33 "Chile—Total Fertility Rate," World Data Atlas, Knoema, https://knoema .com/atlas/Chile/topics/Demographics/Fertility/Fertility-rate.

34 For Mexico's fertility rate, see "Mexico—Total Fertility Rate," World Data Atlas, Knoema, https://knoema.com/atlas/Mexico/Fertility-rate; "Mexico—Total Fertility Rate," World Data Atlas, Knoema, https://knoema.com/atlas/ Mexico/topics/Demographics/Fertility/Fertility-rate.

35 Philip Jenkins, "A Secular Latin America?" *Christian Century*, March 20, 2013, 45.

36 *Religion in Latin America: Widespread Change in a Historically Catholic Region* (Washington, D.C.: Pew Research Center, 2014), https://www.pewforum.org/2014/11/13/religion-in-latin-america/.

37 *Religion in Latin America.*

38 *The Age Gap in Religion around the World.*

39 Anna-Catherine Brigida, "Latin America Has Become an Unlikely Leader in LGBT Rights," *Quartz*, June 6, 2018, https://qz.com/1288320/despite-its-catholic-roots-latin-america-has-become-an-unlikely-lgbt-rights/.

40 Philip Jenkins, "Brokering Peace in Colombia," *Christian Century*, January 16, 2019, 44–45.

41 "Colombia Legalises Gay Marriage," *BBC News*, April 29, 2016, https://www.bbc.com/news/world-latin-america-36166888.

42 Linda Pressly, "Chile Church Scandal: 'How I Escaped the Priest Who Abused Me for Decades,'" *BBC News*, September 13, 2018, https://www.bbc.com/news/stories-45486176.

5 The United States

1 David Voas and Mark Chaves, "Is the United States a Counterexample to the Secularization Thesis?" *American Journal of Sociology* 121, no. 5 (2016): 1517–56; Steve Crabtree, "Religiosity Highest in World's Poorest Nations," *Gallup News*, August 31, 2010, https://news.gallup.com/poll/142727/religiosity-highest-world-poorest-nations.aspx; Compare Joey Marshall, "The World's Most Committed Christians Live in Africa, Latin America—and the U.S.," *Fact Tank* (blog), Pew Research Center, August 22, 2018, https://www.pewresearch.org/fact-tank/2018/08/22/the-worlds-most-committed-christians-live-in-africa-latin-america-and-the-u-s/.

2 Pippa Norris and Ronald Inglehart, "Uneven Secularization in the United States and Western Europe," in *Democracy and the New Religious Pluralism*, ed. Thomas Banchoff (New York: Oxford University Press, 2007), 31–57; Steve Bruce, "Secularisation in the UK and the USA," in *Secularisation in the Christian World*, ed. Callum G. Brown and Michael Snape (Farnham: Ashgate, 2010), 205–18; John Torpey, "American Exceptionalism?" in *The New Blackwell Companion to the Sociology of Religion*, ed. Bryan S. Turner (Oxford: Wiley-Blackwell, 2010), 141–59; John Torpey, "Religion and Secularization in the United States and Western Europe," in *The Post-secular in Question: Religion in Contemporary Society*, ed. Philip S. Gorski, David Kyuman Kim, John Torpey, and Jonathan VanAntwerpen (New York: New York University Press, 2012), 279–306.

3   Grace Davie, *Europe: The Exceptional Case; Parameters of Faith in the Modern World* (London: Darton, Longman & Todd, 2002); Joel Kotkin, *The Next Hundred Million: America in 2050* (New York: Penguin, 2010).

4   Peter Berger, Grace Davie, and Effie Fokas, *Religious America, Secular Europe? A Theme and Variations* (Burlington, Vt.: Ashgate, 2008).

5   "Demography and the West: Half a Billion Americans?" *Economist*, August 22, 2002, https://www.economist.com/special-report/2002/08/22/half-a-billion-americans. For the boomer generation, see Richard A. Easterlin, *The American Baby Boom in Historical Perspective* (Cambridge, Mass.: National Bureau of Economic Research, 1962); Cheryl Russell, *Demographics of the U.S.: Trends and Projections*, 4th ed. (Ithaca, N.Y.: New Strategist, 2012).

6   Lyman Stone, "Number 2 in 2018: Baby Bust—Fertility Is Declining the Most among Minority Women," *Institute for Family Studies* (blog), December 31, 2018, https://ifstudies.org/blog/number-2-in-2018-baby-bust-fertility-is-declining-the-most-among-minority-women; Alia Wong, "The Misplaced Fears about the United States' Declining Fertility Rate," *Atlantic*, May 17, 2019, https://www.theatlantic.com/family/archive/2019/05/real-lessons-americas-declining-fertility-rate/589651/; Gretchen Livingston, "Is U.S. Fertility at an All-Time Low? Two of Three Measures Point to Yes," *Fact Tank* (blog), Pew Research Center, May 22, 2019, https://www.pewresearch.org/fact-tank/2019/05/22/u-s-fertility-rate-explained/; Jacqueline Howard, "US Fertility Rate Falls to 'All-Time Low,' CDC says," *CNN*, July 24, 2019, https://edition.cnn.com/2019/07/24/health/fertility-rate-births-2018-cdc-study/index.html. For the recent U.S. experience as an example of the Second Demographic Transition, see Ron J. Lesthaeghe and Lisa Neidert, "The Second Demographic Transition in the United States: Exception or Textbook Example?" *Population and Development Review* 32, no. 4 (2006): 669–98; Jennifer B. Kane, "A Closer Look at the Second Demographic Transition in the U.S.: Evidence of Bidirectionality from a Cohort Perspective (1982–2006)," *Population Research Policy Review* 32, no. 1 (2013): 47–80.

7   Livingston, "Is U.S. Fertility at an All-Time Low?"; Gretchen Livingston and Deja Thomas, "Why Is the Teen Birth Rate Falling?" *Fact Tank* (blog), Pew Research Center, August 2, 2019, https://www.pewresearch.org/fact-tank/2019/08/02/why-is-the-teen-birth-rate-falling/.

8   Lyman Stone, *Declining Fertility in America* (Washington, D.C.: American Enterprise Institute, 2018), https://www.aei.org/publication/declining-fertility-in-america/.

9   Philip Jenkins, *Rethinking a Nation: The United States in the 21st Century* (London: Red Globe, 2019).

10 Stone, "Number 2 in 2018: Baby Bust."

11 "Americans' Religious Values," Pew Research Center, June 7, 2012, https://www.pewforum.org/2012/06/07/americans-religious-values/; Pew Research Center, *"Nones" on the Rise* (Washington, D.C.: Pew Research Center, 2012), https://www.pewforum.org/2012/10/09/nones-on-the-rise/; Frank Newport, "Most Americans Still Believe in God," *Gallup News*, June 29, 2016, https://news.gallup.com/poll/193271/americans-believe-god.aspx; Dalia Fahmy, "Americans Are Far More Religious than Adults in Other Wealthy Nations," *Fact Tank* (blog), Pew Research Center, July 31, 2018, https://www.pewresearch.org/fact-tank/2018/07/31/americans-are-far-more-religious-than-adults-in-other-wealthy-nations/; Jonathan Evans, "U.S. Adults Are More Religious than Western Europeans," *Fact Tank* (blog), Pew Research Center, September 5, 2018, https://www.pewresearch.org/fact-tank/2018/09/05/u-s-adults-are-more-religious-than-western-europeans/. For doubting the existence of God, see "41d: I Never Doubt the Existence of God," American Values Survey: Question Database, Pew Research Center, https://www.people-press.org/values-questions/q41d/i-never-doubt-the-existence-of-god/#total. For church attendance, see C. Kirk Hadaway and Penny Long Marler, "How Many Americans Attend Worship Each Week? An Alternative Approach to Measurement," *Journal for the Scientific Study of Religion* 44, no. 3 (2005): 307–22; Frank Newport, "Church Leaders and Declining Religious Service Attendance," *Gallup News*, September 7, 2018, https://news.gallup.com/opinion/polling-matters/242015/church-leaders-declining-religious-service-attendance.aspx. For the never-doubters, see "41d: I Never Doubt the Existence of God." For the view that faith is still thriving in the United States, see Glenn T. Stanton, *The Myth of the Dying Church: How Christianity Is Actually Thriving in America and the World* (New York: Worthy, 2019).

12 *U.S. Public Becoming Less Religious* (Washington, D.C.: Pew Research Center, 2015), https://www.pewforum.org/2015/11/03/u-s-public-becoming-less-religious/; *In U.S., Decline of Christianity Continues at Rapid Pace* (Washington, D.C.: Pew Research Center, 2019), https://www.pewforum.org/2019/10/17/in-u-s-decline-of-christianity-continues-at-rapid-pace/. For falling attendance rates, see Gerald F. Seib, "Cradles, Pews and the Societal Shifts Coming to Politics," *Wall Street Journal*, June 24, 2019, https://www.wsj.com/articles/cradles-pews-and-the-societal-shifts-coming-to-politics-11561382477.

13 Jeffrey M. Jones, "U.S. Church Membership Down Sharply in Past Two Decades," *Gallup News*, April 18, 2019, https://news.gallup.com/poll/248837/church-membership-down-sharply-past-two-decades.aspx. For the wider Latino context, see *Religion in Latin America: Widespread Change in a Historically Catholic Region* (Washington, D.C.: Pew Research Center, 2014), https://www.pewforum.org/2014/11/13/religion-in-latin-america/.

14 Chaves is quoted from "American Devotion to Religion Is Waning, According to New Study," UCL News, University College London, March 10, 2016, https://www.ucl.ac.uk/news/2016/mar/american-devotion-religion-waning-according-new-study. Derek Thompson, "Three Decades Ago, America Lost Its Religion. Why?" *Atlantic*, September 2019, https://www.theatlantic.com/ideas/archive/2019/09/atheism-fastest-growing-religion-us/598843/. For recent academic debates over interpreting these figures, see Landon Schnabel and Sean Bock, "The Persistent and Exceptional Intensity of American Religion: A Response to Recent Research," *Sociological Science* 4 (2017): 686–700; David Voas and Mark Chaves, "Even Intense Religiosity Is Declining in the United States," *Sociological Science* 5 (2018): 694–710; Robert D. Putnam and David E. Campbell, *American Grace: How Religion Divides and Unites Us* (New York: Simon & Schuster, 2010).

15 Ryan Burge, "Is Religious Decline Inevitable in the United States?" *Christianity Today*, April 17, 2019, https://www.christianitytoday.com/edstetzer/2019/april/is-religious-decline-inevitable-in-united-states.html. For the continuing significance of independent congregations, usually of an evangelical or Pentecostal nature, see John Gordon Melton, Holly Folk, and David Bromley, "'The Others': Hiding in Plain Sight; Finding and Counting America's Invisible Churches" (paper presented at the annual conference of the Society for the Scientific Study of Religion, Las Vegas, October 26–28, 2018). For general problems with surveys and polling data, see Robert Wuthnow, *Inventing American Religion: Polls, Surveys, and the Tenuous Quest for a Nation's Faith* (New York: Oxford University Press, 2015).

16 *"Nones" on the Rise*; *U.S. Religious Landscape Survey: Religious Affiliation: Diverse and Dynamic* (Washington, D.C.: Pew Research Center, 2008), https://www.pewforum.org/2008/02/01/u-s-religious-landscape-survey-religious-affiliation/; *America's Changing Religious Landscape: Christians Decline Sharply as Share of Population; Unaffiliated and Other Faiths Continue to Grow* (Washington, D.C.: Pew Research Center, 2015), https://www.pewforum.org/2015/05/12/americas-changing-religious-landscape/;

Michael Hout and Claude S. Fischer, "Why More Americans Have No Religious Preference: Politics and Generations," *American Sociological Review* 67, no. 2 (2002): 165–90; Robert P. Jones, Daniel Cox, Betsy Cooper, and Rachel Lienesch, *Exodus: Why Americans Are Leaving Religion—and Why They're Unlikely to Come Back* (Washington, D.C.: Public Religion Research Institute, 2016), https://www.prri.org/research/prri-rns-poll-nones-atheist-leaving-religion/; *In U.S., Decline of Christianity Continues at Rapid Pace.*

17 Michael Lipka, "A Closer Look at America's Rapidly Growing Religious 'Nones,'" *Fact Tank* (blog), Pew Research Center, May 13, 2015, https://www.pewresearch.org/fact-tank/2015/05/13/a-closer-look-at-americas-rapidly-growing-religious-nones/; Becka A. Alper, "Why America's 'Nones' Don't Identify with a Religion," *Fact Tank* (blog), Pew Research Center, August 8, 2018, https://www.pewresearch.org/fact-tank/2018/08/08/why-americas-nones-dont-identify-with-a-religion/; "Religious 'Nones' Are Gaining Ground in America, and They're Worried about the Economy, Says New Study," *Religion News Service*, November 16, 2017, https://religionnews.com/2017/11/16/religious-nones-are-gaining-ground-in-america-and-theyre-worried-about-the-economy-says-new-study/; Gabe Bullard, "The World's Newest Major Religion: No Religion," *National Geographic*, April 22, 2016, https://news.nationalgeographic.com/2016/04/160422-atheism-agnostic-secular-nones-rising-religion/. Peggy Wehmeyer is quoted from her essay "As I Worship on Easter, I'll Wrestle with the Same Question: How Do I Keep Believing This?" *Dallas Morning News*, April 21, 2019, https://www.dallasnews.com/opinion/commentary/2019/04/21/as-i-worship-on-easter-i-ll-wrestle-with-the-same-question-how-do-i-keep-believing-this/. Michael Shermer is quoted from his article "The Number of Americans with No Religious Affiliation Is Rising," *Scientific American*, April 1, 2018, https://www.scientificamerican.com/article/the-number-of-americans-with-no-religious-affiliation-is-rising/. See also Phil Zuckerman, *Faith No More: Why People Reject Religion* (New York: Oxford University Press, 2011).

18 *"Nones" on the Rise*; Stephen Asma, "Religiously Unaffiliated 'Nones' Are Pursuing Spirituality, But Not Community," *Los Angeles Times*, June 7, 2018, https://www.latimes.com/opinion/op-ed/la-oe-asma-nones-spirituality-20180607-story.html; *In U.S., Decline of Christianity Continues at Rapid Pace.*

19 Quoted from *"Nones" on the Rise*. See also James Emery White, *The Rise of the Nones: Understanding and Reaching the Religiously Unaffiliated* (Grand Rapids: Baker Books, 2014); Elizabeth Drescher, *Choosing Our*

Religion: The Spiritual Lives of America's Nones (New York: Oxford University Press, 2016).

20 Barry A. Kosmin and Seymour P. Lachman, *One Nation under God: Religion in Contemporary American Society* (New York: Harmony, 1993).

21 John Fea, Laura Gifford, R. Marie Griffith, and Lerone A. Martin, "Evangelicalism and Politics," *American Historian*, November 2018, https://tah.oah.org/november-2018/evangelicalism-and-politics/; Robert P. Jones, *The End of White Christian America* (New York: Simon & Schuster, 2016); Stephen Bullivant, *Mass Exodus: Catholic Disaffiliation in Britain and America since Vatican II* (Oxford: Oxford University Press, 2019).

22 Alper, "Why America's 'Nones' Don't Identify with a Religion."

23 Alper; Peter Beinart, "Secular Democrats Are the New Normal," *Atlantic*, March 15, 2019, https://www.theatlantic.com/ideas/archive/2019/03/betos-announcement-shows-triumph-secular-democrats/585001/; Amelia Thomson-DeVeaux and Daniel Cox, "The Christian Right Is Helping Drive Liberals Away From Religion," *FiveThirtyEight*, September 18, 2019, https://fivethirtyeight.com/features/the-christian-right-is-helping-drive-liberals-away-from-religion/; Jones, "U.S. Church Membership Down Sharply in Past Two Decades."

24 Thomas Pardee, "Obama's Nod to Nonbelievers Sets Accepting Tone," *Chronicle*, February 2, 2009, https://columbiachronicle.com/d7f781d6-d980-5955-af6b-8326dc3514cd.

25 Philip Jenkins, *Mystics and Messiahs: Cults and New Religions in American History* (New York: Oxford University Press, 2000).

26 Philip Jenkins, "Where Have All The Cultists Gone?" *Anxious Bench* (blog), Patheos, June 27, 2014, https://www.patheos.com/blogs/anxiousbench/2014/06/where-have-all-the-cultists-gone/; Philip Jenkins, "Cult Alternatives," *Anxious Bench* (blog), Patheos, June 30, 2014, https://www.patheos.com/blogs/anxiousbench/2014/06/cult-alternatives/.

27 Robert Wuthnow, *After the Baby Boomers: How Twenty- and Thirty-Somethings Are Shaping the Future of American Religion* (Princeton, N.J.: Princeton University Press, 2007), 51–70; Laban Carrick Hill, *America Dreaming: How Youth Changed America in the '60s* (New York: Little, Brown, 2007).

28 Justin McCarthy, "U.S. Support for Gay Marriage Edges to New High," *Gallup News*, May 15, 2017, https://news.gallup.com/poll/210566/support-gay-marriage-edges-new-high.aspx; Lillian Faderman, *The Gay Revolution: The Story of the Struggle* (New York: Simon & Schuster, 2015).

29 José Casanova, "Immigration and the New Religious Pluralism: A European Union/United States Comparison," in Banchoff, *Democracy and the New Religious Pluralism*, 59–83; William Frey, *Diversity Explosion: How New Racial Demographics Are Remaking America* (Washington, D.C.: Brookings Institution Press, 2015); Steve Phillips, *Brown Is the New White: How the Demographic Revolution Has Created a New American Majority* (New York: New Press, 2016).

30 See for instance Timothy Matovina, *Latino Catholicism: Transformation in America's Largest Church* (Princeton, N.J.: Princeton University Press, 2012); Patricia O'Connell Killen and Mark Silk, eds., *The Future of Catholicism in America* (New York: Columbia University Press, 2019).

31 Pippa Norris and Ronald Inglehart, *Sacred and Secular: Religion and Politics Worldwide*, 2nd ed. (New York: Cambridge University Press, 2011); Pippa Norris, "Existential Insecurity and the Geography of Religiosity," in *The Changing World Religion Map: Sacred Places, Identities, Practices and Politics*, ed. Stanley D. Brunn (Dordrecht: Springer Netherlands, 2015).

32 Maggie Fox, "Infant Mortality Rates Fall 15 Percent in U.S.," *NBC News*, March 21, 2017, https://www.nbcnews.com/health/health-news/infant-mortality-rates-fall-15-percent-u-s-n736366.

33 Monica Duffy Toft, "Wombfare: The Religious and Political Dimensions of Fertility and Demographic Change," in *Political Demography: How Population Changes Are Reshaping International Security and National Politics*, ed. Jack A. Goldstone, Eric P. Kaufmann, and Monica Duffy Toft (Boulder: Paradigm, 2011), 213–25.

34 "Infant Mortality," Centers for Disease Control and Prevention, last modified March 27, 2019, https://www.cdc.gov/reproductivehealth/maternalinfanthealth/infantmortality.htm.

35 Jenkins, *Rethinking a Nation*. For the 2016 election, see Seib, "Cradles, Pews and the Societal Shifts Coming to Politics." For Washington State, see Patricia O'Connell Killen and Mark Silk, *Religion and Public Life in the Pacific Northwest: The None Zone* (Walnut Creek, Calif.: Altamira, 2004). Joel Connelly, "'Nones' Most Numerous in State's Religious Landscape, Pew Research Center Survey Says," *Seattle Post-Intelligencer*, August 2, 2019, https://www.seattlepi.com/local/politics/article/Nones-most-numerous-in-state-s-religious-14274465.php.

36 Steve Sailer, "Happy White Married People Vote Republican, So Why Doesn't the GOP Work on Making White People Happy?" *VDARE*, February 28, 2013, https://vdare.com/articles/happy-white-married-people-vote-republican-so-why-doesn-t-the-gop-work-on-making-white-people

-happy; Monica Duffy Toft, "Identicide: How Demographic Shifts Can Rip a Country Apart," *The Conversation* (blog), April 24, 2019, https://theconversation.com/identicide-how-demographic-shifts-can-rip-a-country-apart-113018.

37   Patrick Fisher, *Demographic Gaps in American Political Behavior* (Boulder: Westview Press, 2014).

38   Callum G. Brown, *Religion and the Demographic Revolution: Women and Secularisation in Canada, Ireland, UK and USA since the 1960s* (Woodbridge: Boydell Press, 2012); Brian Clarke and Stuart Macdonald, *Leaving Christianity: Changing Allegiances in Canada since 1945* (Montreal: McGill-Queen's University Press, 2017). For the diversity of continuing practice—and its strongly individualized nature—see Hillary Kael, ed., *Everyday Sacred: Religion in Contemporary Quebec* (Montreal: McGill-Queen's University Press, 2017).

39   For another view of long-term prospects, see Eric Kaufmann, "Why Is Secularization Likely to Stall in America by 2050? A Response to Laurie DeRose," *Institute for Family Studies* (blog), July 24, 2019, https://ifstudies.org/blog/why-is-secularization-likely-to-stall-in-america-by-2050-a-response-to-laurie-derose.

6 Africa

1   Haroon Bhorat and Finn Tarp, eds., *Africa's Lions: Growth Traps and Opportunities for Six African Economies* (Washington, D.C.: Brookings Institution Press, 2016).

2   For the state of the art in academic study of these issues, see several of the essays in Jack A. Goldstone, Eric P. Kaufmann, and Monica Duffy Toft, eds., *Political Demography: How Population Changes Are Reshaping International Security and National Politics* (Boulder: Paradigm, 2011). See also Jack A. Goldstone, "Africa 2050: Demographic Truth and Consequences," Winter Series 119, Governance in an Emerging New World, Hoover Institution, January 14, 2019, https://www.hoover.org/research/africa-2050-demographic-truth-and-consequences.

3   Matt Rosenberg, "Predicting the 20 Most Populous Countries in 2050," *ThoughtCo* (blog), last modified June 29, 2019, https://www.thoughtco.com/most-populous-countries-in-2050-1435117. For Africa's demographic circumstances, see Christopher Caldwell, "The Coming Migration Out of Sub-Saharan Africa," *National Review*, August 8, 2019, https://www.nationalreview.com/magazine/2019/08/26/the-coming-migration-out-of-sub-saharan-africa/.

4   Alexandra Beatty, *Recent Fertility Trends in Sub-Saharan Africa: Workshop Summary* (Washington, D.C.: National Academies Press, 2016). These topics are explored by multiple essays in the collection edited by Hans Groth and John F. May, *Africa's Population: In Search of a Demographic Dividend* (Cham: Springer International, 2017).

5   Emmanuel Jimenez and Muhammad Ali Pate, "Reaping a Demographic Dividend in Africa's Largest Country: Nigeria," in Groth and May, *Africa's Population*, 33–51; David Shapiro, Basile O. Tambashe, and Anatole Romaniuk, "The Third Biggest African Country: The Democratic Republic of the Congo," in Groth and May, *Africa's Population*, 71–86; Gilles Pison, "There's a Strong Chance That One-Third of All People Will Be African by 2100," *The Conversation* (blog), October 10, 2017, https://theconversation.com/theres-a-strong-chance-that-one-third-of-all -people-will-be-african-by-2100-84576. For a rank order of the highest fertility rates, see "Country Comparison: Total Fertility Rate," The World Factbook, Central Intelligence Agency, https://www.cia.gov/library/ publications/the-world-factbook/rankorder/2127rank.html. In my discussion I am not including a couple of tiny island nations like Cabo Verde or the Solomon Islands. The other non-African nations in the ranks of the highest-fertility nations include Afghanistan, Iraq, Yemen, Jordan, and the Palestinian territories (the West Bank and the Gaza Strip). I should note that the Palestinian figures are controversial, and their accuracy is open to debate.

6   "Country Comparison: Infant Mortality Rate," The World Factbook, Central Intelligence Agency, https://www.cia.gov/library/publications/the -world-factbook/rankorder/2091rank.html; Pablo Viguera Ester, Alberto Torres, José M. Freire, Valentín Hernández, and Ángel Gil, "Factors Associated to Infant Mortality in Sub-Saharan Africa," *Journal of Public Health in Africa* 2, no. 2 (2011): e27.

7   Philip Jenkins, *The Next Christendom: The Coming of Global Christianity*, 3rd ed. (New York: Oxford University Press, 2011).

8   "Country Comparisons: Median Age," The World Factbook, Central Intelligence Agency, https://www.cia.gov/library/publications/the-world -factbook/fields/343rank.html.

9   Blessing Mberu, Donatien Béguy, and Alex C. Ezeh, "Internal Migration, Urbanization and Slums in Sub-Saharan Africa," in Groth and May, *Africa's Population*, 315–32; John Vidal, "The 100 Million City: Is 21st Century Urbanisation Out of Control?" *Guardian*, March 19, 2018, https:// www.theguardian.com/cities/2018/mar/19/urban-explosion-kinshasa-el -alto-growth-mexico-city-bangalore-lagos; Mark R. Montgomery, Rich-

ard Stren, Barney Cohen, and Holly E. Reed, eds., *Cities Transformed: Demographic Change and Its Implications in the Developing World* (Washington, D.C.: National Academies Press, 2003).

10 John F. May, Jean-Pierre Guengant, and Vincent Barras, "Demographic Challenges of the Sahel Countries," in Groth and May, *Africa's Population*, 165–77.

11 "GDP Ranked by Country 2019," World Population Review, http://worldpopulationreview.com/countries/countries-by-gdp/.

12 Bhorat and Tarp, *Africa's Lions*.

13 John R. Weeks and Debbie L. Fugate, eds., *The Youth Bulge: Challenge or Opportunity?* (New York: International Debate Education Association, 2012).

14 The phrase "notoriously religious" derives from John S. Mbiti, *African Religions and Philosophy* (London: Heinemann, 1969), 1.

15 "How Religious Commitment Varies by Country among People of All Ages," in *The Age Gap in Religion around the World* (Washington, D.C.: Pew Research Center, 2018), 50–58, https://www.pewforum.org/2018/06/13/how-religious-commitment-varies-by-country-among-people-of-all-ages/.

16 Jenkins, *The Next Christendom*; Philip Jenkins, *The New Faces of Christianity: Believing the Bible in the Global South* (New York: Oxford University Press, 2006).

17 "Sub-Saharan Africa," in *The Future of World Religions: Population Growth Projections, 2010–2050* (Washington, D.C.: Pew Research Center, 2015), 163–65, https://www.pewforum.org/2015/04/02/sub-saharan-africa/.

18 Philip Jenkins, "Reformation in Ethiopia," *Christian Century*, November 27, 2013, 45; Assefa Hailemariam, "The Second Biggest African Country Undergoing Rapid Change: Ethiopia," in Groth and May, *Africa's Population*, 53–69.

19 *Christ's New Homeland—Africa: Contribution to the Synod on the Family by African Pastors*, trans. Michael J. Miller (San Francisco: Ignatius, 2015).

20 *The Future of World Religions*; Patrick Wintour, "Niger's President Blames Explosive Birth Rate on 'a Misreading of Islam,'" *Guardian*, October 17, 2019, https://www.theguardian.com/global-development/2019/oct/17/nigers-president-blames-explosive-birth-rate-on-a-misreading-of-islam.

21 Jenkins, *The Next Christendom*.

22 Philip Jenkins, "The Catholic Surge in Africa," *Christian Century*, March 15, 2017, 45.

23 Christopher S. Chivvis, *The French War on Al Qa'ida in Africa* (New York: Cambridge University Press, 2016); Barak Mendelsohn, *The Al-Qaeda Franchise: The Expansion of al-Qaeda and Its Consequences* (New York: Oxford University Press, 2016); Alexander Thurston, *Boko Haram: The History of an African Jihadist Movement* (Princeton, N.J.: Princeton University Press, 2018); Serge Michailof, *Africanistan: Development or Jihad* (New Delhi: Oxford University Press, 2018).

24 Elliott D. Green, "Demographic Change and Conflict in Contemporary Africa," in Goldstone, Kaufmann, and Toft, *Political Demography*, 238–51; Ragnhild Nordås, "The Devil in the Demography? Religion, Identity and War in Côte d'Ivoire," in Goldstone, Kaufmann, and Toft, *Political Demography*, 252–66; Siri Aas Rustad, Gudrun Østby, and Henrik Urdal, "Conflicts and the Demographic Transition: Economic Opportunity or Disaster?" in Groth and May, *Africa's Population*, 483–96.

25 Henrik Urdal, "Youth Bulges and Violence," in Goldstone, Kaufmann, and Toft, *Political Demography*, 117–32; Deborah Jordan Brooks, Stephen G. Brooks, Brian D. Greenhill, and Mark L. Haas, "The Demographic Transition Theory of War: Why Young Societies Are Conflict Prone and Old Societies Are the Most Peaceful," *International Security* 43, no. 3 (2018–2019): 53–95.

26 James Copnall, *A Poisonous Thorn in Our Hearts: Sudan and South Sudan's Bitter and Incomplete Divorce* (London: Hurst, 2014).

27 See for instance Ruth Marshall, *Political Spiritualities: The Pentecostal Revolution in Nigeria* (Chicago: University of Chicago Press, 2009).

28 Thurston, *Boko Haram*.

29 Robin Wright, "Baghdadi Is Back—and Vows That ISIS Will Be, Too," *New Yorker*, April 29, 2019, https://www.newyorker.com/news/news-desk/baghdadi-is-backand-vows-that-isis-will-be-too; Michailof, *Africanistan*.

30 Richard Matthew, "Demography, Climate Change, and Conflict," in Goldstone, Kaufmann, and Toft, *Political Demography*, 133–46.

31 Philip Jenkins, "Climate Change and Religion around Africa's Great Lakes," *Christian Century*, November 22, 2017, 44–45.

32 Simon Gregson, Tom Zhuwau, Roy M. Anderson, and Stephen K. Chandiwana, "Apostles and Zionists: The Influence of Religion on Demographic Change in Rural Zimbabwe," *Population Studies* 53, no. 2 (1999): 179–93.

33 Tom A. Moultrie, "A Case of an Almost Complete Demographic Transition: South Africa," in Groth and May, *Africa's Population*, 87–99; Philip Jenkins, "Secular South Africa?" *Christian Century*, February 5, 2014, 37.

7 Two-Tier Islam

1   Relatively pacific Jordan is the other Islamic nation in this list.

2   Hans Groth and Alfonso Sousa-Poza, eds., *Population Dynamics in Muslim Countries: Assembling the Jigsaw* (Heidelberg: Springer Berlin Heidelberg, 2012).

3   David P. Goldman, *How Civilizations Die (and Why Islam Is Dying Too)* (Washington, D.C.: Regnery, 2011); Jay Winter and Michael Teitelbaum, *The Global Spread of Fertility Decline: Population, Fear, and Uncertainty* (New Haven, Conn.: Yale University Press, 2013); Farzaneh Roudi-Fahimi and Mary Mederios Kent, "Fertility Declining in the Middle East and North Africa," Population Reference Bureau, January 24, 2008, https://www.prb.org/menafertilitydecline/; Marcia C. Inhorn, "The Arab World's 'Quiet' Reproductive Revolution," *Brown Journal of World Affairs* 24, no. 2 (2018): 147–59; Inaara Gangji and Muhammad Chaudary, "The Arab World's Silent Reproductive Revolution," *Al Jazeera*, April 16, 2019, https://www.aljazeera.com/news/2019/04/arab-world-silent-reproductive-revolution-190416060958876.html.

4   For proportions defining religion as very important in their lives, see "How Religious Commitment Varies by Country among People of All Ages," in *The Age Gap in Religion around the World* (Washington, D.C.: Pew Research Center, 2018), 50–58, https://www.pewforum.org/2018/06/13/how-religious-commitment-varies-by-country-among-people-of-all-ages/. For differing forms of secularism in the Islamic world, see Mirjam Künkler, John Madeley, and Shylashri Shankar, eds., *A Secular Age beyond the West: Religion, Law and the State in Asia, the Middle East and North Africa* (Cambridge: Cambridge University Press, 2018).

5   Philip Jenkins, "The World's Fastest Growing Religion: Comparing Christian and Muslim Expansion in the Modern Era," in *The Changing World Religion Map: Sacred Places, Identities, Practices and Politics*, ed. Stanley D. Brunn (Dordrecht: Springer Netherlands, 2015), 1767–79; *The Changing Global Religious Landscape* (Washington, D.C.: Pew Research Center, 2017), https://www.pewforum.org/2017/04/05/the-changing-global-religious-landscape/.

6   Ferguson is quoted from Philip Jenkins, *God's Continent: Christianity, Islam, and Europe's Religious Crisis* (New York: Oxford University Press, 2007), 9; Ajami from Jenkins, 8. For the stress on high fertility in the future growth of Islam, see "Sub-Saharan Africa," in *The Future of World Religions: Population Growth Projections, 2010–2050* (Washington, D.C.: Pew Research Center, 2015), 163–65, https://www.pewforum.org/2015/04/02/sub-saharan-africa/.

7   Pakistan and Bangladesh formed a united nation until the latter fought a bloody war of independence in 1971.

8   Jenkins, "The World's Fastest Growing Religion"; Tilak Devasher, *Pakistan: Courting the Abyss* (Noida: Harper Collins, 2016).

9   For debates over gender in Islamic nations, see Ellen Chesler and Terry McGovern, eds., *Women and Girls Rising: Progress and Resistance around the World* (New York: Routledge, 2016); Yanyi K. Djamba and Sitawa R. Kimuna, eds., *Gender-Based Violence: Perspectives from Africa, the Middle East, and India* (Cham: Springer International, 2015).

10 Lena Masri, "'Two Is Enough,' Egypt Tells Poor Families as Population Booms," *Reuters*, February 20, 2019, https://www.reuters.com/article/us-egypt-population/two-is-enough-egypt-tells-poor-families-as-population-booms-idUSKCN1Q91RJ; Raf Sanchez, "Egypt in Desperate Bid to Curb Birth Rate as Population Nears 100 Million," *Telegraph*, March 14, 2019, https://www.telegraph.co.uk/global-health/climate-and-people/egypt-desperate-bid-curb-birth-rate-population-nears-100-million/; John R. Weeks and Debbie L. Fugate, eds., *The Youth Bulge: Challenge or Opportunity?* (New York: International Debate Education Association, 2012).

11 For religious politics in the country, see Khalil al-Anani, *Inside the Muslim Brotherhood: Religion, Identity, and Politics* (New York: Oxford University Press, 2016); Scott W. Hibbard, *Religious Politics and Secular States: Egypt, India, and the United States* (Baltimore: Johns Hopkins University Press 2010).

12 "Female Genital Mutilation (FGM)," World Health Organization, https://www.who.int/reproductivehealth/topics/fgm/prevalence/en/; Ngianga-Bakwin Kandala and Paul Nzinga Komba, *Female Genital Mutilation around the World: Analysis of Medical Aspects, Laws and Practice* (Cham: Springer International, 2018); Annette Langer, "Genital Mutilation in Egypt," *Spiegel*, March 23, 2018, https://www.spiegel.de/international/tomorrow/genital-mutilation-in-egypt-stop-taking-your-daughters-to-be-mutilated-a-1199322.html.

13 Fred C. Abrahams, *Modern Albania: From Dictatorship to Democracy in Europe* (New York: New York University Press, 2015).

14 James Buchan, *Days of God: The Revolution in Iran and Its Consequences* (New York: Simon & Schuster, 2013); Janet Afary, *Sexual Politics in Modern Iran* (New York: Cambridge University Press, 2009). For the post-revolutionary regime, see Annabelle Sreberny and Massoumeh Torfeh, eds., *Cultural Revolution in Iran: Contemporary Popular Culture in the Islamic Republic* (London: I.B. Tauris, 2013); Michael Axworthy,

Revolutionary Iran: A History of the Islamic Republic (Oxford: Oxford University Press, 2013).

15 I draw heavily throughout this chapter on Mohammad Jalal Abbasi-Shavazi, Peter McDonald, and Meimanat Hosseini-Chavoshi, *The Fertility Transition in Iran: Revolution and Reproduction* (Dordrecht: Springer, 2009); Seemeen Saadat, Sadia Chowdhury, and Amir Mehryar, *Fertility Decline in the Islamic Republic of Iran, 1980–2006* (Washington, D.C.: World Bank, 2010); Philip Jenkins, "Infertile Crescent," *New Republic*, November 5, 2007, 10–13.

16 Mahmood Monshipouri, ed., *Inside the Islamic Republic: Social Change in Post-Khomeini Iran* (New York: Oxford University Press, 2016). For the role of education in shaping demographic patterns, see Eric P. Kaufmann and Vegard Skirbekk, "'Go Forth and Multiply': The Politics of Religious Demography," in *Political Demography: How Population Changes Are Reshaping International Security and National Politics*, ed. Jack A. Goldstone, Eric P. Kaufmann, and Monica Duffy Toft (Boulder: Paradigm, 2011), 194–211. For gender issues across the region, see Valerie J. Hoffman, ed., *Making the New Middle East: Politics, Culture, and Human Rights* (Syracuse: Syracuse University Press, 2019).

17 "Iran's Falling Marriage, Birth Rates Spell Trouble for Country's Demographics," *bne IntelliNews*, September 16, 2016, https://www.intellinews .com/iran-s-falling-marriage-birth-rates-spell-trouble-for-country-s -demographics-106037/; Ramin Mostaghim and Sarah Parvini, "'White Marriage' a Growing Trend for Young Couples in Iran," *Los Angeles Times*, May 29, 2015, https://www.latimes.com/world/middleeast/la-fg -iran-white-marriage-20150529-story.html.

18 Ahmadinejad is quoted from David P. Goldman, "The Strategic Implications of Iran's STD Epidemic," *Middle East Forum*, January 30, 2015, https://www .meforum.org/5000/strategic-implications-iran-std; For Khamenei, see "Iran Back Flip on Population Likely as Ayatollah Khamenei Calls for Change," *South China Morning Post*, April 16, 2014, https://www.scmp.com/news/ world/article/1484410/iran-back-flip-population-likely-ayatollah-khamenei -calls-change.

19 Richard Cincotta and Karim Sadjadpour, *Iran in Transition: The Implications of the Islamic Republic's Changing Demographics* (Washington, D.C.: Carnegie Endowment for International Peace, 2017), https:// carnegieendowment.org/2017/12/18/iran-in-transition-implications-of -islamic-republic-s-changing-demographics-pub-75042.

20 Cincotta and Sadjadpour, *Iran in Transition*; Richard Cincotta, "The Age-Structural Theory of State Behavior," Oxford Research Encyclopedia of

Politics, August 22, 2017, https://oxfordre.com/politics/view/10.1093/
acrefore/9780190228637.001.0001/acrefore-9780190228637-e-327.

21 Misagh Parsa, *Democracy in Iran: Why It Failed and How It Might Succeed* (Cambridge, Mass.: Harvard University Press, 2016); Reuel Marc Gerecht, "Tehran's Own Worst Enemy," *Wall Street Journal*, June 20, 2017, https://www.wsj.com/articles/tehrans-own-worst-enemy-1498000880.

22 David Blair, "Friday Prayers in the Islamic Republic of Iran—but Where Are the Worshippers?" *Telegraph*, August 1, 2015, https://www.telegraph
.co.uk/news/worldnews/middleeast/iran/11776241/Friday-prayers-in-the
-Islamic-Republic-of-Iran-but-where-are-the-worshippers.html; Shashank Bengali and Ramin Mostaghim, "Iran's 'City of Mullahs' Has a Surprising Side," *Los Angeles Times*, September 8, 2017, https://www.latimes.com/world/middleeast/la-fg-iran-religion-20170908-story.html.

23 Reuel Marc Gerecht, "The Secular Republic of Iran," *Wall Street Journal*, January 4, 2018, https://www.wsj.com/articles/the-secular-republic-of-iran
-1515111062.

24 Sohrab Ahmari, *From Fire, by Water: My Journey to the Catholic Faith* (San Francisco: Ignatius, 2019), 62.

25 Roxana Saberi, "Growing Popularity of Sufism in Iran," *BBC News*, April 25, 2006, http://news.bbc.co.uk/2/hi/4907406.stm; Loes Witschge, "Iran's Gonabadi Dervishes: A 'Long History' of Persecution," *Al Jazeera*, February 27, 2018, https://www.aljazeera.com/indepth/features/iran
-gonabadi-dervishes-long-history-persecution-180227193000395.html.

26 Neha Thirani Bagri, "'Everyone Treated Me Like a Saint'—in Iran, There's Only One Way to Survive as a Transgender Person," *Quartz*, April 19, 2017, https://qz.com/889548/everyone-treated-me-like-a-saint-in-iran-theres-only
-one-way-to-survive-as-a-transgender-person/.

27 Leonid Bershidsky, "Democracy in Iran? The Demographics Say Yes," *Bloomberg*, January 2, 2018, https://www.bloomberg.com/news/articles/
2018-01-02/democracy-in-iran-the-demographics-say-yes.

28 Patrick Crowley, ed., *Algeria: Nation, Culture and Transnationalism, 1988–2015* (Liverpool: Liverpool University Press, 2017).

29 Mary-Jane Deeb, "The Society and Its Environment: Family Planning," in *Algeria: A Country Study*, ed. Helen Chapin Metz (Washington, D.C.: Federal Research Division, Library of Congress, 1994), 105–6, http://countrystudies.us/algeria/61.htm.

30 Mounira M. Charrad, ed., *States and Women's Rights: The Making of Postcolonial Tunisia, Algeria, and Morocco* (Berkeley: University of California Press, 2001).

31 Crowley, *Algeria*.

32 Dina Temple-Raston, "The Female Quran Experts Fighting Radical Islam in Morocco," *Atlantic*, February 12, 2018, https://www.theatlantic.com/international/archive/2018/02/the-female-quran-experts-fighting-radical-islam-in-morocco/551996/.

33 Bershidsky, "Democracy in Iran?"; Richard P. Cincotta and John Doces, "The Age-Structural Maturity Thesis: The Impact of the Youth Bulge on the Advent and Stability of Liberal Democracy," in *Political Demography: How Population Changes Are Reshaping International Security and National Politics*, ed. Jack A. Goldstone, Eric P. Kaufmann, and Monica Duffy Toft (Boulder: Paradigm, 2011), 98–116; "Tunisia Predicted: Demography and the Probability of Liberal Democracy in the Greater Middle East" (event held at the Wilson Center, Washington, D.C., March 24, 2011), https://www.wilsoncenter.org/event/tunisia-predicted-demography-and-the-probability-liberal-democracy-the-greater-middle-east.

34 Wai Mun Hong, "Demographic Pressure, Social Demands, and Instability in the Maghreb," in *The Lure of Authoritarianism: The Maghreb after the Arab Spring*, ed. Stephen J. King and Abdeslam M. Maghraoi (Bloomington: Indiana University Press, 2019), 68–93.

35 Ursula Lindsey, "Some Gains, Many Sacrifices: Women's Rights in Tunisia," *Al-Fanar Media*, July 10, 2017, https://www.al-fanarmedia.org/2017/07/scholars-debate-legacy-state-feminism-chances-overcoming-islamist-secularist-divide/; Ursula Lindsey, "Is Tunisia Ready for Gender Equality?" *New York Review of Books*, April 4, 2019, https://www.nybooks.com/articles/2019/04/04/tunisia-ready-gender-equality/; Noa Avishag Schnall, "A Queer Film Festival in Tunisia—Where Being Gay Is Illegal," *New York Times*, May 14, 2019, https://www.nytimes.com/2019/05/14/arts/tunisia-gay-lgbt-queer-film-festival.html; Simon Speakman Cordall, "Meet the Man Hoping to Become the Muslim World's First Openly Gay President," *Independent*, July 14, 2019, https://www.independent.co.uk/news/world/middle-east/tunisia-lgbt-gay-president-candidate-mounir-baatour-shams-a9003656.html.

36 Anne Booth, *Economic Change in Modern Indonesia: Colonial and Post-Colonial Comparisons* (Cambridge: Cambridge University Press, 2016).

37 "Indonesia: Fresh Wave of Anti-LGBT Rhetoric, Arrests," *Human Rights Watch*, October 29, 2018, https://www.hrw.org/news/2018/10/29/indonesia-fresh-wave-anti-lgbt-rhetoric-arrests.

38 Theodore Friend, *Indonesian Destinies* (Cambridge, Mass.: Belknap Press of Harvard University Press, 2003).

39 "Saudi Arabia Population 2019," *World Population Review*, http://worldpopulationreview.com/countries/saudi-arabia-population/.

40 Gillian Duncan, "Fertility Rates in the UAE Dropping Significantly and Rapidly, According to Report," *National*, June 5, 2018, https://www .thenational.ae/uae/fertility-rates-in-the-uae-dropping-significantly-and -rapidly-according-to-report-1.737198.

41 Vivian Nereim, "Saudi Religious Police Return to Streets of Riyadh," *Independent*, June 26, 2017, https://www.independent.co.uk/news/world/ middle-east/saudi-arabia-religious-police-riyadh-islam-mohammed-bin -salman-vision-2030-a7808796.html.

42 Philip Jenkins, "Christians in the Gulf," *Christian Century*, March 16, 2016, 45; Mehdi Chowdhury and S. Irudaya Rajan, eds., *South Asian Migration in the Gulf: Causes and Consequences* (Cham: Palgrave Macmillan, 2018).

8 Go Forth and Divide

1 Derek Thompson, "The Doom Loop of Modern Liberalism," *Atlantic*, October 24, 2017, https://www.theatlantic.com/business/archive/2017/10/ immigration-modern-liberalism/543744/.

2 Olga Khazan, "A Surprising Reason to Worry about Low Birth Rates," *Atlantic*, May 26, 2018, https://www.theatlantic.com/health/archive/2018/ 05/a-surprising-reason-to-worry-about-low-birth-rates/561308/.

3 Vijay Prashad, ed., *Strongmen: Putin, Erdoğan, Duterte, Trump, Modi* (New York: O/R Books, 2018); Jan-Werner Müller, "Populism and the People," *London Review of Books*, May 23, 2019, 35–37, https://www.lrb .co.uk/v41/n10/jan-werner-muller/populism-and-the-people; David Kaye, "Strongmen and Fragile Democracies," *Los Angeles Review of Books*, June 22, 2017, https://lareviewofbooks.org/article/strongmen-and-fragile -democracies/; Monica Duffy Toft, "Differential Demographic Growth in Multinational States: Israel's Two-Front War," *Journal of International Affairs* 56, no. 1 (2002): 71–94; Toft, "Identicide: How Demographic Shifts Can Rip a Country Apart," *The Conversation* (blog), April 24, 2019, https://theconversation.com/identicide-how-demographic-shifts-can-rip-a -country-apart-113018.

4 Jack A. Goldstone, Eric P. Kaufmann, and Monica Duffy Toft, eds., *Political Demography: How Population Changes Are Reshaping International Security and National Politics* (Boulder: Paradigm, 2011).

5 For "demographic disintegration," see Toft, "Differential Demographic Growth in Multinational States." See also Robert Fisk, *Pity the Nation: The Abduction of Lebanon*, 4th ed. (New York: Thunder's Mouth Press/ Nation Books, 2002).

6   Soner Cagaptay, *Erdogan's Empire: Turkey and the Politics of the Middle East* (London: I.B. Tauris, 2019).

7   Cihan Tuğal, *The Fall of the Turkish Model: How the Arab Uprisings Brought Down Islamic Liberalism* (London: Verso, 2016); Soner Cagaptay, *The New Sultan: Erdogan and the Crisis of Modern Turkey* (London: I.B. Tauris, 2017).

8   Jeremy F. Walton, *Muslim Civil Society and the Politics of Religious Freedom in Turkey* (New York: Oxford University Press, 2017).

9   "Turkey Total Fertility Rate by Province 2013," Wikimedia Commons, March 22, 2015, https://commons.wikimedia.org/wiki/File:Turkey_total _fertility_rate_by_province_2013.png.

10 Mehmet Ali Eryurt and İsmet Koç, "Demography of Ethnicity in Turkey," in *The International Handbook of the Demography of Race and Ethnicity*, ed. Rogelio Sáenz, David G. Embrick, and Néstor P. Rodríguez (Dordrecht: Springer Netherlands, 2015), 483–502.

11 Helen Lewis, "Why We Should Fear Populists Like Orbán and Erdogan Who Want Women to Be Baby Machines," *New Statesman*, February 13, 2019, https://www.newstatesman.com/politics/feminism/2019/02/why-we -should-fear-populists-orb-n-and-erdogan-who-want-women-be-baby.

12 "If you have a young population" is from Norma Cohen and Funja Guler, "Erdogan's Call to Increase Birth Rate Draws Sceptical Response from Women," *Financial Times*, September 30, 2013, https://www.ft.com/ content/8dd59f9c-1ed5-11e3-b80b-00144feab7de; "Recep Tayyip Erdogan Tells Turks in Europe to Have 5 Children," *NDTV*, March 18, 2017, https://www.ndtv.com/world-news/recep-tayyip-erdogan-tells-turks-in -europe-to-have-5-children-1670780.

13 Basharat Peer, *A Question of Order: India, Turkey, and the Return of Strongmen* (New York: Columbia Global Reports, 2017).

14 Michael Walzer, *The Paradox of Liberation: Secular Revolutions and Religious Counterrevolutions* (New Haven, Conn.: Yale University Press, 2015).

15 Bidyut Chakrabarty and Sugato Hazra, *Winning the Mandate: The Indian Experience* (New Delhi: SAGE, 2016), 16.

16 Lars Tore Flåten, *Hindu Nationalism, History and Identity in India: Narrating a Hindu Past under the BJP* (Abingdon: Routledge, 2017); Walter K. Andersen and Shridhar D. Damle, *Messengers of Hindu Nationalism* (London: Hurst, 2019); Sonia Faleiro, "Absent Opposition, Modi Makes India His Hindu Nation," *New York Review of Books*, July 29, 2019, https://www.nybooks.com/daily/2019/07/29/absent-opposition-modi -makes-india-his-hindu-nation/.

17 Philip Jenkins, "Intolerance in India," *Christian Century*, October 5, 2010, 45.

18 Eliza Griswold, "The Violent Toll of Hindu Nationalism in India," *New Yorker*, March 5, 2019, https://www.newyorker.com/news/on-religion/the-violent-toll-of-hindu-nationalism-in-india; Cherian George, *Hate Spin: The Manufacture of Religious Offense and Its Threat to Democracy* (Cambridge, Mass.: MIT Press, 2016); K. S. Komireddi, *Malevolent Republic: A Short History of the New India* (London: Hurst, 2018).

19 Shailaja Chandra, "Three States Hold the Key," *Indian Express*, July 15, 2016, https://indianexpress.com/article/opinion/columns/india-polpulation-family-planning-emergency-india-births-rate-total-fertility-rate-2914318/; "UP, MP, Bihar Have Highest Fertility Rates, Shows UN Report: How Fertile Are Indian States?" *India Today*, November 12, 2018, https://www.indiatoday.in/education-today/gk-current-affairs/story/un-report-fertility-rates-india-1386951-2018-11-12; Jay Winter and Michael Teitelbaum, "Population and Politics in India," chap. 5 in *The Global Spread of Fertility Decline: Population, Fear, and Uncertainty* (New Haven, Conn.: Yale University Press, 2013); Krishnamurthy Srinivasan, *Population Concerns in India: Shifting Trends, Policies, and Programs* (New Delhi: SAGE, 2017).

20 Conveniently summarized at Wikipedia, s.v. "List of Indian States and Union Territories by GDP," last modified October 26, 2019, 16:17, https://en.wikipedia.org/wiki/List_of_Indian_states_and_union_territories_by_GDP.

21 "Why India's South Confounds the Otherwise All-Conquering Narendra Modi," *Economist*, June 22, 2019, https://www.economist.com/asia/2019/06/22/why-indias-south-confounds-the-otherwise-all-conquering-narendra-modi.

22 Wikipedia, s.v. "List of Languages by Number of Native Speakers in India," last modified October 23, 2019, 04:52, https://en.wikipedia.org/wiki/List_of_languages_by_number_of_native_speakers_in_India.

23 Walzer, *The Paradox of Liberation*; Paul Morland, *Demographic Engineering: Population Strategies in Ethnic Conflict* (Abingdon: Routledge, 2016).

24 Colin Shindler, *Israel, Likud and the Zionist Dream: Power, Politics, and Ideology from Begin to Netanyahu* (New York: St. Martin's Press, 1995).

25 Nachman Ben-Yehuda, *Theocratic Democracy: The Social Construction of Religious and Secular Extremism* (New York: Oxford University Press, 2010); Gadi Taub, *The Settlers: And the Struggle over the Meaning of Zionism* (New Haven, Conn.: Yale University Press, 2010); Avi Shilon,

Menachem Begin: A Life, trans. Danielle Zilberberg and Yoram Sharett (New Haven, Conn.: Yale University Press, 2012).

26 Toft, "Differential Demographic Growth in Multinational States"; Alon Tal, *The Land Is Full: Addressing Overpopulation in Israel* (New Haven, Conn.: Yale University Press, 2016).

27 Yoav Peled and Horit Herman Peled, *The Religionization of Israeli Society* (Abingdon: Routledge, 2019).

28 "Benjamin Netanyahu Says Israel Is 'Not a State of All Its Citizens,'" *Guardian*, March 10, 2019, https://www.theguardian.com/world/2019/mar/10/benjamin-netanyahu-says-israel-is-not-a-state-of-all-its-citizens.

29 "Religious Commitment and Practices," in *Religious Belief and National Belonging in Central and Eastern Europe* (Washington, D.C.: Pew Research Center, 2017), 69–81, https://www.pewforum.org/2017/05/10/religious-commitment-and-practices/; Philip Jenkins, "Resurrected Cathedrals," *Christian Century*, April 19, 2011, 45.

30 Walter Laqueur, *Putinism: Russia and Its Future with the West* (New York: Thomas Dunne, 2015).

31 Ilan Berman, "Russia's Fraught Demographic Future," Russia in Decline, Jamestown Foundation, September 13, 2016, https://jamestown.org/program/ilan-berman-russias-fraught-demographic-future/; Amie Ferris-Rotman, "Putin's Next Target Is Russia's Abortion Culture," *Foreign Policy*, October 3, 2017, https://foreignpolicy.com/2017/10/03/putins-next-target-is-russias-abortion-culture/; Anatoly G. Vishnevsky, "Family, Fertility, and Demographic Dynamics in Russia: Analysis and Forecast," in *Russia's Demographic "Crisis,"* ed. Julie DaVanzo and Gwendolyn Farnsworth (Santa Monica: RAND, 1996), 1–35, https://www.rand.org/pubs/conf_proceedings/CF124/CF124.chap1.html; Tatiana Karabchuk, Kazuhiro Kumo, and Ekaterina Selezneva, *Demography of Russia: From the Past to the Present* (London: Palgrave Macmillan, 2017).

32 Dominic Rubin, *Russia's Muslim Heartlands: Islam in the Putin Era* (London: Hurst, 2018).

33 "Islam in Russia," *Al Jazeera*, March 7, 2018, https://www.aljazeera.com/indepth/features/islam-russia-180307094248743.html; "Putin Unveils Plan to Boost Birth Rates in Russia," *News24*, November 28, 2017, https://www.news24.com/World/News/putin-unveils-plan-to-boost-birth-rates-in-russia-20171128.

34 "Putin: Christianity is the Foundation of the Russian State," *CBN News*, July 29, 2018, https://www1.cbn.com/cbnnews/cwn/2018/july/putin-christianity-is-the-foundation-of-the-russian-state; Robert Duncan, "Holy Russia? Believers Debate Putin's Record as a Christian Leader,"

Compass, October 17, 2017, https://www.thecompassnews.org/2017/10/holy-russia-believers-debate-putins-record-christian-leader/.

35 Jeremy W. Lamoreaux and Lincoln Flake, "The Russian Orthodox Church, the Kremlin, and Religious (Il)liberalism in Russia," *Palgrave Communications* 4 (2018): 115, https://www.nature.com/articles/s41599-018-0169-6.

36 Jason le Miere, "Same-Sex Marriage as Immoral as Nazi Laws, Russian Putin Ally Says," *Newsweek*, May 30, 2017, https://www.newsweek.com/same-sex-marriage-russia-gay-617565.

37 Chrissy Stroop, "Putin Wants God (or at Least the Church) on His Side," *Foreign Policy*, September 10, 2018, https://foreignpolicy.com/2018/09/10/putin-wants-god-or-at-least-the-church-on-his-side/.

38 Gilles Kepel, *The Revenge of God: The Resurgence of Islam, Christianity and Judaism in the Modern World*, trans. Alan Braley (University Park: Pennsylvania State University Press, 1991).

9 Living in a Low-Fertility World

1 Darrell Bricker and John Ibbitson, *Empty Planet: The Shock of Global Population Decline* (New York: Crown, 2019); Wolfgang Lutz, Warren C. Sanderson, and Sergei Scherbov, eds., *The End of World Population Growth in the 21st Century: New Challenges for Human Capital Formation and Sustainable Development* (London: Earthscan, 2004).

2 J. M. Keynes, "Some Economic Consequences of a Declining Population," *Eugenics Review* 29, no. 1 (1937): 13–17.

3 For religious futures see Vegard Skirbekk, Eric Kaufmann, and Anne Goujon, "Secularism, Fundamentalism, or Catholicism? The Religious Composition of the United States to 2043," *Journal for the Scientific Study of Religion* 49, no. 2 (2010): 293–310, 293.

4 For secular efforts to adapt to these new conditions, see John Burns and Chris Porter, *Big Shifts Ahead: Demographic Clarity for Businesses* (Charleston, S.C.: Advantage, 2016).

5 Philip Jenkins, *The Next Christendom: The Coming of Global Christianity*, 3rd ed. (New York: Oxford University Press, 2011).

6 David Voas, "The Continuing Secular Transition," in *The Role of Religion in Modern Societies*, ed. Detlef Pollack and Daniel V. A. Olson (New York: Routledge, 2008), 25–48.

7 Callum G. Brown, *Becoming Atheist: Humanism and the Secular West* (London: Bloomsbury Academic, 2017).

8 Eric Kaufmann, *Shall the Religious Inherit the Earth? Demography and Politics in the Twenty-First Century* (London: Profile Books, 2011); Conrad Hackett, Marcin Stonawski, Michaela Potančoková, Brian J. Grim,

and Vegard Skirbekk, "The Future Size of Religiously Affiliated and Un-affiliated Populations," *Demographic Research* 32 (2015): 829–42; "Sub-Saharan Africa," in *The Future of World Religions: Population Growth Projections, 2010–2050* (Washington, D.C.: Pew Research Center, 2015), 163–65, https://www.pewforum.org/2015/04/02/sub-saharan-africa/.

9   Quoted in Philip Jenkins, "Euro Skepticism: Why Benedict XVI Tried, and Failed, to Evangelize Europe," *New Republic*, February 13, 2013, https://newrepublic.com/article/112404/why-pope-benedict-failed-evangelize-europe.

10 The following discussion is drawn from Philip Jenkins, *God's Continent: Christianity, Islam, and Europe's Religious Crisis* (New York: Oxford University Press, 2007).

11 Jenkins, *God's Continent*.

12 The quote is from Mark Mather, "Aging in the United States," Population Reference Bureau, January 13, 2016, https://www.prb.org/aging-unitedstates-fact-sheet/; "Older People Projected to Outnumber Children for First Time in U.S. History," United States Census Bureau, March 13, 2018, https://www.census.gov/newsroom/press-releases/2018/cb18-41-population-projections.html.

13 "For the First Time, 1 Person in 5 in Japan Is 70 or Older," *Japan Times*, September 17, 2018, https://www.japantimes.co.jp/news/2018/09/17/national/number-women-japan-aged-least-65-years-old-tops-20-million-first-time/#.XJT6GdF7mEk.

14 See for instance Daniel B. Kaplan and Barbara J. Berkman, "Religion and Spirituality in Older Adults," MSD Manual: Professional Version, last modified May 2019, https://www.msdmanuals.com/en-gb/professional/geriatrics/social-issues-in-the-elderly/religion-and-spirituality-in-older-adults.

15 Larkin's poem can be found at Philip Larkin, "Church Going," World Poetry Database, https://www.shigeku.org/xlib/lingshidao/waiwen/larkin.htm. See also Philip Jenkins, "Church Going . . . Going . . . Not Gone . . . ," *Aleteia* (blog), December 30, 2015, https://aleteia.org/2015/12/30/church-going-going-not-gone/.

INDEX

racism, 8, 20, 106
Radcliff, Pamela Beth, *Modern Spain*, 211n39
Rajasthan, India, 172
Ramasamy, E. V., 173
Ramos, Joshua, 206n35
Rashtriya Swayamsevak Sangh, 170
Raspail, Jean, 47; *The Camp of the Saints*, 8, 203n12
Reagan, Ronald, 165
recessions, 39, 100
refugees, 17, 47
Reher, David S., "Baby Booms, Busts, and Population Ageing in the Developed World," 208n13
Reich, Emil, 28; *Germany's Swelled Head*, 207n2
Religion and the Demographic Revolution (Brown), 21, 206n32, 209n26, 232n38
Religion in Britain since 1945 (Davie), 70, 219n45
religiosity, 12–14, 17, 55, 186; in Africa, 128, 139; gender and, 11; of immigrants, 17; in Iran, 151; in Islamic societies, 142, 146; in United States, 15, 23, 69, 101–3
Republican Party, 102, 106, 107, 117
resentment, generational, 17
Restrepo, Pascual, "Secular Stagnation?," 211n37
Revelation, book of, 49
Revenge of God, The (Kepel), 181, 245n38
Riley, Nancy E., *International Handbook on Gender and Demographic Processes*, 203n15, 210n30
Romania, 35, 36
Rome, Italy, 73
Rosta, Gergely, *Religion and Modernity*, 201n1, 213n1, 216n17
Roy, Olivier, *Is Europe Christian?*, 213n1
RSS: *see* Rashtriya Swayamsevak Sangh

Rubin, Dominic, *Russia's Muslim Heartlands*, 244n32
rural areas, 34, 59, 80, 81, 85–86, 110, 133
Russia, 24, 59, 164, 177–81, 185
Rwanda, 133

Saadat, Seemeen, *Fertility Decline in the Islamic Republic of Iran, 1980–2006*, 238n15
Sadjadpour, Karim, *Iran in Transition*, 155, 238n19
Sáenz, Rogelio, *The International Handbook of the Demography of Race and Ethnicity*, 211n43
"saffron wave," 170–71
Sandbrook, Dominic, *White Heat*, 217n30
Sanders, Bernie, 152
Santiago de Compostela, Spain, 73
Sanzenbacher, Geoffrey T., *Is the Drop in Fertility Temporary or Permanent?*, 204n21
Sardon, Jean-Paul, *Childbearing Trends and Prospects in Low-Fertility Countries*, 208n12, 209n19
Saudi Arabia, 23–24, 142, 144, 145, 157–59, 160
Saunders, Doug, *The Myth of the Muslim Tide*, 205n28
scandals, 66, 67–68, 87, 88–89, 95–96, 106, 111
Scandinavia, 4, 7, 29, 34, 37, 55
Scharping, Thomas, *Birth Control in China, 1949–2000*, 224n30
schisms, 46, 131, 174, 198
Schleifer, Cyrus, 204n21
science fiction, 17, 19
Second Demographic Transition (SDT), 7, 10, 20, 22, 100, 203n11
Second Vatican Council, 66
secular drift, 4, 101
secularity, 13, 50, 101–3, 139, 144, 177
secularization, 3, 22–24, 69–71, 72–73, 74, 142, 189; demography

and, 20–21; in East Asia, 84, 96; in
Europe, 48, 49; in Japan, 85; in Latin
America, 96; in South Africa, 139; in
United States, 101–3, 117–18
security, 14–15, 113–14, 150, 186
segregation, 117
seminaries, 53, 54
Seoul, South Korea, 87
Sephardim, 174
Seshadri, Ananth, "The Baby Boom
and Baby Bust," 208n12
Sevilla, Jaypee, *The Demographic
Dividend*, 210n32
"sex recession," 41, 210n34
sexual minorities, 10
sexual revolutions, 21, 62; opposition
to, 63–64
sexuality, 22, 30, 33; alternative, 37,
110; attitudes toward, 42–44, 53,
61–62, 68, 81, 197; in media, 80
Shah of Iran, 149, 150, 153
Shall the Religious Inherit the Earth?
(Kaufmann), 21–22, 190, 206n35,
245n8
Sharma, Sonya, *Women and Religion
in the West*, 204n19
Shermer, Michael, 104, 107
Shindler, Colin, *Israel, Likud and the
Zionist Dream*, 243n24
Shinto, 84, 85–86
Shock of Gray (Fishman), 20
Shorto, Russell, 207n1
Sikhs, 170, 173
Silk, Mark, *The Future of Catholicism
in America*, 231n30
Singapore, 38, 80, 89–90
"68ism," 37
Skirbekk, Vegard, 204n21, 206n35
Smith, Stephen, *The Scramble for
Europe*, 211n43
Snape, Michael, *Secularisation in the
Christian World*, 215n11, 218n42
social media, 18, 41, 80, 109

social revolutions, 9, 30, 37, 48, 92,
93–94, 110
social safety nets, 14, 32
social welfare, 15, 16, 29, 31, 32, 37,
42, 114
socialism, 32, 142
Somalia, 38, 133
Sousa-Poza, Alfonso, *Population
Dynamics in Muslim Countries*,
236n2
South Africa, 123, 124, 138–39
South Asia, 23, 38, 59, 82
South Korea, 8, 38, 80, 81, 86–88
South Sudan, 133
Southeast Asia, 55, 83–84
Southern Europe, 34
Soviet Union, 175, 178
Spain, 34, 36, 42, 43, 44, 45, 51, 53,
54; TFR in, 31, 43
Spengler: *see* Goldman, David P.
spirituality, noninstitutional, 72–75,
96, 105, 152, 191
Sri Lanka, 83
stability, 14, 16, 150
Stanley, Brian, *Christianity in the
Twentieth Century*, 218n39
state weakness, 124–25, 133–34
Sterilia, 7, 121, 202n8
Stonawski, Marcin, 206n35
Stone, Lyman, *Declining Fertility in
America*, 201n3, 226n8
Strauss, Rebecca, *The Graying of the
Great Powers*, 205n30
Strhan, Anna, *Religion and the Global
City*, 220n53
Sudan, 133
Sufi orders, 127, 135, 152, 193
Swaziland, 139
Sweden, 31, 36, 37, 45, 56
Sylva, Douglas A. Sylva, *Population
Decline and the Remaking of Great
Power Politics*, 206n30
Syria, 155, 166, 179